Advances in Fisheries Bioeconomics

Efforts to effectively conserve and manage marine resources are facing increasing complexity of environmental and governance challenges. To address some of these challenges, this book presents advancements in fisheries bioeconomics research that provide significant ideas for addressing emerging environmental and fisheries management issues.

Advances in Fisheries Bioeconomics gives insights into innovative approaches dealing with these issues, as well as novel ideas on changes in fisheries management paradigms. With contributions from leading experts in the field, this book offers an examination of a number of topics, including: ecosystem-based fisheries management; by-catch management and discard bans; the number of players in the fisheries game; the effects of ocean acidification; and the trends and impacts of eco-labelling and eco-certification of fisheries. Through integrating resource biology and ecology with the economics of fishers' behaviour, the authors provide valuable analysis of the current issues in fisheries management.

This book will be of interest to those on advanced courses in fisheries science, natural resource biology and ecology, and environmental and natural resource economics. It will also appeal to researchers, policymakers and advocacy groups around the world.

Juan Carlos Seijo is Professor of Fisheries Bioeconomics, School of Natural Resources, Marist University of Merida, Mexico.

Jon G. Sutinen is Distinguished Professor Emeritus of Environmental and Natural Resource Economics, University of Rhode Island, USA.

Routledge Explorations in Environmental Economics

Edited by Nick Hanley
University of Stirling, UK

For a full list of titles in this series, please visit www.routledge.com/series/REEE

Advances in Fisheries Bioeconomics

Theory and Policy

**Edited by Juan Carlos Seijo
and Jon G. Sutinen**

Routledge
Taylor & Francis Group

LONDON AND NEW YORK

First published 2018 by Routledge

2 Park Square, Milton Park, Abingdon, Oxfordshire OX14 4RN

52 Vanderbilt Avenue, New York, NY 10017

Routledge is an imprint of the Taylor & Francis Group, an informa business

First issued in paperback 2020

British Library Cataloguing-in-Publication Data
A catalogue record for this book is available from the British Library

Library of Congress Cataloging-in-Publication Data
A catalog record for this book has been requested

ISBN: 978-1-138-56746-7 (hbk)
ISBN: 978-0-367-59127-4 (pbk)

Typeset in Bembo
by Swales & Willis Ltd, Exeter, Devon, UK

Contents

Figures

Tables

Contributors

Peder Andersen, Department of Food and Resource Economics, University of Copenhagen, Denmark

Lee G. Anderson, Maxwell P. and Mildred H. Harrington Professor Emeritus, School of Marine Science and Policy, College of Earth, Ocean, and Environment, University of Delaware, Newark, Delaware, USA

John F. Caddy, Via Cervialto 3, Aprilia 04011, Latina, Italy

Anthony Charles, School of the Environment and School of Business, Saint Mary's University, Halifax, Nova Scotia, Canada

Kevern L. Cochrane, Department of Ichthyology and Fisheries Science, Rhodes University, Grahamstown, South Africa

Rögnvaldur Hannesson, Professor Emeritus, Department of Economics, Norwegian School of Economics, Bergen, Norway

Anna Schuhbauer, Fisheries Economics Research Unit, Institute for the Oceans and Fisheries and Liu Institute for Global Studies, University of British Columbia, Vancouver, Canada

Juan Carlos Seijo, School of Natural Resources, Marist University of Merida, Mexico

Lisa Ståhl, Section for Environment and Natural Resources, University of Copenhagen, Denmark

Jon G. Sutinen, Professor Emeritus, Department of Environmental and Natural Resource, Economics, University of Rhode Island

U. Rashid Sumaila, Fisheries Economics Research Unit, Institute for the Oceans and Fisheries, University of British Columbia, Vancouver, Canada

Raul Villanueva, School of Natural Resources, Marist University of Merida, Mexico

Acknowledgements

We greatly appreciate the support of the inter-institutional PhD Program in Bioeconomics of Fisheries and Aquaculture offered by Marist University of Merida, the Northwest Center of Biological Research (CIBNOR) and the Interdisciplinary Center of Marine Sciences of the National Polytechnic Institute (CICIMAR-IPN) for jointly organizing the international symposium where papers included in this book were presented. This academic event was organized as part of the twentieth anniversary of Marist University and 200 years of Marist education in 79 countries. Special thanks to Dr Elisa Serviere, Dr German Ponce, Karla Barrera, Margarita Soberanis and Jose Diaz for their valuable organizing and logistic capacity and support. This book would not have been possible without the orientation, understanding and technical support of Andy Humphries and Laura Johnson of Routledge, Taylor & Francis. We also want express our gratitude and appreciation to Miguel Angel Cabrera for his support in formatting and reviewing equations and figures included in the book.

1   Introduction

Juan Carlos Seijo and Jon G. Sutinen

Economic considerations have long shaped policies directed at conserving and managing fisheries and other natural resources. Efforts to systematically integrate economic and biological elements into what has come to be known as bioeconomics began in the 1950s. Bioeconomics has evolved into a sophisticated tool commonly practised by natural and social scientists that advise fishery policymakers. Bioeconomics is a rich and robust framework that has stood up well over time, proving its ability to incorporate new dimensions and complexities.

Today's fishery managers face a far more complex set of issues than in the 1950s, when bioeconomics first emerged. Contemporary management issues are challenging bioeconomic analysts like never before. The chapters in this book demonstrate many of the ways in which bioeconomics is responding to address such issues by providing insights to innovative approaches that address emerging complex environmental and fisheries management issues, including novel ideas involving changes in fisheries management paradigms. This book presents advancements in fisheries bioeconomics research to address some of these challenges.

The subject area covered by the book is both taught and researched at a large number of universities. The book is relevant to advanced courses in fisheries science, natural resource biology and ecology, and environmental and natural resource economics. It is also relevant to the global community of scholars, policymakers and advocacy groups, a community that spans both developed and developing countries in all parts of the world.

Following this introduction, leading experts in the fields of fisheries bioeconomics examine the theory and policy implications of several contemporary fisheries issues. Summaries of Chapters 2 through 10 follow below.

In Chapter 2, Rögnvaldur Hannesson applies basic non-cooperative game theory to illustrate how countries exploiting a common fishery may totally annihilate the fish stock. Hannesson shows as the number of players (countries) increases, theory predicts conservation of the fish stock becomes less likely, leading to extinction. This prediction is challenged by Hannesson, who asks whether this necessarily means that fish stocks are increasingly likely to be exploited to extinction as the number of players increase. Would not players (countries) prefer to avoid annihilation of their fisheries even if no single one of them is dominant enough to conserve the stock in its own interest? He examines this question in some detail with evidence from an actual fishery.

In Chapter 3, Jon G. Sutinen and Peder Andersen present the theory and policy implications of recovering enforcement costs in fisheries. Services such as research, enforcement, decision-making and administration services are essential ingredients of regulatory programmes directed at the management of common pool resources. The recovery of fishery management costs from the fishing industry is becoming increasingly common among the fishing nations of the world. Although some aspects of cost recovery mechanisms are well studied and documented, there remain some important implications for fisheries policy that have not been adequately studied. To partially address this gap in knowledge, this chapter investigates how cost recovery in the form of a royalty influences producer behaviour and optimal policy for managing a fishery. Sutinen and Andersen build on their earlier economic analysis of fisheries law enforcement to examine the economic and policy consequences of using a royalty on production to recover the costs of enforcement services for fisheries management.

In Chapter 4, John F. Caddy challenges the conventional approach to fishery management that focuses on harvesting those cohorts that have matured and spawned at least once while protecting juveniles. This conventional approach may be appropriate when there is no shortage of mature fish, but this is not the case in many world fisheries today. Instead, the mature cohorts of many demersal fisheries have been fished down to low levels, leading to an intense focus in the literature on models that define the minimum number of spawners needed to replace the population. In a very rich and comprehensive discussion, Caddy replaces the assumption of a constant natural mortality for all age groups, with a more realistic declining mortality rate at age for juveniles, combined with an expanded life cycle model. With estimates for the Mediterranean hake fishery, Caddy simulates the outcomes of the conventional approach (harvesting older fish) compared with a multi-gear allocation approach that harvests juveniles and conserves spawning fish.

In Chapter 5, Juan Carlos Seijo and Raul Villanueva present the theory of ocean acidification effects on fisheries targeting calcifier species. Organisms in benthic and neritic environments are susceptible to changes in saturation of carbonates, and even small changes in concentrations of CO_2 in oceanic waters can cause negative impacts in calcifier organisms, such as molluscs, echinoderms and crustaceans, as well as ecologically valuable critical habitats such as corals. To deal with the possible effects of ocean acidification (OA), Seijo and Villanueva present equilibrium and dynamic bioeconomic frameworks and trajectories to account for the OA stressor affecting marine species and the likely performance of their fisheries over time in data-limited fisheries contexts. Questions addressed in this chapter include: (1) How do we incorporate analytically in bioeconomic models the effect of ocean acidification on calcifier species in data-limited situations with available catch and effort data to determine bioeconomic reference points with ocean acidification? (2) What is the possible dynamic bioeconomic effect of OA on calcifier species with different renewability capacities? Seijo and Villanueva address these questions with a bioeconomic biomass dynamic model in which OA effects are built into the natural growth of biomass function. They use the model to explore the OA effect on fisheries targeting species with different renewability capacity.

In Chapter 6, Peder Andersen and Lisa Ståhl examine the prevalent problem of unwanted by-catch. By-catch is often discarded, resulting in direct food waste, and indirectly influences biodiversity, stock abundance and long-term catch. To minimize by-catch problems, fisheries management regulations such as restricting the legal minimum sizes of landed fish, mesh size and closed areas are applied. A more dramatic approach to reduce the discards of unwanted catches requires landing of all caught fish, independent of size and quality. This has been part of the fishery policy in Norway and Iceland for years. By 2015, the European Common Fisheries Policy Reform instituted a landing obligation (discard ban), one of the most significant changes of the Common Fisheries Policy since 1983. Despite this major change in the governance of EU fisheries, there is a lack of theoretical as well as empirical analyses of the consequences of a landing obligation policy. Andersen and Ståhl address this gap in knowledge with a simple model for analysing fleet behaviour under a landing obligation regime and an empirical analysis of the economic impact of implementing an LO for the Danish fishery, a multispecies fishery regulated by ITQs.

In Chapter 7, Rashid Sumaila and Anna Schuhbauer discuss the distributional implications of subsidies in industrial and small-scale fisheries. They use a simple bioeconomic model to explain why fisheries subsidies are generally seen to lead to overcapacity and overfishing. Next, Sumaila and Schuhbauer summarize the latest estimates of fisheries subsidies in the literature, showing that the amount of taxpayer dollars given to the fishing sector is large.

In Chapter 8, Kevern Cochrane discusses the trends and impacts of eco-labelling and eco-certification of fisheries. Environmental concerns about the sustainability of fisheries and aquaculture globally have fuelled a demand, especially in developed countries, for seafood products that are certified as having come from sustainable sources. This in turn has driven growth in the number of schemes offering certification and labelling services. The success of these schemes can be measured by the growing number of fisheries that are certified or are seeking certification. Reliable certification schemes provide an incentive to fisheries to comply with globally recognized sustainability standards, but at the same time the concepts and practice have generated conflict and confusion among scientists, consumers and retailers. This chapter examines some of the biggest challenges being faced, which include concerns that developing countries and small-scale fisheries are disadvantaged, criticism of the sustainability standards that are applied, and confusion in the marketplace because of the proliferation of schemes and a lack of transparency on performance.

In Chapter 9, Lee G. Anderson argues that, at its core, the primary function of fisheries management in the single stock case is the determination of the annual allowable harvest, which most often is based on the selection of a target stock size and a control rule that specifies a harvest path that causes the target stock size to be achieved or maintained. The selection of the target stock and the control rule are policy decisions. Anderson describes a procedure for the ecosystem-based fisheries management (EBFM) approach based on setting a multidimensional target space and a control rule for a multidimensional harvest path to lead to a vector of stock sizes within the target stock space. He uses economic principles to describe the nature of the target stock space, based on a broadly defined metric for measuring the value of the bundle of sustainable production from the set of stocks, and that considers the value of output trade-offs from different harvest production bundles.

In Chapter 10, Anthony Charles examines the emerging practice of bio-socio-economic analysis to support fishery management programmes. According to Charles, there are five prominent ingredients of bio-socio-economics: (1) incorporating and assessing multiple fishery objectives, and dealing with the resulting conflicts; (2) recognizing and analysing distributional impacts of fishery policy and practice; (3) human dimensions of fisheries governance and rights in the commons; (4) consideration of behavioural and labour dynamics in fisheries, including fisher response to regulations and the role of labour markets; and (5) interactions of fisheries and fishing communities (including underlying values, objectives, knowledge, institutions and functions). After describing these ingredients, Charles discusses two specific examples of bio-socio-economic models and analysis (one with a combination of multiple objectives and labour dynamics, and another involving dynamics of fishing communities and the nature of distributional impacts). Lastly, the discussion shifts from model-based analysis to fishery policy analysis, explaining how the bio-socio-economic perspective can produce improved fishery policy.

Finally, in Chapter 11, Jon G. Sutinen and Juan Carlos Seijo summarize the major results and conclusions of this volume, and propose some topics for future research to further advance the application of bioeconomics to global fisheries issues.

2 The number of players in a fisheries game

Curse or blessing?

Rögnvaldur Hannesson

Introduction

In a non-cooperative game, the players look for the best response to what they think the other players will do. This is known as the Nash-Cournot equilibrium solution, applied in the seminal papers by Clark (1980) and Levhari and Mirman (1980). In equilibrium, no participant can improve his position; all players do exactly what they are expected to do, and all players apply the best response to these actions. The outcomes of these games in the fisheries context are known to be potentially disastrous, especially when the number of players is large (Hannesson, 2007). It is tempting, therefore, to conclude that a large number of countries sharing a fish stock is a recipe for disaster. We argue that this is not necessarily so. Taking a far-sighted view and realizing the disastrous consequences of uncoordinated and aggressive playing, countries might cooperate, albeit in an informal and implicit way, with the risk of common ruin maintaining cooperation as in infinitely repeated games.[1] Furthermore, the sustainable but non-cooperative outcomes in games with dominant players might have pay-offs that are perceived as sufficiently unfair to the dominant player to dissuade him from seeking such outcomes even if apparently in his best interest.

We shall begin with a simple two-country model, applying the Nash-Cournot approach as in Clark (1980) and Levhari and Mirman (1980). In this setting, 'bad' outcomes, and possibly total annihilation of the fish stock, are likely to occur unless one country is sufficiently dominant. To obtain a non-cooperative solution with a viable stock, one country must have a sufficiently large share of the stock to provide an incentive for conservation. We derive this critical share for the case of stock-independent cost per unit of fish caught, a case where stock extinction can result from a non-cooperative play. In a multi-country setting, one country is less likely to be sufficiently dominant, and hence stock extinction would seem all the more likely. Yet when we look at a real-world fishery (the Northeast Atlantic mackerel fishery) characterized by at least five players, none of whom seems sufficiently dominant, and where stock sensitivity of unit landings cost seems unimportant, this prediction is not borne out; the countries participating in this fishery seem to be following a rather moderate catch strategy.

A simple model

Consider a simple model where the surplus growth of a fish stock (G) depends on how much of the stock (S) is left behind after fishing. Ignoring individual growth and natural mortality during fishing, the stock left after fishing in year t is:

$$S_t = X_t - Y_t \qquad (2.1)$$

where X_t is the stock at the beginning of year t and Y_t is the amount fished during year t. The stock is shared between two countries such that a share β_i of the stock always comes to country i's waters at the beginning of each year. The fish stay in each country's waters while the fishing takes place and then migrate out of the national waters to breed and grow as a unit.[2] Therefore, the stock in each country's waters at the beginning of year $t+1$ will be:

$$\beta_i X_{t+1} = \beta_i \left[S_{t,i} + S_{t,-i} + G \left(S_{t,i} + S_{t,-i} \right) \right] \qquad (2.2)$$

Suppose that the cost per unit of fish caught is independent of the size of the stock from which it is taken. Then, if the price is independent of the catch volume, the rent per unit of fish caught, or the net price of fish (p), will also be a constant that can be ignored. We can find the rent-maximizing stock to be left behind either by maximizing the present value of rent over two periods with respect to the stock to be left behind after the first period, or by maximizing the present value of rents over an infinite time horizon with respect to the stock to be left behind after fishing in all periods. Both give the same answer, because as long as all parameters remain unchanged, the optimal stock to be left after fishing in any period will be the same. Taking the first approach, the maximization problem for country i is:

$$Maximize\, V_i = \beta_i X - S_i + \frac{1}{1+r} \left\{ \beta_i \left[S_i + S_{-i} + G \left(S_i + S_{-i} \right) \right] - S_i^* \right\} \qquad (2.3)$$

where r is the discount rate and S_i^* is the stock to be left in the next period, which is a decision to be taken in the next period, but, as already stated, will be equal to the optimal value of S_i in any period, as long as no parameters change. The first-order condition for maximum is:

$$\beta_i \left[1 + G' \left(S_i + S_{-i} \right) \right] \le 1 + r \qquad (2.4)$$

The interpretation of this is straightforward. Suppose we have strict equality. The expression on the left shows the return for country i from leaving behind a weight unit of fish. This will generate a surplus growth of $G'(S)$, and at the beginning of the next period $1 + G'(S)$ units will return, whereof country i will get a share β_i. But since the β_i's are unequal except when both countries get an equal share of the returning stock, there is no way the maximum condition can hold with strict equality for all. The minor country will always want to leave behind a smaller stock than the dominant country (the country with the largest β_i). But it can never leave behind less than nothing, so we will end up with a solution where the dominant country does all the conservation necessary for ensuring the availability of fish in all future periods.

But even the dominant country might not have strong enough incentives to leave any fish behind. To get a solution for the dominant country with a strict equality and a viable stock, we need:

$$\beta_i \left[1 + G'(0) \right] > 1 + r \tag{2.5}$$

That is, the return on saving some of the stock as it approaches extinction must be greater for the dominant country than the return on fishing it out and invest the money for the going rate of return (r). This is a variant of the condition that Colin Clark famously demonstrated in the early 1970s, now appearing in a two-country setting instead of applying to a fishery with a sole owner (Clark, 1973).

This is a demanding condition. Maximum growth rates of fish stocks are probably high, but unlikely to be way above 100 per cent. Figure 2.1 shows the critical dominant country share as a function of the maximum growth rate of the stock, for discount rates of 1 versus 10 per cent. These arguably reasonable upper and lower limits of the discount rate do not lead to widely different critical values of the dominant country critical stock share. For a maximum growth rate of the stock of 10 per cent and a discount rate of 10 per cent, even a dominant country stock share close to 100 per cent would not be enough to ensure the viability of the stock; leaving anything behind

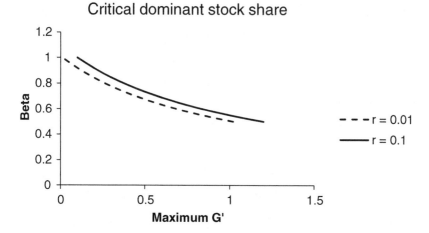

Figure 2.1 Sensitivity of dominant country critical share to the maximum growth rate of the fish stock.

would simply be a bad investment. With a discount rate of only 1 per cent, the dominant country's share would still have to be over 90 per cent to ensure that leaving some fish behind would be a good investment. To ensure a viable stock if both countries are equal, the maximum growth rate would have to be over 100 per cent with a discount rate of 1 percent, and 120 per cent with a discount rate of 10 per cent.

It is instructive to look at how the catches of the dominant versus the minor country change as the dominant country's share of the stock changes. This is shown in Figure 2.2, for a logistic growth function with a maximum growth rate of 0.5, a carrying capacity of the environment of 1, and a discount rate of 5 per cent. As a sole owner, the dominant country would leave behind a stock of 0.45 and its sustainable catch would be 0.12375. As its share of the stock falls, it leaves less and less behind, and nothing at all if its share is below the critical level of 0.7. Its catch would fall monotonically to zero as its share of the stock falls. The minor country's sustainable catch increases as its share increases up to a maximum for a dominant country share of slightly over 80 per cent. At this point, the minor country catches more fish than the dominant country. It does so as the dominant country's share falls below 87 per cent, and the difference continues to widen, until the minor country catches almost five times as much fish as the dominant country when the latter's share has fallen to 74 per cent. Whether or not this would be considered 'fair' is a legitimate question, but the point is that the minor country knows that the dominant country is better off leaving some fish behind to ensure a continued fishery for itself, and the minor country would be able to take advantage of that.

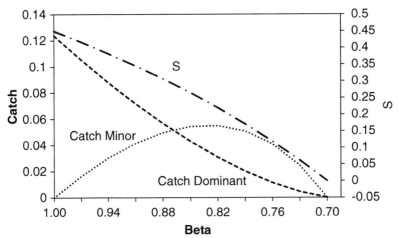

Figure 2.2 Catches of the dominant and the minor country and the stock left behind by the dominant country as functions of the dominant country's share of the stock (β), for a logistic growth function with a maximum growth rate of 0.5 and a rate of interest of 5 per cent.

More countries

Now suppose there are three or more countries sharing a fish stock. As the number of countries increases, it becomes less and less likely that any one of them is sufficiently larger than all the others to have a strong enough incentive to preserve the stock. In that case, no country can be relied upon to conserve the stock in its own interest. Furthermore, as the critical share of the dominant country increases (cf. Figure 2.1), it becomes even less likely that one single country of three or more would have such a dominant share.

Consider again the critical share determined by Equation 2.5. Let $G'(0)$ be 1, implying a maximum growth rate of 100 per cent. Assume an interest rate of 10 per cent. According to Figure 2.1, the dominant country would have to have a share of at least 55 per cent. Then suppose there are three countries each with an equal share of one-third. None of them would have an incentive to conserve the stock for its own benefit. Applying the best response to the other two's actions, a mutually consistent solution would be one where no one leaves anything behind and the stock would be wiped out.

But would not the three (or whatever the number is) be smarter than mutually fishing one another out of existence? Note that this situation is fundamentally different from the one where one nation has an incentive to preserve the stock in its own interest, no matter how small a catch it would leave for the country in question and no matter how egregious the free-riding gains for the minor player or players. With no single country being critically dominant in the sense of Equation 2.5, leaving nothing behind brings no free-riding gains, but mutual annihilation.

An example: the Northeast Atlantic mackerel

The story of the Northeast Atlantic mackerel indicates that nations sharing a fish stock without any single one being sufficiently dominant are indeed smarter than fishing one another out of existence. The four main countries participating in this fishery are the EU, Norway, the Faroe Islands and (since 2007) Iceland.[3] The modelling approach above seems basically adequate for the mackerel fishery, except that the numerical model needs to be a lot more complicated; an age-structured one with recruitment fluctuations. The countries in question seem to care little about fishing costs as possible determinants of an optimal fishing strategy, focusing instead on setting an overall fish quota, so as to avoid over-exploitation, and on the sharing of this overall fish quota. It thus makes sense to model their behaviour as maximizing the present gross value of fish catches over time at a low and possibly zero discount rate.

Before 2007, the two main participants in the mackerel fishery, Norway and the EU, had agreed on setting and sharing an overall catch quota. Later, the Faroe Islands, a minor partner, joined this agreement. Russia as a non-coastal state was accommodated through the North East Atlantic Fisheries Commission. This agreement was upended when the mackerel began to appear in the Icelandic economic zone in significant quantities in 2007. Attempts at including Iceland in this agreement have failed. None of the other three has a large enough share of the stock to act as a conservationist in its own interest; models of the mackerel fishery (Hannesson, 2013a, 2013b, 2013c, 2014) show that a strategy of best response to other players' actions produces a consistent solution where the mackerel stock is nearly annihilated.

Yet we do not see such self-destructive strategy applied in practice. Since 2015, there has been an agreement in place between three parties, the EU, Norway and the Faroe Islands, with Iceland an outsider. The overall catch quota set by the agreeing parties appears moderate, and so does the unilateral quota the Icelanders have set for themselves. The same can be said for the unilateral quotas the countries set for themselves before a partial agreement was restored; the fishing mortality of the mackerel stock has been fairly steady since 2006, immediately before the mackerel agreement broke down (see Figure 2.3), and appears lower than required to take the maximum sustainable yield (Hannesson, 2013a, 2013b, 2013c, 2014). Despite increasing landings, the stock has been increasing since 2006 (see Figure 2.4). This is very different from the outcome we would expect from an unfettered competition where each player seeks the best response to other players' moves. Hence, the fishing strategies of the parties seem more adequately described as a moderate and sustainable exploitation, maintained by fear of mutually assured destruction of the fishery in case any single party were to apply the strategy of best short-term reply to the others' actions.

Figures 2.5 and 2.6 show the outcomes from a model of the mackerel stock under optimal management (cooperation) versus competition (a non-cooperative game). The objective of optimal management is assumed to be maximum

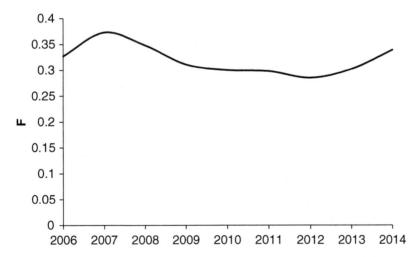

Figure 2.3 Fishing mortality (F) of Northeast Atlantic mackerel, 2006–2014.
Source: ICES (2015).

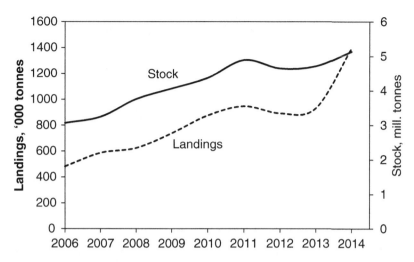

Figure 2.4 Landings and stock of Northeast Atlantic mackerel, 2006–2014.
Source: ICES (2015).

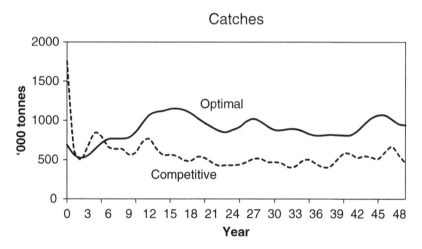

Figure 2.5 Catches of mackerel over a 50-year period under optimal management
versus a non-cooperative game.

long-term yield without discounting, whereas in a non-cooperative game each
participant would maximize his catch per year, given what the others take.
The instrument is fishing mortality generated by each country's fishing fleet
or, in the case of overall optimization, the overall fishing mortality.[4] In a non-
cooperative game, each participant would fish with maximum intensity, which
would quickly wipe out the stock. In the outcomes shown in Figures 2.5
and 2.6 we have set an arbitrary upper limit of 2.0 on each country's fishing

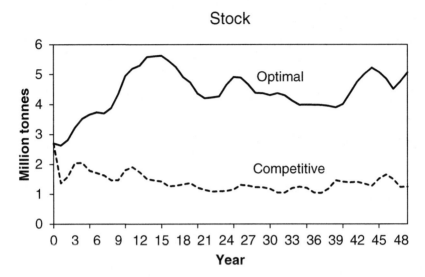

Figure 2.6 The stock of mackerel over a 50-year period under optimal management versus a non-cooperative game.

mortality (to wipe out the stock, fishing mortality would have to be infinite, which is probably unrealistic). All parties except the EU, which is the dominant party, would fish with this intensity, while the EU would apply a fishing mortality of 1.479 in its own zone, which is still pretty high. As we see from Figure 2.5, the total catch in a non-cooperative game would be almost 2 million tonnes in the first year, dropping quickly thereafter to 400,000–600,000 tonnes and then fluctuating between these limits because of random fluctuations in recruitment to the stock. The stock itself (see Figure 2.6) would drop from an initial level of 2.7 million tonnes to between 1 and 2 million tonnes, between which it would then fluctuate because of the random variations in recruitment. With optimal management, the catches would fluctuate between 800,000 and 1.2 million tonnes, and the stock itself would fluctuate between 4 and 5.5 million tonnes. The first years show unusually small catches and a small stock, due to an assumed small stock in the beginning. It bears mentioning that the outcome under a non-cooperative game could be a lot worse if an upper limit had not been imposed on the fishing mortality each player's fleet is able to generate.

The actual development of the fishery, shown in Figures 2.3 and 2.4, is in fact fairly similar to what happens under optimal management in Figures 2.5 and 2.6. These figures are not directly comparable; the results in Figures 2.5 and 2.6 come from a model with an input different from the reality shown in Figures 2.3 and 2.4, but what seems evident is that the countries fishing the mackerel have not engaged in a war of all against all, as predicted by the non-cooperative game model. The unilateral or partially agreed quotas that the countries have set themselves seem to have been moderate enough to justify the label 'quasi-cooperation', despite all the rhetoric the parties have engaged in.

Conclusion

The outcome of a fisheries game when each party seeks the best reply to other parties' actions is stark; without a sufficiently dominant single party, it may end in a destruction of the fishery. This is particularly likely to happen when the cost per weight unit of fish is independent of the stock size. Stock-dependent costs make it uneconomical even in the short run to fish stocks to extinction, but our purpose here is to show what could happen in the worst of circumstances.

The fact that a sufficiently dominant party would have an incentive to conserve the stock in its own interest invites the conclusion that a situation where there are many parties to the fishery would be particularly prone to produce a bad outcome where stocks are fished to extinction. Yet this might be a premature conclusion. The example of the Northeast Atlantic mackerel indicates that countries can engage in informal and implicit cooperation rather than mutual destruction of their fisheries. The latter, needless to say, would not be in the long-term interest of anyone. A dominant party able to conserve a stock through its unilateral actions could, on the other hand, be engaged in in a thankless task; the free-rider could in some circumstances gain a much greater benefit from such efforts than the dominant party itself. This is likely to arouse resentment, perhaps to the point of unwillingness by the dominant party to engage in any conservation at all. So, it is a bit doubtful if sustainable exploitation would be more difficult to achieve when no single party is dominant; A large number of players in a fisheries game is not necessarily a curse; it could be a blessing.

Notes

1 The notion of far-sighted equilibrium is discussed in de Zeeuw (2008).
2 This formulation of the problem is due to Robert McKelvey (e.g. see Golubtsov and McKelvey, 2007).
3 The EU is treated as one country because of its Common Fisheries Policy. Scotland is a major participant in the mackerel fishery, but was in the period discussed part of the EU together with the rest of the United Kingdom. What implications the British exit from the EU will have on fisheries policy is unknown at the time of writing (late 2016), and in any case irrelevant for the analysis in this chapter.
4 For details about the model, see Hanneson (2015).

References

Clark, C.W. (1973). Profit maximization and the extinction of animal species. *Journal of Political Economy*, 81: 950–961.
Clark, C.W. (1980). Restricted access to common-property fishery resources: a game-theoretic analysis. In: P.-T. Liu (ed.), *Dynamic Optimization and Mathematical Economics*. New York: Plenum, pp. 117–132.

de Zeeuw, A. (2008). Dynamic effects on the stability of international environmental agreements. *Journal of Environmental Economics and Management*, 55: 163–174.

Golubtsov, P.V. and McKelvey, R. (2007). The incomplete information split-stream fish war: examining the implications of competing risks. *Natural Resource Modeling*, 20: 263–300.

Hannesson, R. (2007). Incentive compatibility of fish-sharing agreements. In: T. Bjørndal, D.V. Gordon, R. Arnason and U.R. Sumaila (eds), *Advances in Fisheries Economics: Festschrift in Honour of Professor Gordon R. Munro*. Oxford: Blackwell, pp. 196–206.

Hannesson, R. (2013a). Sharing a migrating fish stock. *Marine Resource Economics*, 2: 1–17.

Hannesson, R. (2013b). Zonal attachment of fish stocks and management cooperation. *Fisheries Research*, 140: 249–254.

Hannesson, R. (2013c). Sharing the Northeast Atlantic mackerel. *ICES Journal of Marine Science*, 70: 259–269.

Hannesson, R. (2014). Does threat of mutually assured destruction produce quasi-cooperation in the mackerel fishery? *Marine Policy*, 44: 342–350.

Hannesson, R. (2015). Management of shared stocks: Northeast Atlantic mackerel, Norwegian spring spawning herring, and blue whiting. A report from the Nordic project 'Pelagisk krise'. Unpublished manuscript.

ICES (International Council for the Exploration of the Sea) (2015). *Report of the Working Group on Widely Distributed Fish Stocks (WGWIDE)*. Copenhagen: ICES.

Levhari, D. and Mirman, L.J. (1980). The great fish war: an example using a dynamic Cournot-Nash solution. *Bell Journal of Economics*, 11(1): 322–334.

3 Consequences of recovering enforcement costs in fisheries

Jon G. Sutinen and Peder Andersen

Introduction

Governments spend significant financial resources on fisheries management, especially on enforcement, research and management administration (Andersen and Sutinen, 2003; Sutinen and Andersen, 2003). For many of the world's fishing nations, the large government expenditures on fishery management services impose significant burdens on both taxpayers and the regulated fishing community (Shrank et al., 2003). The shift towards user charges accelerated in the 1980s and is penetrating fishery management. Some countries have changed the way they finance and provide fishery management. Countries such as Australia, Canada and New Zealand have applied cost recovery mechanisms to fisheries, agriculture, food quality, transportation, telecommunications and other sectors.

Three reasons appear to drive the recovery of the costs of fishery management. One is to raise revenue. Recent trends in reducing general taxes and downsizing government has placed greater budgetary pressures on government agencies to fund their programmes. Another is fairness. The third is economic efficiency. Elsewhere, we explain how user charges can potentially alleviate some forms of governmental failure (Andersen and Sutinen, 2003). User fees and other cost recovery mechanisms tend to encourage governments to provide goods and services at least cost. However, payers such as the fishing industry often expect to influence the provision the management services subject to cost recovery, which is commonly captured in the phrase 'user pays, user says'. Recognizing these effects, Andersen and Sutinen (2003) conclude that applying user charges to the financing of fishery management has the potential to have profound effects on the performance of fisheries.

There are several issues to be resolved when designing cost recovery programmes for fisheries. Since there are multiple methods for recovering costs, it's important to consider the advantages and disadvantages of the different types of user charges and financing mechanisms. This chapter examines the issue by formally considering the application of a royalty to recover the cost of enforcement in a fishery. To this end, we develop a novel model by modifying and extending our earlier bioeconomic analysis of fisheries law enforcement (Sutinen and Andersen, 1985) to account for cost recovery with a royalty.

In the next section, we develop a formal model of cost recovery in a fishery. We use the model to analyse how the use of a royalty to recover enforcement costs affects bioeconomic outcomes and fishery management policies. The chapter concludes with a summary of our principal results and a discussion of other policy and research issues.

A bioeconomic model of fisheries law enforcement

We begin our analysis with a basic static bioeconomic model of a singles species fishery that is in full bioeconomic equilibrium, and managed by a fisheries management authority and fisheries enforcement agency. The management authority regulates the fishery with a set of controls that restrict firms' standardized effort for a fixed the number of firms ($N = \bar{N}$).[1] Each firm's effort cannot legally exceed $\bar{e}$, the target level of firm effort.[2] The enforcement agency provides enforcement services, such as surveillance, in an amount represented by S.

If detected and convicted of exceeding $\bar{e}$, the violating firm is penalized an amount given by:

$$\gamma = \gamma\left(e - \bar{e}\right)$$

where:

$$\gamma \begin{cases} > 0 \; if \; e > \bar{e} \\ = 0 \; otherwise \end{cases}$$

and $\gamma_e \geq 0$, $\gamma_{ee} \geq 0$, for $e > \bar{e}$ (subscripts denote partial derivatives).

We assume imperfect enforcement, such that the enforcement agency is not capable of detecting and convicting every firm in violation of the regulation. As a consequence, the probability of detection and conviction is $0 \leq \theta < 1$, the level of which is given by $\theta = \theta(S)$, where S represents enforcement services, $S \geq 0$, $\theta(0) = 0$, and $\theta_S > 0, \theta_{SS} \leq 0$.

Firm outcomes

Each firm's profits without penalties and cost recovery are given by:

$$\pi = PaeX - c\left(e\right) \tag{3.1}$$

where P is the ex-vessel price of fish, *a* the catchability coefficient, X the stock size, and c(e) is the production cost function, where $c_e > 0$ and $c_{ee} > 0$. We assume price, P, is constant.

If detected and convicted of violating the regulation ($e > \bar{e}$), the firm's profits are $PaeX - c\left(e\right) - \gamma\left(e - \bar{e}\right)$, and if not detected and convicted its profits are $PaeX - c(e)$. Therefore, the firm's expected profits are:

$$E\{\pi\} = \theta(S)\left[PaeX - c(e) - \gamma(e - \bar{e})\right] + \left[1 - \theta(S)\right]\left[PaeX - c(e)\right] \quad (3.2)$$

$$E\{\pi\} = PaeX - c(e) - \theta(S) \cdot \gamma(e - \bar{e}) \quad (3.3)$$

Assuming the firm maximizes expected profits with respect to fishing effort, the firm's level of effort, e, is determined by the first-order condition:

$$PaX - c_e(e) \begin{cases} = \theta(S) \cdot \gamma_e(e - \bar{e}) \; for \, e > \bar{e} & (3.4a) \\ \leq \theta(S) \cdot \gamma_e(e - \bar{e}) \; for \, e = \bar{e} & (3.4b) \end{cases}$$

With imperfect enforcement and no cost recovery, each firm sets its effort level where marginal profits are less than or equal to the expected marginal penalty, according to Equation 3.4. Figure 3.1 illustrates a firm's solution to Equation 3.4a, and Figure 3.2 illustrates the solution to Equation 3.4b without cost recovery.

It is evident from Equation 3.4 that each firm's effort level depends on enforcement services, S, and stock size, X. In other words:

$$e = e(S, X) \quad (3.5)$$

where $e_S \leq 0, e_X \geq 0$ in four combinations (see Appendix A). More surveillance decreases each firm's amount of illegal effort, and an increase in the stock size increases illegal effort.

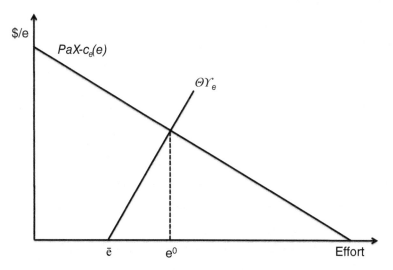

Figure 3.1 Firm's effort costly, increasing expected marginal penalty.

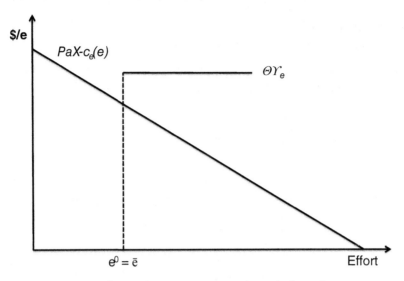

Figure 3.2 Firm's effort costly, constant expected marginal penalty.

With cost recovery, each firm pays a royalty $rPaeX$, where $(0 < r < 1)$, used to cover enforcement costs. A firm's expected profits with royalty payment become:

$$E\{\pi\} = (1-r)PaeX - c(e) - \theta(S) \cdot \gamma(e - \overline{e})$$
(3.6)

and the first-order condition is:
(3.7a)

$$(1-r)PaX - c_e(e)\begin{cases} = \theta(S) \cdot \gamma_e(e - \overline{e}) \ for \ e > \overline{e} \\ \leq \theta(S) \cdot \gamma_e(e - \overline{e}) \ for \ e \leq \overline{e} \end{cases}$$
(3.7b)

Figure 3.3 illustrates the solution to Equation 3.7a, showing that applying a royalty decreases illegal effort from e^0 to e^1, *ceteris paribus*. Since each firm's effort level depends on the royalty rate, r, as well as on enforcement services and stock size, the firm's effort function is:

$$e = e(r, S, X)$$
(3.8)

where $e_r \leq 0$, and $e_s \leq 0$, $e_X \geq 0$, as before (see Appendix B).

Aggregate outcomes with cost recovery

Aggregating each firm's level of effort, as given by Equation 3.8, across the $\overline{N}$ firms in the fishery results in the aggregate effort function:

$$\overline{N} \cdot e(r, S, X) = F(S, r, X)$$
(3.9)

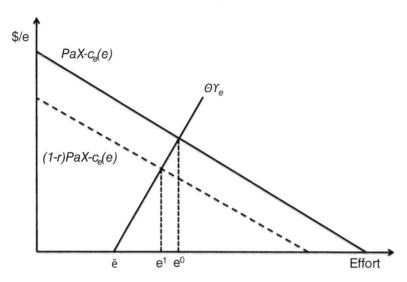

Figure 3.3 Firm's effort – with royalty, $r > 0$.

The fishery's population equilibrium function, $X = X(F)$ (where $X_F < 0$), can be used to eliminate the fish stock variable, X, so that the aggregate equilibrium effort function becomes:

$$F = F(S,r) \tag{3.10}$$

It is readily shown that $F_S < 0$ *and* $F_r < 0$. An increase in enforcement services, S, and/or in the royalty rate, r, decreases the aggregate equilibrium level of effort in the fishery, which in turn increases the equilibrium stock size, X.

The fleet's total penalty is represented by $\Gamma\left(F - F^T\right) = N \cdot \gamma\left(e - e^T\right)$, where $F^T = \bar{N} \cdot e^T$ is the management agency's target level of aggregate effort.

Aggregate expected profits for the fishing fleet when paying a royalty, r $R(F)$, are given by:

$$E\{\Pi\} = (1-r) \cdot R(F) - C(F) - \theta(S) \cdot \Gamma\left(F - F^T\right) \tag{3.11}$$

where $R(F) = P \cdot SY(F)$ and the sustainable yield curve, $SY(F)$, has the conventional property that $SY_F \gtreqless 0 \, as \, F \lesseqgtr F_{MSY}$, the maximum sustainable yield level of fishing effort. The aggregate production cost function is $C(F)$, where $C_F > 0$, $C_{FF} > 0$.

The fleet's level of aggregate effort is determined by the following first-order condition:

$$(1-r)R_F = C_F + \theta(S)\Gamma_F \tag{3.12}$$

The fleet applies an aggregate level of effort where the marginal revenue net of the royalty equals the marginal cost of production plus the marginal expected aggregate penalty. The aggregate outcome determined by Equation 3.12 is illustrated in Figure 3.4.

Inserting $F = F(S, r)$ into Equation 3.11 gives profits for the fleet in terms of the policy variables S and r.

$$E\{\Pi\} = (1-r) \cdot R(S,r) - C(S,r) - \theta(S) \cdot \Gamma(F(S,r) - F^T) \qquad (3.13)$$

This formulation shows how the policy variables, r and S, determine aggregate equilibrium outcomes. It combines the aggregate effort function $F(S,r)$, where $r = 0$, with the standard sustainable revenue function, $P \cdot SY(F)$, and the total cost function for the fishing fleet. When there are no enforcement services, i.e. $S = 0$, and no cost recovery, i.e. $r = 0$, the unregulated level of aggregate fishing effort is $F^0 = F(0, 0)$, the level of aggregate equilibrium effort that results when $S = 0$. A positive level of enforcement services, $S^1 > 0$, applied to the fishery results in an equilibrium level of aggregate effort of $F^1 < F^0$.

Enforcement costs

Enforcement costs are denoted by $E(S)$, where $E_S > 0$ and $E_{SS} \geq 0$, $S > 0$. Inserting the inverse form of the aggregate effort function, Equation 3.10, into $E(S)$ yields the following form of the enforcement cost function:

$$E(F,r) \qquad (3.14)$$

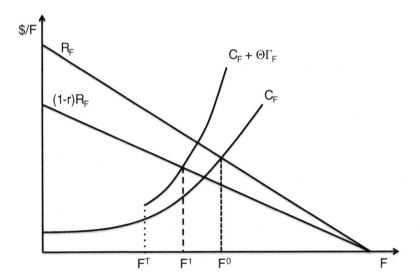

Figure 3.4 Outcomes with royalty.

where

$$E_F = E_S \cdot S_F < 0; E_r = E_S \cdot S_r < 0$$

In other words, allowing an increase in the aggregate equilibrium effort requires lower enforcement cost, and an increase in the royalty rate reduces enforcement costs, *ceteris paribus*.

Optimal management policy with full cost recovery

This section examines the conditions for optimal management policy in which full recovery of enforcement costs is required. For the case of full cost recovery, optimal policy must satisfy the constraint:

$$r \cdot R(F) = E(F, r) \tag{3.15}$$

To derive optimal policy, we maximize net social benefits[3] subject to the constraint:

$$Max \, \Pi = R(F) - C(F) - E(F, r) \tag{3.16}$$

$$s.t. \quad r \cdot R(F) = E(F, r)$$

The first-order conditions for this optimization problem are:

$$R_F - C_F - E_F + \lambda [rR_F - E_F] = 0 \tag{3.17}$$

$$-E_r + \lambda [R(F) - E_r] = 0 \tag{3.18}$$

$$rR(F) - E(F, r) = 0 \tag{3.19}$$

Combining Equations 3.17 and 3.18 gives the condition for this case as:

$$R_F = C_F + E_F - E_r / [R(F) - E_r] \tag{3.20a}$$

Solving Equations 3.19 and 3.20a simultaneously gives both the MEY level of aggregate effort, F^{***}, and royalty rate, r^{***}, for the case of full cost recovery. Recall that $E_F < 0$ and $E_r < 0$, hence R_F is larger and the optimal effort, F, lower than with less than full cost recovery.

It's useful to compare this MEY effort level with two other cases. The MEY effort, F^*, for the case of costless, perfect enforcement, is determined by:

$$R_F = C_F \tag{3.20b}$$

and the MEY effort, F^{**}, for costly, imperfect enforcement without full cost recovery – and with or without a royalty payment – the MEY level of aggregate effort:

$$R_F = C_F + E_F \tag{3.20c}$$

It is clear from Equations 3.20a–c that $F^* < F^{***} < F^{**}$. Figure 3.5 illustrates these optimal outcomes.

In other words, using a royalty to cover enforcement costs yields a lower optimal effort level and larger stock size than without a royalty. The use of a royalty has a double dividend in the form of economic efficiency and conservation benefits (a larger stock size) for over-exploited fisheries.

Summary and conclusions

This chapter develops a novel model for analysing the use of a royalty to recover the costs of enforcement in a fishery. A basic static bioeconomic model of fisheries law enforcement is used to derive the economic, biological and fishery management policy consequences for this type of user charge. We find that using a royalty has multiple advantages, including a conservation benefit that has not been explicitly noted in studies of cost recovery mechanisms. This result is further evidence that who pays and how they pay for management services influences policies and the economic performance of a fishery.

Our analysis has a number of limitations and raises a number of additional issues for future research. Perhaps most importantly, our analysis of cost

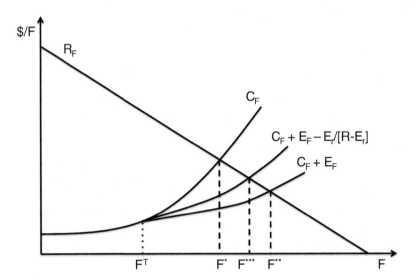

Figure 3.5 Comparison of optimal outcomes.

recovery includes only enforcement costs, while in practice there are many other types of management costs (research, observers, administrative, etc.). The results are derived for the economically optimal case, whereas in practice fisheries policy rarely approaches an economic optimum. In addition, there is no consideration of dynamics. The basic model used here produces results only for long-run, static equilibriums. A more appropriate model for practical policy analysis should consider short-run outcomes in a dynamic setting.

Also, we have assumed here that only licensed quota holders operate in the fishery, whereas in practice unlicensed, unauthorized producers may participate and have to be monitored by enforcement operations.

A couple of other issues are worth noting. Some countries are devolving authority to manage fisheries to user groups such as cooperatives, producer organizations and community organizations, together with the responsibility of providing some of the management services. User groups are arranging and paying for fisheries research, enforcement and other services, and bear the cost of those services. The model developed here is not likely to be appropriate for user group management. Instead, the user group may be best viewed as a club in the sense of Buchanan (1965), in which the group joins together voluntarily to manage and reap mutual benefits from sharing the fishery resource (Andersen and Sutinen, 2004). The effects of royalties found here would seem to apply to such cases of user group management, but further research is warranted to investigate this matter in greater depth.

The last issue is an empirical one. Evidence suggests that the cost recovery rates may be small in many or most cases. In the US, the amount of recovered costs is limited to no more than 3 per cent of total revenue. It is not clear whether such low rates of cost recovery, in the form of royalties, would have a significant impact on behaviour and outcomes in practice. Further studies on these issues are needed.

Appendices

Appendix A: no cost recovery

Derivation of the signs requires considering four cases. For case I, (3.4a) where $e > \bar{e}$ (shown in Figure 3.1), differentiating (1a) yields $e_s < 0$ and $e_X > 0$. For case II, (3.4a) where $e = \bar{e}$, differentiation results in $e_s = 0$ and $e_X > 0$. Case III, (3.4b) where $e = \bar{e}$ (shown in Figure 3.2), differentiation results in $e_s = 0$ and $e_X = 0$. And case IV, (3.4b) where $e < \bar{e}$, differentiation results in $e_s = 0$ and $e_X > 0$.

Cases	First-order conditions	where	$e_S(S, X)$	$e_X(S, X)$
I	(1a) $PaX - c_e(e) = \theta(S) \cdot \Gamma_e(e - \bar{e})$	$e > \bar{e}$	<0	>0
II	Same as I	$e = \bar{e}$	$= 0$	> 0
III	(1b) $PaX - c_e(e) < \theta(S) \cdot \Gamma_e(e - \bar{e})$	$e = \bar{e}$	$= 0$	$= 0$
IV	Same as III	$e < \bar{e}$	$= 0$	> 0

Appendix B: cost recovery with a royalty

Signing the partial derivatives of (3.8) also must consider four cases.

Cases	First-order conditions	where	$e_r(r, S, X)$	$e_s(S, X)$	$e_x(S, X)$
V	(2a) $(1-r)PaX - c_e(e) = \theta(S)\cdot\Gamma_e(e-\bar{e})$	$e > \bar{e}$	< 0	< 0	> 0
VI	Same as I	$e = \bar{e}$	$= 0$	$= 0$	> 0
VII	(2b) $(1-r)PaX - c_e(e) < \theta(S)\cdot\Gamma_e(e-\bar{e})$	$e = \bar{e}$	$= 0$	$= 0$	$= 0$
VIII	Same as III	$e < \bar{e}$	$= 0$	$= 0$	> 0

Notes

1 The number of firms is assumed constant to simplify the analysis presented herein. In addition, we assume identical firms merely to simplify the notation and exposition. The results obtained herein, however, hold for the case of heterogeneous firms and varying number of firms.
2 We assume that the management authority uses a suite of regulations (any combination of input and/or output controls) to set an upper bound on effort at a target level of standardized effort.
3 Penalty fees are not included in net social benefits since they are transfers from fishing firms to the general treasury (Sutinen and Andersen, 1985).

References

Andersen, P. and Sutinen, J.G. (2003). Financing fishery management: principles and economic implications. In: W. Shrank, R. Arnason and R. Hannesson (eds), *The Cost of Fisheries Management*. Hampshire: Ashgate, pp. 45–63.

Andersen, P. and Sutinen, J.G. (2004). *Finance Mechanisms for Governing the Commons: Paying for Research, Enforcement, Decision-Making and Administration*. Twelfth Biennial Conference of the International Institute of Fisheries Economics and Trade, 21–30 July, Tokyo, Japan.

Buchanan, J.M. (1965). An economic theory of clubs. *Economica*, 32(125): 1–14.

Shrank, W., Arnason, R. and Hannesson, R. (eds) (2003). *The Cost of Fisheries Management*. Hampshire: Ashgate.

Sutinen, J.G. and Andersen, P. (1985). The economics of fisheries law enforcement. *Land Economics*, 61(4): 387–397.

Sutinen, J.G. and Andersen, P. (2003). Fisheries management costs: findings and challenges for future research. In: W. Shrank, R. Arnason and R. Hannesson (eds), *The Cost of Fisheries Management*. Hampshire: Ashgate, pp. 279–284.

4 Conserving spawners and harvesting juveniles

Is this a better alternative to postponing capture until sexual maturity?

John F. Caddy

Introduction

This chapter searches for an approach to monitoring the reproductive performance of a generalized high fecundity finfish stock while fishing for juveniles. Current assessments frequently use stock–recruit relationships that require information on the abundance of adult fish, but such data may not be available for fisheries on juveniles. Given the high fecundity of many demersal fishes, a revival of 'old-fashioned' fecundity per recruit calculations was explored in Caddy (2015). Using recent estimates of F-at-age for a multi-gear Mediterranean hake fishery, and a vector of natural mortality rates for juveniles based on Caddy (1991), it became obvious that limits of safety were being approached when fishing mortalities for juveniles were close to $F = 1.0$. Since an offshore fishery for adults was also operating, the fishery risked infringing an intergenerational break-even point based on an idea of Charnov (1993), namely that reproductive performance should not be allowed to decline in successive generations. This defines a new limit reference point approach (e.g. Caddy and Mahon, 1995), but is not a specific prediction of the number of spawners in the next generation, which would be difficult to estimate. In order to maintain an adequate spawning population, it is pointed out that for Mediterranean hake, a significant proportion of offshore grounds should be closed as spawning refugia. Exploitation rates on adults should be kept at a low level, in addition to overall capacity limits being placed on gears targeting recruiting juveniles. This objective is aided by a steeply declining rate of natural mortality for juveniles, and the offshore migration of maturing fish out of the area of action of small mesh trawls (see Figure 4.1).

Market sizes, culinary preferences and bioeconomic factors

Small fish are prominent on Mediterranean markets. For demersal fishes, this has been affected in recent decades by exploitation on mature fishes on previously untrawled areas (natural refugia), where in the past spawners received some protection from the uneven nature of the terrain. Market demand for

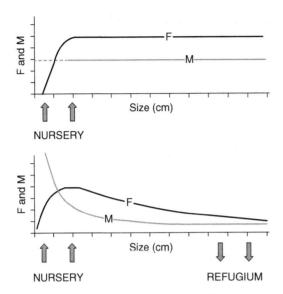

Figure 4.1 The conventional assumptions on availability of fish and their natural mortality rates at size are shown in schematic fashion in the upper cartoon, and protection of nursery areas may be included in conventional management frameworks. In reality, M diminishes with age, and adult catchability on inshore grounds in the Mediterranean also declines sharply, due in part to characteristics of fine mesh gear, and in part to an offshore migration (lower cartoon).

fresh fish is high, with high prices paid for smaller fish (e.g. retail sale of juvenile hake 18–24 cm, headless at €17.5/kg, October 2015 price in a supermarket south of Rome, Italy), since under a long culinary tradition, fish dishes in the Mediterranean are often served with several small fish on a plate. There is a close linkage between fishers, markets and customer demand for fresh fish, including the need to serve tourists traditional dishes in one of the world's prime tourist areas.

An alternative paradigm for sustainability was suggested when bioeconomic factors and a vector of higher natural mortality rates for juveniles were considered. A study of the bioeconomics of a small mesh fishery for juvenile Mediterranean hake (Caddy and Seijo, 2002) showed that a relatively high market price for juveniles plays a significant role in the economic performance of this fishery. The last-cited paper for a small-scale fishery was based on the interaction between two variables: (1) age-specific market value (landed weight of age-specific species multiplied by age-specific price); and (2) the species reproductive production at different ages, which results from multiplying the probability of survival to maturity by the average fecundity at age.

The contrast between age-specific optima for these two variables is evident (see Figure 4.2). The highest percentage share of market value for the

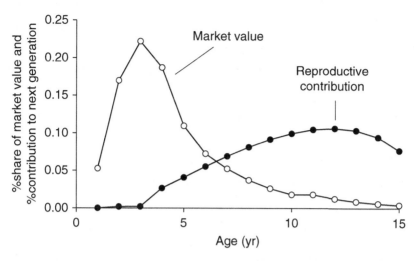

Figure 4.2 From Caddy and Seijo (2002), illustrating that in the fishery for juvenile hake, there is a contrast of objectives in setting an exploitation pattern, between maximizing juvenile yield, and sustaining the eventual reproductive performance of survivors producing the next generation. This calls for protective measures on the older spawners.

hake species occurs at age 3, while the highest percentage share of the species reproductive contribution takes places at age 12. This chapter investigates these assertions in more detail.

A brief comparison between Mediterranean and Atlantic fisheries

An early study (Doumenge, 1968) identified a common life history pattern for many demersal fish species. These often start life in nearshore nurseries and migrate offshore to spawn. In this respect, the Mediterranean hake is somewhat different, with young fish congregating in deeper shelf areas prior to offshore movement when maturity approaches (see Abella et al., 2005). This recognition by assessment scientists supports a new approach to fisheries management called the 'refugium paradigm'. Note that in the 1970s–1980s, despite heavy inshore trawling, recruitment to the juvenile bottom fish stock continued without rigorous effort control or quotas. Mediterranean shelves (unlike the North Atlantic) have few large trawlable areas such as the Gulf of Lyons and Adriatic Sea, so that a significant proportion of the stock area was unavailable to easily damaged fine mesh trawls.

The relevant phenomena in both North Sea and Mediterranean fisheries are worth contrasting. In the Mediterranean, bottom trawls (predominantly 40 mm stretch-mesh cod ends) are used in the inshore fishery. These rarely take mature fish (for hake, maturity occurs at age 5). This is in part because large fish are not readily catchable with fine mesh gear, but mainly because hake (as with some other groundfish), start to migrate at age 3+ to pre-spawning aggregations on rough bottom along the shelf edge and slope, where a steeply sloping and rocky sea floor makes fishing with unmodified trawls impractical in the Mediterranean, and illustrates the possibility of incorporating spatially defined juvenile nursery areas and adult refugia into the management system.

As noted in Caddy (2012), the geographical characteristics of Mediterranean shelves differ considerably from the wider shelves of the Northeast Atlantic. In contrast to the North Sea floor of predominantly granular sediments pre-adapted to trawling, relatively few smooth bottom areas exist in the Mediterranean. The predominantly narrow shelf is delimited by a steep drop-off marked by rocky outcrops. High fishing mortalities for age 3+ hake may be overestimated if emigration rates from inshore waters and high natural mortality rates are not considered. In the northern Mediterranean, F's from inshore trawling decline by the age of maturity, although long-lining and gill-nets target larger fish offshore (e.g. Aldebert et al., 1993). Hence, even quite high juvenile F's affect the stock for only two to three years (see Caddy, 2015) and are not necessarily the main cause of reproductive overfishing, although effort control of this fishery is essential.

Deepwater trawling in the Mediterranean is mainly aimed at red shrimp, but also catches mature fish of several species. This practice began in shelf edge waters more than two decades ago, and longlining and gill netting are also carried out in deeper waters. What was an ecologically diverse natural refugium and an offshore habitat for mature fishes has apparently been damaged by offshore trawling in some areas (see Puig et al., 2012), and the Mediterranean trawl fishery for juvenile hake also seems to be in decline over the recent decade. One feasible hypothesis for this phenomenon is reduced recruitment as a result of over-exploitation of the spawning stock, and/or impacts on the offshore refugium. The conclusion is that the previously under-regulated Mediterranean fishery applied little trawling effort to rocky areas of the shelf edge, unwittingly creating an offshore refugium for adults, which in turn led to regular inshore recruitment. Establishing a more formal refugium or marine protected area for adults now has become a key factor in a plan to restore a sustainable fishery, as long as effort control keeps juvenile fishing mortality below a reference point for intergenerational spawner survival. In summary, if an offshore refugium for spawners could be realized, harvesting juveniles in moderation would be sustainable using balanced harvesting or related strategies that capture larger juveniles, while conserving adults for reproduction.

Do changes in predation rate with age resemble frequencies in a musical scale? If so, why?

Before going into detail on the mortality rate of juvenile fishes, I suggest a brief digression to show that M-at-age vectors (Caddy, 1991) closely resemble the fundamental characteristics of musical scales. This leads to a reflection on the role of a declining encounter frequency with size with predators in contributing to the level of predation-at-age, M_t, which declines rapidly towards the conventional assumption of 'constant M' as they grow in size towards maturity. The 'harmonic' criteria typical of musical scales were first developed by Pythagoras (see Figure 4.3b), and a 'musical analogy' is proposed between how sound frequencies decline with cumulative wavelengths, and how predation rates experienced by different sizes of prey decline with successive stages in the life history. Thus, the concept of a musical scale closely parallels in form the transition in marine ecosystems from high-frequency predator–prey interactions and high M's-at-size for planktonic larvae, to low-frequency interactions and relatively low predation rates typical of mature marine organisms. A 'musical analogy' for the risk of death with age resulted from fitting the reciprocal mortality model to a musical scale sent to the author by a well-known musician, Aubrey Meyer. The same hyperbolic relationship can be fitted to both phenomena (see Figure 4.3):

Musical frequency = 0.003 + 1.03 / (cumulative wavelengths)

This 'musical model' is a useful analogy to a model of natural mortality at age described in the simple model of M-at-age described below.

Figure 4.3 illustrates that a characteristic of time intervals spent in different life history stages is also consistent with the theory of Pythagoras on the physical properties of a musical scale. On this point, Caddy (2003) suggested that the time intervals in the crustacean intermoult could be described by a 'gnomonic' spacing. If these time intervals also apply to successive life history stages of marine animals, it is more reasonable than the 'constant M assumption' through the life history, to assume the same probability of loss by natural mortality in each of the successively longer gnomonic intervals.

A factor of general relevance, then, is that juvenile fish experience a much higher natural mortality rate at age than mature fish. M_t might even equal or exceed the juvenile fishing mortality for the first few years in the juvenile hake fishery. Thus, with an intensive juvenile fishery, a significant proportion of ages 0+ and 1–2-year-old fish die from predation or other density-dependent factors if not caught (see Figure 4.3). Inevitably, significant losses in numbers from predation would also result from delaying harvests to a larger size, as a result of a transition to larger mesh sizes. Another factor to consider is that a moderate juvenile fishery may have a positive density-dependent effect on growth (e.g. Papaconstantinou and Stergiou, 1988). By increasing individual food availability, a moderate level of fishing mortality on juveniles could increase the net growth rate of survivors. The conventional management approach advocated for North Atlantic fisheries, namely to increase the size at capture towards that of maturity, does not therefore seem relevant for trawl fisheries on juveniles. In the case of Mediterranean hake, this would require a delay in exploitation of approximately two years from first availability, and inevitably would require a movement of the fishery to the ecologically sensitive shelf edge and slope.

Recent fishing mortality rates for juvenile demersal fish of F ≈ 0.9 in the northern Mediterranean are of the same order of magnitude as the M's-at-age predicted for age 1–2 juveniles, and a fecundity-recruit approach with the reciprocal M-at-age formulation predicts that few survivors make it to maturity under the current mortality rates prevailing (Caddy, 2015). An example from assessment of another gadoid fishery (Caddy, 2015) illustrated that the natural mortality rates for age 0+ to 3+ North Sea cod, as determined from their presence as prey in stomach contents of predators (Sparholt, 1990), was also fitted adequately by the 'reciprocal equation' (Caddy, 1991; Abella et al., 1997).

M declines sharply with age towards a more constant level for adults

An M-at-age vector portrayed in any one of the models described below represents changes in predation-at-size or predation-at-age, and could be integrated into the existing body of assessment theory. It would be a logical starting point for yield, trophic and reproductive modelling of marine fisheries, and for studies on exploited ecosystems where detailed trophic information is unavailable.

I described three alternative models for juvenile M-at-age, which start from different basic assumptions but give mutually consistent results. These are illustrated in Figures 4.3a, 4.3c and 4.3d. Summarizing the three models, we have:

1   the 'reciprocal model';
2   the gnomonic model; and
3   the fractal model.

One variation arises when we assume that a fractal environment determines the appropriate model for M_t for a species dependent on physical cover. This is relevant for reef-dwelling organisms that may never leave the coral reef; a habitat which, like many others, has landscape components and fractal characteristics (e.g. Burrough, 1981; Caddy, 2007). Although M_t declines initially with size while growth is fast, decapod crustaceans (Caddy, 1986) and larger reef fish will eventually experience rising predation rates as large crevice availability seriously declines, and stunting and strongly inflected growth curves may result. One model suggested for this process resembles the 'ring-a-ring o' roses' children's game, in which one of a ring of chairs is removed whenever the music stops. The dancing children are then fewer than the available chairs, and a child without a chair is expelled from the game. The analogy between this game and the battle between reef fishes for a limited number of large reef crevices to allow them to avoid predation was originally suggested by Sale (1978). One example consistent with a fractal dimension D of 2–3 is typical of semi-enclosed crevices in a reef habitat. If migration is not an option in this situation, individual growth will either remain stunted (Caddy, 2013) or predation will occur. See the reanalysis of Munro's (1983) Pedro Reef study for evidence of how fractal constraints apply in a multispecies reef community (Caddy, 2011).

Free-living species may also show diminishing log frequencies with size, probably in part reflecting habitat characteristics and the intensity of predation fields they generate (e.g. Caddy and Stamatopoulos, 1991). To locate a suitable habitat configuration that reduces predation, a cohort is obliged to migrate to deeper water, caves in canyon walls, and areas with larger cover units. This migration may be accompanied by higher predation risk from sharks and other large predators. As maturity approaches, such migrations seem typical of many reef fish and decapod crustacean life histories. The requirement to locate themselves in areas with a high frequency of large

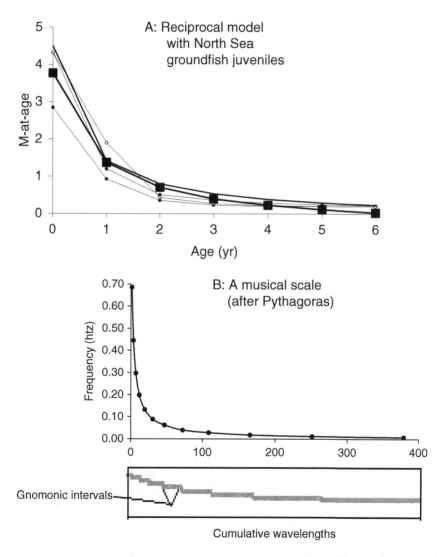

Figure 4.3 (continued)

(continued)

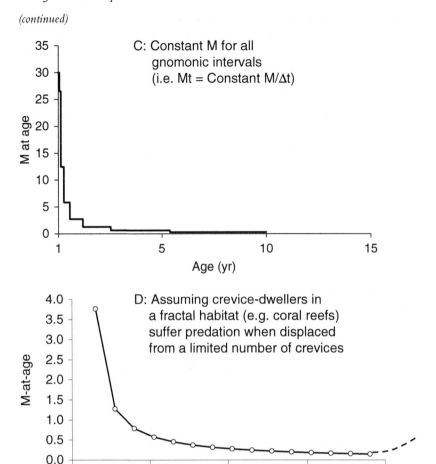

Figure 4.3 Three approaches to modelling M-at-age for juvenile fish or invertebrate populations, and a musical analogy: (a) M-at-age vectors for four species of North Sea demersal fishes showing an overall fitting (black squares) by $M_t = A + B / t$; (b) fitting frequency against cumulative wavelength, for a musical scale; (c) M-at-age by gnomonic interval for eight life history stages; and (d) predicted M's-at-age for cover-dependent species in a fractal landscape, assuming that only those 'under cover' survive. (redrawn from Caddy, 2012). In all three approaches, juvenile values for M_t descend rapidly to a close to constant value with maturity, although the fractal model supposes a rise in M_t occurs for older organisms when dislodged from the few crevices of suitable size in a fractal surface, such as a coral reef.

crevices (a relatively infrequent or localized habitat in the marine environment) must be a significant constraint on adult population size and a cause of population bottlenecks (Caddy, 2011). This would justify artificially increasing the frequency of large crevices in adult refugia as a habitat amelioration measure, as well as offering more conventional protection by management from fishing for mature organisms. The log frequency at size data for some apparently 'free-living' species (e.g. hake) also shows a higher rate of decline for older fish, apparently reflecting offshore migration to a spawning area. Even in the absence of crevices as a predator protection measure, predation interactions of juveniles of another species, silver hake, are apparently mediated by shelter within sand ripples on the bottom (Auster et al., 2003).

The gnomonic model

The concept of a gnomonic time interval was proposed as a possible way of modelling the progressive decline in natural mortality rates of highly fecund marine organisms throughout life (Caddy, 1996). Dividing the life history into progressively longer time intervals with age, and assuming equal numbers of predatory attacks in each interval, would result in a mortality curve declining, as in Figure 4.3. Thus, the same risk of death, G, is supposed to occur over progressively longer intervals for successive life history stages, Δ_i, and leads to a declining mortality rate when expressing predation rate on an annual basis. A simulation of the life history on this basis starts with a short 'seed' interval, a, to which further time intervals are added that increase in duration throughout life, which means that the lifespan $t_n = \Sigma \Delta_i$ is made of summed intervals (from $i = 1 \rightarrow n$), starting with $\Delta_1 = a$, a brief interval early in the life history that could correspond to the time from spawning to hatching. Progressively longer intervals are added of duration Δ_i ($i = 2, 3 \ldots n$), each set equal to $a \cdot t_{i-1}$, where t_{i-1} is the life history duration up to and including the last interval. This strategy was first modelled for intermoult intervals of crustaceans where the gnomonic concept was first explicitly tested (Caddy, 2003), but has been further developed by colleagues. Thus, the discovery for loliginid squids (Royer et al., 2002), by Mexican scientists for different penaeid shrimps (Ramírez-Rodríguez and Arreguín-Sánchez, 2003; Araneta-Garza et al., 2016), for sardines (Martínez-Aguilar et al., 2005), and for red grouper (Giménez-Hurtado et al., 2009) show that some invertebrates and finfish have life history stages with durations close to those predicted by the gnomonic approach. This was frankly surprising; I expected gnomonic time divisions to be arbitrarily located within the life history. That natural gnomonic time intervals are a feature of a variety of life histories in the marine environment has not yet been considered an important element in either marine biology or stock management.

Frequent misconceptions as to the relationship between age and survival rate

An axiom of the Beverton and Holt approach was that harvesting immature fish is inappropriate before a cohort has matured and spawned at least once. The targeting of sexually mature fish, the sale of fish as fillets and steaks, and a widespread aversion to exploiting juveniles are all features of this 'North Sea paradigm'. As explained above, such an assumption may have been relevant for the North Sea fishery in the 1940s–1960s when exploitation recommenced

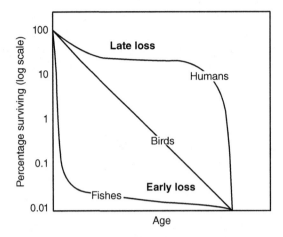

Figure 4.4 Generalized survivorship curves for mammals (e.g. fishermen!), birds and European hake (modified after Larkin, 1978). The prevailing mortality pattern for a species shapes its life history strategy, and should be taken into account in harvesting. Many fish have a very high fecundity, but the vast majority of offspring die long before maturity. On the other hand, fishermen (long-lived mammals) survive much longer, and instinctively protect the few offspring they produce. This habit, they may believe (erroneously), should also apply to the much more abundant offspring of high-fecundity fishes.

after a four- to five-year pause during hostilities, after which it was presumably believed that there was no shortage of mature fish. This is not the case nowadays in many demersal fisheries.

As pointed out by Larkin (1978), our compulsion to protect juveniles of high-fecundity finfish that produce several hundred thousand eggs per mature female per year may stem from our strong human instinct to protect the 1–5+ offspring we produce in a lifetime. Figure 4.4, modified from Larkin (1978), contrasts the life history strategies of fish and mankind very clearly. For fishers to assume that protection of all the spawning products of a highly fecund fish is a top priority, while not protecting the few individuals surviving to maturity, seems illogical. It is encouraged by the infrequent use of fecundity data in fish stock assessment. Recognizing that for many highly fecund commercial species, the probability of a female egg reaching maturity and spawning is of the order of 1:250,000+, which makes arrival at maturity a low-probability achievement, with obvious negative implications for fishery managers.

The long-term disadvantages of harvesting older fish

Penttila and Gifford (1976) described the growth rate of cod from Georges Bank by von Bertalanffy parameters $K = 0.120$ and $L_\infty = 148.1$ cm. Compared with this recent study, in 1605 English explorers off the New England coast (reported in Bakeless, 1961) caught cod 'three to five feet in length' (91–152 cm, or close to a modern estimate of L_∞) 'so fast as the hook came down' (Bakeless, 1961: 211), noting that, 'He is a very bad fisher cannot kill in one day with his hook and line, one, two, or three hundred cods' (Bakeless, 1961: 222). This simple contrast with later data on maximum sizes suggests that the average size of cod taken on handlines on the virgin stock was close to the theoretically maximum size (L_∞) nowadays, hence the value of L_∞ must have been higher. Evidently, the average size and abundance of cod in the Northwest Atlantic have both substantially declined over the last 400 years. Over this period, intensive fisheries for mature cod have exerted a continual selection pressure, removing potentially larger specimens in favour of relatively stunted, early-maturing fish.

An experimental confirmation of this selective effect by fisheries on mature individuals was demonstrated in an aquarium by Conover et al. (2005) for a small species, the silverside. He showed that selective harvesting of larger individuals over several generations resulted in progeny, which, as adults were significantly smaller and weaker, produced smaller and fewer eggs, and had reduced foraging and predator avoidance capabilities than their ancestors. This is attributed to selective harvesting of mature animals, leading to a genome for a species that reaches maturity earlier at a smaller size.

The few large surviving spawners of fisheries for adults have been referred to as BOFFFFs ('big, old, fat, female, fertile fish'), and according to Hixon et al. (2014: 2172), they 'not only produce far more eggs than smaller females, even after accounting for body size, but also often produce larger or better provisioned eggs and larvae that grow faster and are better capable of withstanding starvation'. BOFFFFs also enjoy longer spawning seasons, can outlive unfavourable reproduction conditions, and be ready to 'spawn profusely' next season – a strategy referred to as the 'storage effect'. It seems from this that there is a major selective advantage in avoiding full exploitation of older spawners.

Estimating yield and fecundity per recruit when M declines with age

A simple equivalent to the yield/recruit model is to use the Thompson-Bell calculation (Ricker, 1975) and substitute a vector of M_t for the constant parameter value M. One application of this can be envisaged: to simulate a 'balanced harvesting' approach where F's for older fish are kept at a lower level than for younger fish, in parallel to what happens to M with age. A marked contrast exists between the results, both with the constant M assumption and when a more realistic M-at-age vector is used in overall yield per recruit, or in gear selectivity calculations. Here, due to high predation rates on juveniles, the summed yield per recruit is obviously much lower for survivors of a given number of age 0+ pre-recruits, and the optimum mesh size is smaller (Caddy, 2015).

As noted by Schmalz et al. (2016: 1), there is a 'fundamental conflict between harvesting fish and conserving their biomass'. The current study uses data on

F-at-age to complete the life cycle, and seeks a limited fishing mortality that results in an intergenerational equivalence between the spawning potentials of successive generations. The basic requirement for fishery conservation is that the net effect of all fisheries on the stock should not closely approach or exceed what can be called a 'Charnov equilibrium point'. This occurs when the number of mature females in the maternal generation (and their net fecundity or number of offspring) is the same in the following generation. Since estimating the number of mature females in successive years offers practical difficulties, the simulation in Caddy (2015) compared the number of 0+ pre-recruits in the fishery in successive years. This situation can be visualized in Figure 4.5.

The high predation rates on a 'cloud' of larval and juvenile stages of high-fecundity species not only contribute to the low probability of individual survival to maturity, but planktonic feeding by small fish on abundant small particle food means that they themselves contribute to the trophic requirements of later life history stages, often cannibalistic. Obviously, the major unknown for most species is the mortality rate of the eggs and planktonic larvae. A range of species-specific mortality rates between egg and the end of the larval stage have been estimated (for some examples, see Dahlberg, 1979). Generalizing from these data, pelagic marine fishes seem to have the lowest survival rates of eggs

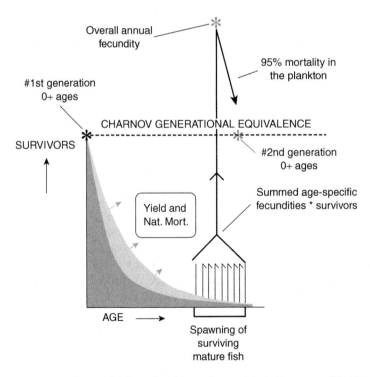

Figure 4.5 Illustrating the role of fecundity, and its influence on life history survival of successive generations of pre-recruits, using the reciprocal model for M_t, to define the Charnov equilibrium point between successive generations.

and larvae. Some freshwater fishes show higher values, resembling the estimate from egg to pre-recruit for another hake species of 95–97 per cent mortality (Garavelli et al., 2012), which is used here. Given order of magnitude estimates for mortality of eggs and pre-recruits, together with recent estimates of fishing mortality on a cohort, and natural mortality rates at age coming from the reciprocal model (Caddy, 2015), this allows a preliminary model of a closed life history. It also gives a tentative estimate of the Charnov equilibrium point (i.e. the intergenerational ratio between pre-recruit numbers in successive years). Apart from its management implications, this type of simulation confirms that integrating estimates of F-at-age for mature fishes with the reciprocal model for natural mortality rate at age offers an insight into the reproductive constraints on a population. Even though density-dependent effects prevent specific estimates of future reproductive success, an estimate of the relative values of reproductive output for each fishing strategy is useful in judging how close that strategy takes us to the output for the next generation imposed by age-specific fecundities and natural mortalities at age.

Indirect mortalities of juvenile fish from fishing reduce yield from the population

Research in Northern Europe and North America has shown that there is often a significant mortality of small fish after passing through trawl cod ends. Exhaustion from swimming in the trawl mouth, plus physical damage in the net, leads to the loss of glycogen reserves and increases the risk of predation subsequent to escapement. Minimum legal sizes of capture and/or of landing also increase discarding of dead juvenile fish. These factors render doubtful the assumption that all escaping small fish will survive and contribute to a higher yield at a larger mesh size.

Protecting juveniles can best be accomplished by reducing seasonal effort over nursery areas and prohibiting discarding (fish are assumed to be dead once on deck). Damage to escapees while passing through the mesh is the conventional cause of indirect fishing mortality, but higher predation on weakened juveniles after escapement through the cod end also results in higher fishing mortality rates than are easily measurable. Studies on survival of juvenile fishes through cod end meshes in the North Atlantic (e.g. Sangster et al., 1996) showed that physiological stress occurs due to exhaustion of glycogen reserves after prolonged swimming in front of the foot rope of a trawl (mentioned in a review by Caddy and Seijo, 2011). Simulations with these higher incidental mortalities of juveniles reaching 20 per cent or more for the first age group show that the advantages of increasing the mesh size of trawls are likely to be much lower than when incidental, uncaptured mortalities are ignored.

Indirect mortalities of juveniles

Precision navigational and fish-finding equipment, and trawls designed to avoid hang-ups on rocky bottom, allow fishing in 'high-risk' areas near outcrops (i.e. in the foraging arenas of the organisms sheltering there). This high-risk strategy also leads to a high frequency of 'net hangs' in rocky areas, as documented by Link and Demarest (2003). Outcrops strung with non-biodegradable synthetic netting that 'ghost fish' resident ichthyofauna have been documented. They can only be partly counteracted by a properly regulated MPA, by measures to recover lost nets, or by regulations banning equipment designed for rough bottom to avoid using dragged nets in rocky refugia.

Balanced harvesting

Targeting mature fish with a high exploitation rate is 'unnatural' in that a high fishing rate on adults is incompatible with the lower natural risk of death due to predation the older cohorts are adapted to. A 'utopian' strategy for food web exploitation to counter this risk was suggested by Caddy and Sharp (1986), namely to harvest a constant proportion of the total production of each of 1, 2, 3 . . . *n* component species, or *n* component age groups, so that an exploitation ratio, E_n, is maintained constant:

$$E_n = F_1 / \left(F_1 + M_1 \right) = F_2 / \left(F_2 + M_2 \right) = ...F_n / \left(F_n + M_n \right) \tag{4.1}$$

This philosophy, which exploits juveniles at a higher rate than adults, is now called 'balanced harvesting' (BH) (for more details, see Garcia et al., 2011; Law et al., 2012; Kolding et al., 2016). Thus, the harvest rates for components of a food web should remain proportional to a species or age group's natural mortality rate at size *n*, to keep the exploitation ratio, E_n, for all species or ages as closely as possible constant.

A simulation of a theoretical population subject to different exploitation strategies by Law et al. (2012) showed that if the number of fish caught in a given size class was kept proportional to that class size in the population's size spectrum, this strategy produced the highest sustainable yields, with the least disruption to the theoretical population. However, Suuronen (2005) concluded that achieving true balanced harvesting, mixes of gears and fishing methods would have to be much more selective; this would pose significant engineering challenges. Some serious practical difficulties exist in applying BH, especially as a multispecies management measure. In all cases, it depends for its success on locating empirical but safe limit reference points for F_t / M_t, and the ability to allocate the catch by different fleet/gear components to achieve it. Obviously, gear selectivities have to be known over a species size range and age, and gear-specific harvests kept in balance. However, this general approach seems worthwhile in single-species fisheries, and for modelling purposes allows F_t's to be defined in terms of an M-at-age model such as discussed here.

A first step towards introducing a form of balanced harvest in practice would be possible if a market for juvenile fishes and by-catch species already existed. This was developed in the past in the Mediterranean and tropical areas, where local cuisines appreciate small fish. Promoting better use of by-catch and juvenile fishes where markets for juveniles exist could be part of a feasible strategy for single-species fisheries. The question remains as to whether balanced harvesting is feasible. The main criterion, as described below, is how to compare different overall allocation strategies for realizing the Charnov equilibrium in a multi-gear approach. Several strategies for reducing the risk of reproductive overfishing in a multi-gear single-species fishery were tested to judge how effective they were in avoiding management approaches that do not take into account the Charnov equilibrium.

Simulating harvesting strategies in a multi-gear single-species fishery

Even if juveniles are unfished, high levels of natural mortality imply that few age 1+ fish survive predation, and the probability of a recruit reaching sexual maturity is very low. A fishery for juveniles is, for the most part, harvesting fish that under natural conditions would not subsequently survive predation. In fact, a moderate exploitation of juveniles could reduce pressure on their food resources and allow the survivors to grow more rapidly to a reproductive age, as implied by the observations of Papaconstantinou and Stergiou (1988) of density-dependent growth.

Different harvesting strategies for single-species fisheries have been investigated with estimates of the fishing mortality rate on age groups harvested by different fishing gears, using the method of length cohort analysis for Gulf of Lions hake (e.g. Aldebert et al., 1993). My objective was to see if BH could conserve spawning potential by fishing strategy alone in a single-species multi-gear fishery, with a multi-gear fishery similar to Figure 4.6, using calculations of the form given in Table 4.1.

Fish age composition and resulting fishing mortality vectors are shown in Table 4.1, assuming that spawning occurs after harvesting. The hypothetical example in Figure 4.6 simulates a multi-gear fishery for hake, where a fine mesh trawl fishery is aimed at juveniles, and three other gears harvest progressively larger animals surviving fisheries on smaller individuals, a commonplace situation. Parameters used for these estimates are included in Table 4.2. The key issue is how could management measures for the four fisheries determine catch allocations for each gear component, and affect the overall fecundity of the stock?

Fishing mortalities corresponding to balanced harvesting

One advantage to simulating fisheries resembling balanced harvesting is that fishing mortalities are predefined by the natural mortality vector. Certainly, fishing mortalities at age can be varied, but fitting a large number of different models for each of the M-at-age vectors used would open up many more options to explore than can be discussed here. Adding stochasticity would render the current task of illustrating the principles involved still more difficult.

The approach adopted was to start with 50,000 female age 0+ pre-recruits subject to age-specific natural and fishing mortality rates throughout their life history, using the rationale of Caddy (2015), notably to follow female survivors through four contemporaneous fisheries with different relative fishing mortalities

Table 4.1 Setting overall F-at-age (F) = M_t for female hake except for age 1 (see ★)

Age (yr)	M-at-age	Small mesh trawl	Standard trawl	Gill net	Long-line	Net F-at-age	No. female survive	Individual weight (g)	Catch (kg)	Residual biomass (kg)	Spawn biomass (kg)	Fecundity (No*10⁴)	# Eggs (No*10⁶)
							50,000						
1	1.54	1.54				0.31★	7,832	16		126		0	
2	0.84	0.42	0.42			0.84	1,450	111	354	161		0	
3	0.61	0.30	0.30			0.61	429	308	157	132		0	
4	0.49	0.25	0.25			0.49	160	593	80	95		0	
5	0.42	0.14	0.14	0.14		0.42	69	937	43	64	64	36	25
6	0.38		0.13	0.13	0.13	0.38	32	1,311	24	43	43	50	16
7	0.34		0.11	0.11	0.11	0.34	16	1,691	14	28	28	64	10
8	0.33			0.16	0.16	0.33	9	2,059	8	18	18	77	7
9	0.30			0.15	0.15	0.30	5	2,405	5	12	12	90	4
10	0.28			0.14	0.14	0.28	3	2,720	3	7	7	101	3
11	0.27			0.13	0.13	0.27	2	3,003	2	5	5	111	2
12	0.26				0.26	0.26	1	3,254	1	3	3	120	1

Net F of age 1 is set at F(1) = 0.2M(1), assumed caused by indirect fishing mortality (no landings).

SUMMARY:

Wt Catch: 691 kg
Residual Biomass: 694 kg
Spawning Biomass: 180 kg
% biomass mature fish: 24.9%
No. female eggs: 34.1*10⁶
female eggs/ # 0+ of parental generation: 683
With 3% larval survival = 24 age 0+ of next generation.
With 5% larval survival = 34 age 0+ of next generation.

Note: Overall, F's are divided equally between gears. Catch weights at age, residual spawning biomasses (calculated after harvest) and number of eggs produced are summed over age. The total fecundity is expressed per age 0+ pre-recruited females of the maternal generation (50,000). The number of age 0+ females surviving planktonic life is then calculated for two hypothetical larval survival rates, 3 per cent and 5 per cent.

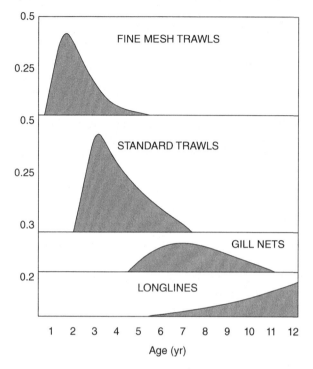

Figure 4.6 Diagram illustrating hypothetical multi-gear fisheries for hake that harvest the stock at relatively low fishing mortality rates by age for each gear; similar to the situation described by Aldebert et al. (1993) for this fishery in French Mediterranean waters.

Table 4.2 Parameters of yield/fecundity calculation

von Bertalanffy	W∞:	4696.4
von Bertalanffy	K:	0.185
Reciprocal M	A:	0.142
Reciprocal M	B:	1.403
Length–weight	a:	0.0041
Length–weight	b:	3.192

at age, to a maximum of 12 years. For mature hake (5–12 years), age-specific fecundities provided by Cesarini (1994) were summed over all mature fish surviving harvests. To gain an estimate of the number of female age 0+ survivors completing the life cycle from the initial fecundity (assuming 50:50 sex ratio), the estimated planktonic survival rate of a South African species of hake was employed (Garavelli et al., 2012). In this first calculation, the fishing mortalities were low. After larval life in the plankton, the 3,207 eggs/initial number of age

0+ fish of the parental generation had been reduced to 96–160 age 0+ female fish of the second generation – corresponding to a considerable increase in numbers.

Assuming the fishing rate for a given age, i, when summed over all gears, g, equals the natural mortality rate for each age, this is expressed by: $\Sigma F_{i,g} = M_i$. Summed F_i's for all gears set equal to M_i effectively corresponds to balanced harvesting of all age groups. Figure 4.8 shows that for Mediterranean hake, this would set the age 1 harvest rate by the first gear as high as $F_1 = M_1 = 1.54$. This 'pure' BH strategy reduces mature fish to 26 per cent of the biomass, and the reproductive potential from this strategy was 6–10 times the parental population of age 0+ fish (i.e., although this is above the Charnov equilibrium point, it corresponds to only a modest yield of 584 kg) (see Figure 4.7).

Figure 4.8 shows the output when catching age 1 fish is discouraged (as in the fishery off Livorno, Italy), but with the same balanced mortalities for all

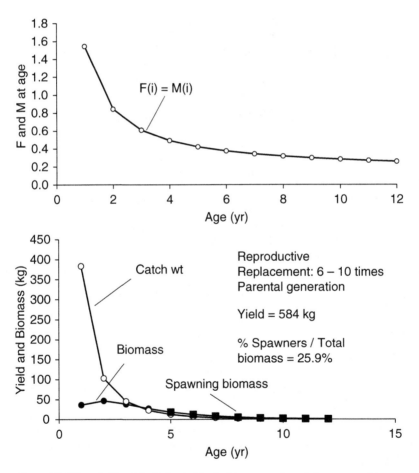

Figure 4.7 (Above): $F_i = M_i$; (Below): Catch, biomass and surviving mature biomass at age for a hake population subject to balanced harvesting of all ages (F_i's = M_i's).

other ages. An incidental mortality of age 1 fish by the small mesh gear, and discards from it, is hypothesized to occur at a level $F_1 = 0.2 \cdot M_1$, but there was no accumulation of age 1 fish in the corresponding yield (i.e. an indirect fishing mortality on age 1 fish was applied that did not show up as yield). A yield of 689 kg was accomplished, and a generous reproductive replacement of 20–34 times the parental 0+ group, with 26 per cent of the biomass consisting of mature fish resulted (i.e. avoiding retention of the first age group, but applying BH for older fish seemed to be a reproductively favourable strategy).

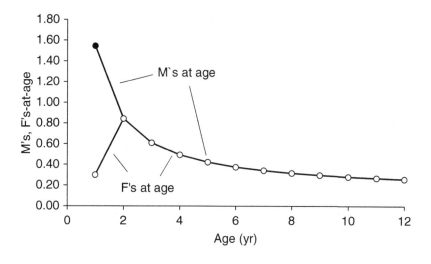

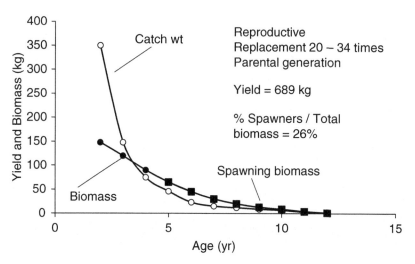

Figure 4.8 (Above): M's and F's at age; (below): Catch, biomass and mature biomass at age for a hake population subject to balanced harvesting of all age groups (F_i's = M_i's), except age 1 fishes, which are killed incidentally at $F_1 = 0.2M_1$ but not landed.

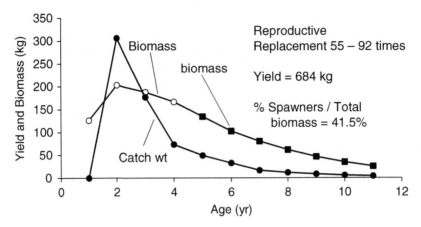

Figure 4.9 Catch, biomass and mature biomass at age for a hake population subject
to balanced harvesting of all age groups (F_i's = M_i's), except age 1 fishes,
which are killed incidentally at $F_1 = 0.2M_1$ but not landed. No longline
fishery is carried out, reducing mortalities on mature fish.

The example shown in Figure 4.9 illustrates the situation when both capture of age 1 is discouraged and a longline fishery is prohibited. A moderate to
high yield, a high reproductive replacement, and a high percentage of mature
fish in the biomass result.

Figure 4.10 illustrates the relative yields by the four gears when balanced
harvest without catches of age 1 was effected. These relative yields could be

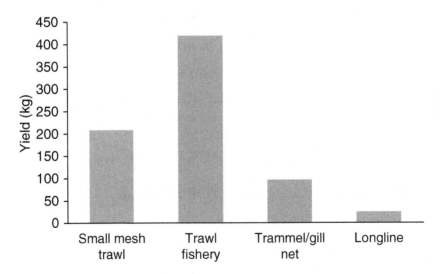

Figure 4.10 Relative yields by gears with balanced harvesting when no age 1 fish
were landed.

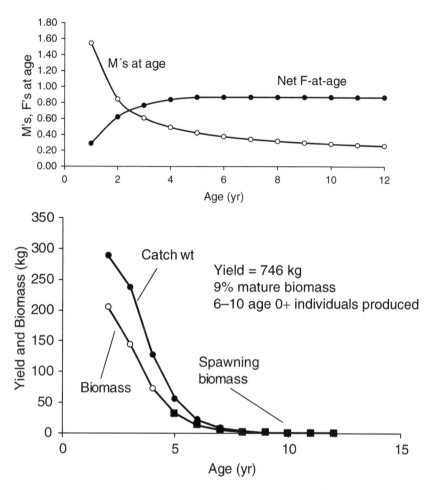

Figure 4.11 (Above): showing a conventional selection ogive for the trawl, with F rising to a plateau, and the reciprocal M-at-age applied. (Below) Yield and biomass at age shown when harvesting is mediated by a conventional trawl selective ogive with preferential harvesting of larger fish.

considered as typical of the relative catch allocations by gear needed to achieve this result (assuming that all catches of age 1 can be avoided, which is not necessarily possible in practice). Figure 4.11 shows the results of harvesting when using the conventional strategy of targeting adult fish. Although the yield is good, only a small spawning biomass remains, with a low Charnov ratio.

Comments on the harvesting strategies tested

Seeking an optimal strategy by the above mechanism would require many more simulations than presented here, but my intention was to explore the methodology (though seeking an optimum for reproductive capacity is clearly a priority). This approach allowed testing each harvesting strategy for its reproductive efficiency as well as for total yield/recruit.

Among the safe strategies found (see Table 4.3) were the original data set of *F*'s at age by gear described first, and the balanced harvest example eliminating capture of age 1 fish while retaining the BH criterion for other ages, and better still when the gear taking the oldest fish was eliminated. A BH strategy taking age 1 fish did not appear to be precautionary, as the yield was dominated numerically by age 1 fish, which are less marketable. The highest percentage of mature biomass (54.3 per cent) surviving was found by setting the sum of fishing mortality at all ages equal to the summed (low value) at ages for the longline fishery. This yielded 721 kg and provided a high percentage increase of recruits, well above the Charnov equilibrium point. It showed that fishing young fish with a lower mortality rate of spawners can yield positive results. Further testing of the balanced harvest approach by setting $F_i = b \cdot M_i$, where $b < 1$, would probably provide high yields, a higher residual spawning biomass, and a high survival rate to the next generation.

Modelling a single-species fishery by balanced harvesting strategy assuming a reciprocal model for M_i does not alone prevent overfishing, and could result in an overall catch largely made up of small juveniles. Nonetheless, seeking to reduce mortalities of age 1 fish to a minimum gave positive results. It seems that the different strategies that were tested vary significantly in their resulting yield and reproductive success, and the introduction of a spawning refugium would be a supplementary precautionary measure.

Table 4.3 Statistics for five runs using the calculation framework in Table 4.1

Key statistics	Original F vector used	Balanced harvesting (BH)	BH, but Age 1 not Harvested	ΣF_{ig} equal for all ages	BH No age 1 landed; no LL fishery
% biomass mature females/total biomass	45.4	25.9	0.28	38.3	47.6
Eggs produced/ 500,000 age 0+ fish	319,863,577	19,854,303	141,857,177	209,973,740	311,053,575
Female eggs produced/ 500,000 age 0+ fish	159,931,789	9,927,151	70,928,589	104,986,895	155,526,787
Female eggs/age 0+ parental generation	3,199	199	1,419	2,100	3,111
Number age 0+ recruits/ 0+ parental generation	96–170	6–10	43–71	63–105	93–156
Total yield (kg)	810	584	979	683	831

Spawner–recruit and life history models

The relationship between adult spawning biomass and recruitment survival discussed in this study is an attempt to avoid reproductive overfishing and define a limit reference point based on spawning potential and natural M-at-age. This is not to deny the density dependence evident in spawner–recruit relationships, although for some organisms environmental factors may be more important (e.g. Caddy and Defeo, 1996). In practice, the use of spawner–recruit models is inevitable if there are a lack of data on earlier life history stages (i.e. the egg → larvae → recruit sequence passed through by early life history stages is poorly defined by most conventional fishery data). A further possible deficiency of the SRR relationship is evident in the current century when climate change appears to be underway (i.e. defining the abundance of recruits as a function of a history of spawning in earlier years implies that an equilibrium relationship exists between spawner and recruit data collected in different years). The productivity per unit stock size is assumed to remain unchanged over time. If global climate changes are occurring, this seems a weak assumption.

A further problem with the exclusive use of SRRs was revealed by analyses carried out on finfish SRRs by Myers (2001). These showed that it is unsafe to assume that spawning populations can be reduced by more than 60–70 per cent and recover easily, and even these figures may be dangerously optimistic (Caddy and Agnew, 2004). Walters and Kitchell (2001) suggested that finfish stock abundance should not fall below 50 per cent of the unfished spawning biomass. These studies sought limits to exploitation, and suggested that it might be wise to define a specific limit reference point (LRP) based on spawning success at the limits of population fecundity. The weak point of the fecundity/recruit approach is, of course, estimating a realistic value for survival in the plankton, but this approach seems more realistic when spawning stocks are reduced in size. The model described here will have to be addressed by research to better estimate realistic combinations of fecundity at age and larval mortalities in the plankton prior to recruitment, at which time stochasticity can be realistically introduced and may explain some of the variance seen in SRRs. At the same time, errors in the typical larval survival rate in the plankton do not seriously compromise judgements as to the relative reproductive performance of different fishing strategies, which is the main objective here.

Aiming for a closed life cycle model of a life history

Several estimates of the Charnov ratio reported so far in this chapter appear improbably high (see values for the Charnov ratio specified in the earlier figures). A subsequent review of the literature on fish biology showed other factors documented by fish biologists that have the potential to affect the Charnov ratio and ideally should be included in the model, even if only as provisional values. Factors that have been documented to influence the effective fecundity of marine finfish populations can be applied in succession to the closed life cycle model shown in Figure 4.12.

CLOSED LIFE CYCLE

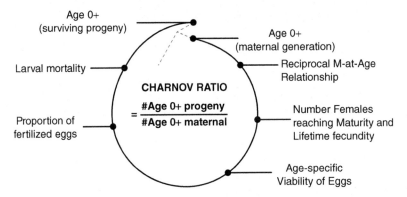

Figure 4.12 Diagram illustrating the closed life cycle model, and the value of the Charnov ratio derived from the ensemble of individual factors affecting the balance between effective fecundity and mortality.

Additional factors applied successively to this experimental version of a closed life history model for a hake stock are as follows.

Low viability of eggs produced by young spawners

Infertile eggs are a common feature of finfish spawning, and are often seen, for example, when artificial fertilization of eggs is practiced in aquaculture. The main factor impacting the quality of progeny in rockfish documented by Berkeley et al. (2004), and authors studying gadoids and other species of broadcast spawners, is the dominant effect of maternal age on egg size and on the rate of larval growth, the body mass of larvae, and their resistance to natural mortality. The viability of eggs produced by the first age group of spawners has been documented to be lower than for older females (e.g. Conover et al., 2005; Hixon et al., 2014). As these authors note, the low effective fecundity of many young spawners means that age truncation caused by harvesting the oldest spawners in a population should have a drastic impact on stock replacement. The values shown in Table 4.4 will be assumed arbitrarily for the net viability of eggs produced by younger spawners.

Infertile and unfertilized eggs

The overall fertility and proportion of eggs fertilized in open water spawnings may be much less than 100 per cent, and this may be partly responsible for the high fecundity needed by externally spawning fish and invertebrates if the Charnov ratio is to remain consistently above unity. Extensive laboratory and

Table 4.4 Relative egg viability at age

Age	Relative egg viability
5	0.25
6	0.5
7	0.75
8–12	1.0

open water studies were carried out in the early half of the twentieth century (summarized for gadoids by Markle and Waiwood, 1985), at a time when fecundity data were believed to be more important than they are considered to be nowadays. Much of the high variability in stock–recruit relationships, for example, would seem to be due to mortality in egg and larval stages, and this was originally seen as reflecting a 'relative inherent weakness of this point in the life chain' for species using external fertilization (Breder and Rosen, 1966). In fact, adaptations to reduce the proportion of unfertilized eggs have evolved; thus, Middaugh and Takita (1983) showed that Atlantic silversides spawn at low current velocities in order to reduce milt dispersion. Unfertilized eggs sink, hence there is only a short time interval available for fertilization in surface waters, and unfertilized eggs may be common. For a provisional idea of the relative impact these factors might have, they are built into the model, so that to the outputs shown in Table 4.5, two other factors are added:

- Hypothetical egg viabilities are low following age at maturity, but from the literature are shown to increase with age of spawners.
- An overall limited probability of 40 per cent egg hatching is applied.

As shown in Table 4.5, these reduce the Charnov ratio. Obviously, the input values can be easily modified in further model runs based on better data or alternative assumptions.

The tentative conclusions drawn from Table 4.5 are that the values for the Charnov ratio under these assumptions would be low, but above unity for unmodified balanced harvesting, and would decline substantially if a low viability of early-age spawners were assumed, and more so if only 40 per cent of eggs were fertilized. The Charnov ratio remains high for balanced harvesting with age 1 conserved under all options, and also when no longline fishery is permitted. The Charnov ratio falls below unity for a fishery on adults if there is only 3 per cent larval survival and the hypothesized viability and fertilization rates apply. Again, indices of future recruitment fall to low levels when adults are targeted.

Refining a reproductive limit reference point

The closed life cycle procedure discussed here is seen as a precautionary method for judging relative spawning potentials from different harvest strategies, and is

Table 4.5 Charnov ratios for different fishing strategies with accumulation of mortality factors during egg production and fertilization

Larval survival in plankton	5%	3%	5%	3%	5%	3%
Fishing strategy	100% egg survival		Low viability eggs of early post-maturity females		Only 40% eggs fertilized	
Balanced harvesting	9.9	6.0	5.7	3.4	2.3	1.4
Balanced harvesting (but no age 1 caught)	34.2	20.5	19.4	11.7	7.8	4.7
Balanced harvesting (no age 1 caught and no longlining)	92	55.2	58.9	35.4	23.6	14.1
Targeting adults with an asymptotic F	8.3	5.0	3.1	1.9	1.2	0.7

aimed at establishing a limit reference point approach to avoiding reproductive overfishing. Over the longer term, this objective should be given a higher priority than maximizing current yield. Defining the Charnov equilibrium point for several fishing strategies should provide a relative judgement between them that can be supplemented by considering the proportion of older mature age groups in the uncaught biomass. What multiple of the Charnov equilibrium point is safe and should be aimed for is uncertain, but small values (e.g. < 5) are of doubtful precautionary value, since once a Charnov ratio of 1:1 between successive generations is approached, most eggs will be produced by first spawners (ages 5–6 for hake), and as explained, compared with older spawners, the viability of their eggs is in doubt.

Given a low Charnov ratio and a low percentage of mature fish surviving, a limited contribution from older spawners is likely in the next generation; hence, if trawl ogives are focused on catching old fish, this is likely to result in reduced recruitment. Calculations with the conventional trawl selection ogive resulted in 9 per cent of mature females surviving and the Charnov ratio dropping close to unity.

Discussion

Implementing adult refugia should lead to improved recruitment of juveniles

Under the refugium concept aimed at conserving the spawning stock, a ban on adding chains to towed gear (e.g. Bellman et al., 2005) or even abandoning trawling over rocky bottom would be a useful management strategy. Establishing a priority for modification of bottom gear without intensive at-sea controls by the management authority has obvious cost advantages for control and surveillance. The use of lighter towed gear also saves algal or coral growths needed for protection of juvenile fish nursery areas or adult refugia from trawl impacts. Measures to periodically remove lost tangle nets from rock outcrops will also be needed (a degree of control of smaller fishing boats using trammel nets to fish rocky areas for larger fish is also called for).

An early definition of a fisheries refugium was:

> A protected enclave within the original distribution range (elsewhere subject to catastrophic mortality by fishing), or a characteristic of the harvesting method, either of which allows a proportion of the stock to survive to maturity and replace the population as a whole.
>
> (Anthony and Caddy, 1980)

A management strategy using the refugium concept was contrasted by Caddy (2014) with the marine protected area (MPA) methodology. Briefly summarized, the boundaries to an MPA are specified in legislation and have to be constantly controlled (Bohnsack, 1996), while a refugium is characterized by its habitat type (e.g. Herrnkind et al., 1997), and may be protected by banning the gear modifications needed to operate there, and not by spatial regulations. In general, a refugium is much larger in extent than an MPA and requires less at-sea surveillance.

The focus of management closures in the Mediterranean (as elsewhere) has been on protecting a small proportion of nearshore 'nursery areas' for juveniles. It is arguable, however, that the presence of unfished natural refugia protecting older spawners explains why nearshore Mediterranean trawl fisheries remained relatively productive in the 1970s and 1980s, despite high rates of exploitation and limited regulatory control.

Effects of heavy bottom trawls and the survival of escapees

For almost a century, fishing fleets trawled the shallow shelf of the northern Mediterranean, but in the 1960s they also began to pursue offshore shrimp resources. Here, intensive trawling with reinforced gear in some areas led to marine shelf and slope habitats 'looking like ploughed fields', thus changing the habitat of deep shelf creatures, according to work published in *Nature* (Puig et al., 2012). Trawling destroys cover that fish need for protection and feeding, and damages biodiversity. Hence, trawling should be limited to flat sedimentary areas without dense epifauna/flora.

One feature of trawl fisheries rarely considered is that on rough bottom, the skipper will often find only a few trajectories without dangerous obstacles, and will repeat trawl sets over these. One relevant feature of this procedure is that such areas act as 'baited' zones, since damaged organisms attract more fish into the area. It also could result in frequent recaptures of small fishes that escaped from previous sets. The implications of this for indirect fishing mortality of escapees need further consideration.

Applying a more realistic M-at-age curve than 'constant M', such that M_t descends rapidly with age, (e.g. Caddy, 1991; Abella et al., 1997), reduces the advantages of a mesh size increase. It also shows that high mortality rates are inevitable during the early life history, hence the need to focus exploitation on age groups prior to maturity, and an even higher priority to establish some form of spatial protection for mature fish within the habitat range. Large increases in mesh size as a unique solution to management problems should be viewed with caution; incidental losses due to predation and indirect mortalities by trawling can be substantial, and a high level of predation on exhausted young fish escapees reduce the predicted advantages of delaying capture of escapees to a larger size, which depend on the assumption of 100 per cent survival of escapees. Protecting small post-recruits (and the essential epifauna/flora of nursery areas they depend on) could, in part, be achieved by seasonal or permanent closure to trawling of some key nursery areas.

From a bioeconomic perspective, the capture of a mature female terminates a train of future benefits from population replenishment by its offspring, which could exceed the value of the parental female captured (e.g. Prager et al., 1987; Caddy and Seijo, 2002). When based on a Y/R analysis with a declining natural mortality vector, a 40 mm minimum stretched mesh size appears to be a reasonable gear regulation for the Mediterranean trawl fishery. It should be supplemented by functioning offshore refugia, which ideally require a ban on rock hopper trawls, and/or an area closure. Inshore closures to protect epifauna and flora required for cover, and protection of post-recruits from predation, are also required in productive areas (Caddy, 2012). Protecting juvenile nursery areas seems a feasible option, rather than legislating for further increases in mesh size. More importantly, legislation to prevent the use of heavy dragged gear would probably be a practical measure. If established to regulate exploitation on adult fish, satellite tracking of vessels could protect offshore closures. From evidence reported by other researchers on the lower viability of eggs produced by first-time spawners, maintaining spawning refugia for older fish seems an important supplementary measure.

Common assessment procedures worldwide are still influenced by the assumptions of the Beverton and Holt paradigm. Summarized briefly, this asserts that postponing harvest until first maturity and avoiding capture of immature fishes will maximize Y/R and conserve fecundity. Recent experience, however, illustrates the importance of conserving older spawners and not relying on spawning by the first maturing age group. The difficulty of achieving this objective has been seriously underestimated. Many trawl fisheries catch but discard small fish, or damage small fish escaping from the trawl, and discarding small fish is an often-overlooked feature of trawling (Alverson et al., 1994). The major decline in mean age of many stocks due to overfishing, as documented by Pauly et al. (1998), means that it is impossible not to capture fish prior to maturity. Unregistered higher natural mortalities of small fish have led to errors in stock demography and its practical consequences. As a result of an incorrect 'constant M-at-age' assumption during yield and gear calculations, the mortalities at age of young fish escaping from fine mesh gears (either due to natural mortality and/or indirect fishing mortalities) have usually been underestimated.

This elaboration of a fecundity/recruit closed life history model could be useful, even if some parameter values such as larval mortality have to be based on informed guesswork. One conclusion of this study is that a high-fecundity strategy is in fact quite resistant to high mortality rates, even when expressed by an M-at-age vector and a relatively high fishing mortality, if it is assumed that 'wastage' of eggs results in no useful output for the species. The difficulty of reducing the next generation to a Charnov ratio of 1:1 suggests that the natural attrition of a cohort from egg to adult could be higher than assumed here. An alternative assumption that is interesting to consider is that external fertilization may be less complete, larval mortalities higher, a significant proportion of eggs infertile, or that egg consumption by zooplankton or pelagic fishes is programmed from an evolutionary perspective. A closed life history model nevertheless allows one to compare relative changes in any of the factors as they affect the Charnov ratio. The different rates of attrition in the egg and larval stages seem unlikely to be affected by the fishing or natural mortality rates applied to age groups already in the fishery; hence, the procedure could be useful for comparing different fishing strategies for their relative reproductive impact, and as a useful source of research directions for marine research.

Broader implications of the closed life history model

McKenzie (2002) noted that unusually low numbers of zooplankton and high abundances of phytoplankton were revealed by recent Northern Atlantic surveys. It seems improbable to account for this effect solely by climate warming. The author believed that these radical changes in the pelagic ecosystem could be largely an effect of recent events in the fisheries sector, as is also implicit in the results presented here. Although juvenile zooplankton are herbivorous, McKenzie (2002) reported that successful reproduction by adult zooplankton species requires some carnivorous feeding of zooplankton species prior to their spawning. The critical food source for zooplankton, at least in part, must consist of the energy-rich pelagic spawn of marine fish and invertebrates (Steidinger and Walker, 1984). As shown here, a miniscule percentage of eggs spawned survive planktonic life to become juveniles. At first sight, this means an almost complete 'wastage' of the 10–20 per cent of body weight of the spawning stock occurs when they extrude eggs and sperm into surface waters! For a moderately large fish stock, this would be somewhere in the range of 5,000 to 10,000 or more tons annually of energy-rich animal cells. From an evolutionary perspective, it makes little sense to suppose that this is all wastage, and not in some ways an advantage to the newly recruiting year class.

The sharp reduction in the proportion of older mature fish in stocks caused by overfishing must have drastically reduced spawning products as a dietary component for zooplankton, in addition to its direct impact on the survival of juvenile fish. We should also ask: Is the uniformly small size of pelagic fish eggs designed to facilitate zooplankton consumption, and if so, is predation of the large majority of fish eggs and sperm by zooplankton and pelagic fishes really a wastage? Or did the evolution of large oceanic populations of trophically linked pelagic and demersal fishes require the reservoir of trophic energy present in fish biomass to be periodically injected downwards into the trophic web? If so, does this enhance the biomass of zooplankton later used as food by hatched fish larvae? Such a mechanism for moving fish biomass downwards in the food web, although contrary to the conventional assumption of bottom-up movement of trophic resources, evidently exists. The consumption of tons of high energy food of the appropriate unit size ensures that a healthy population of copepod nauplii and other small zooplankton organisms are available by the time surviving fish larvae begin to feed.

The classical view of predation on planktonic eggs and larval fish is that a 'critical period' (Hjort, 1914; Cushing, 1990) exists, during which survival of larvae is at risk. For Baltic cod, Voss et al. (2001) found that after regular feeding of larvae begins, a bottleneck marked by a high mortality rate may occur after the larval yolk sack is depleted. This seems to be due to starvation caused by the local absence of a suitable size spectrum of food organisms. In addition to protection of the spawning stocks, fishery managers may consider that factors such as those just described, which affect the health of oceanic food webs, are of particular importance.

References

Abella, A.J., Caddy, J.F. and Serena, F. (1997). Do natural mortality and availability decline with age? An alternative yield paradigm for juvenile fisheries, illustrated by the hake *Merluccius merluccius* fishery in the Mediterranean. *Aquatic Living Resources*, 10: 257–269.

Abella, A.J., Serena, F. and Ria, M. (2005). Distributional response to variations in abundance over spatial and temporal scales for juveniles of European hake (*Merluccius merluccius*) in the Western Mediterranean Sea. *Fisheries Research*, 71: 295–310.

Aldebert, Y., Recasens, L. and Lleonart, J. (1993). Analysis of gear interactions in a hake fishery: the case of the Gulf of Lions (NW Mediterranean). *Scientia Marina*, 57: 207–217.

Alverson, D.L., Freeberg, M.H., Murawski, S.A. and Pope, J.G. (1994). A global assessment of fisheries bycatch and discards. *FAO Fisheries Technical Paper*, 339.

Anthony, V.C. and Caddy, J.F. (eds) (1980). Proceedings of the Canada–U.S. workshop on status of assessment science for N.W. Atlantic lobster (*Homarus americanus*) stocks (St. Andrews, N.B., 24–26 October 1978). Biological Station, St. Andrews, New Brunswick. *Canadian Technical Report of Fisheries and Aquatic Sciences*, 932.

Aranceta-Garza, F., Arreguín-Sánchez, F., Ponce-Díaz, G. and Seijo, J.C. (2016). Natural mortality of three commercial penaeid shrimps (*Litopenaeus vannamei, L. stylirostris* and *Farfantepenaeus californiensis*) of the Gulf of California using gnomonic time divisions. *Scientia Marina*, 80(2): 199–206.

Auster, P.J., Lindholm, J., Schaub, S., Funnell, G., Kaufman, L.S. and Valentine, P.C. (2003). Use of sand wave habitats by silver hake. *Journal Fish Biology*, 62(1): 1–246.

Bakeless, J. (1961). *America as Seen by Its First Explorers*. New York: Dover Publications.

Bellman, M.A., Heppell, S.A. and Goldfinger, C. (2005). Evaluation of a US west coast ground-fish habitat conservation regulation via analysis of spatial and temporal patterns of trawl fishing effort. *Canadian Journal of Fisheries and Aquatic Sciences*, 62: 2886–2900.

Berkeley, S.A., Chapman, C. and Sogard, S.M. (2004). Maternal age as a determinant of larval growth and survival in a marine fish, *Sebastes melanops*. *Ecology*, 85(5): 1258–1264.

Bohnsack, J.A. (1996). Marine reserves, zoning, and the future of fishery management. *Fisheries*, 21: 14–15.

Breder, C.M. and Rosen, D.E. (1966). *Modes of Reproduction in Fishes*. Neptune City, NJ: TFH Publications.

Burrough, P.A. (1981). Fractal dimensions of landscapes and other environmental data. *Nature*, 294: 240–242.

Caddy, J.F. (1986). Modelling stock–recruitment processes in Crustacea: some practical and theoretical perspectives. *Canadian Journal of Fisheries and Aquatic Science*, 43(11): 2330–2344.

Caddy, J.F. (1991). Death rates and time intervals: is there an alternative to the constant natural mortality axiom? *Reviews in Fish Biology and Fisheries*, 1: 109–138.

Caddy, J.F. (1996). Modeling natural mortality with age in short-lived invertebrate populations: definition of a strategy of gnomonic time division. *Aquatic Living Resources*, 9: 197–207.

Caddy, J.F. (2003). Scaling elapsed time: an alternative approach to modelling crustacean moulting schedules? *Fisheries Research*, 63: 73–84.

Caddy, J.F. (2007). *Marine Habitat and Cover: Their Importance for Productive Coastal Fishery Resources*. Oceanographic Methodology Series. Paris: UNESCO Publishing.

Caddy, J.F. (2011). How artificial reefs could reduce the impacts of bottlenecks in reef fish productivity within natural fractal habitats. In: S.A. Bortone, B.F. Pereira, G. Fabi and S. Otake (eds), *Artificial Reefs in Fisheries Management*. Boca Raton, FL: CRC Press, pp. 45–64.

Caddy, J.F. (2012). Why do assessments of demersal stocks largely ignore habitat? *ICES Journal of Marine Science*, 71(8): 2114–2126.

Caddy, J.F. (2013). Fractal environments select for high von Bertalanffy K's in crevice-dwelling fishes. *Ciencia Pesquera*, 21(2): 49–56.

Caddy, J.F. (2014). Why do assessments of demersal stocks largely ignore habitat? *ICES Journal of Marine Science: Journal du Conseil*, 71(8): 2114–2126.

Caddy, J.F. (2015). Criteria for sustainable fisheries on juveniles illustrated for Mediterranean hake: control the juvenile harvest, and safeguard spawning refugia to rebuild population fecundity. *Scientia Marina*, 79(3): 287–299.

Caddy, J.F. and Agnew, D.J. (2004). An overview of recent global experience with recovery plans for depleted marine resources and suggested guidelines for recovery planning. *Reviews in Fish Biology and Fisheries*, 14: 43–112.

Caddy, J.F. and Defeo, O. (1996). Fitting the exponential and logistic surplus yield models with mortality data: some explorations and new perspectives. *Fisheries Research*, 25: 39–62.

Caddy, J.F. and Mahon, R. (1995). Reference points for fisheries management. *FAO Fisheries Technical Paper*, 347.

Caddy, J.F. and Seijo, J.C. (2002). Reproductive contributions foregone with harvesting: a conceptual framework. *Fisheries Research*, 59(1–2): 17–30.

Caddy, J.F. and Seijo, J.C. (2011) Destructive fishing practices by bottom gears: a broad review of research and practice. *Ciencia Pesquera*, 19: 5–58.

Caddy, J.F and Sharp, G.D. (1986). An ecological framework for marine fishery investigations. *FAO Fisheries Technical Paper*, 283.

Caddy, J.F. and Stamatopoulos, C. (1991). Mapping growth and mortality rates of crevice-dwelling organisms onto a perforated surface: the relevance of 'cover' to the carrying capacity of natural and artificial habitats. *Estuarine Coastal and Shelf Science*, 31(1): 87–106.

Cesarini, A. (1994). *Biologia reproduttiva di Merluccius merluccius (Linée 1758) nel Mar Tirreno Settentrionale*. University of Pisa thesis.

Charnov, E.L. (1993). *Life History Invariants: Some Explorations of Symmetry in Evolutionary Ecology*. New York: Oxford University Press.

Conover, D.O., Arnott, S.A., Walsh, M.R. and Munch, S.B. (2005). Darwinian fishery science: lessons from the Atlantic silverside (*Menidia menidia*). *Canadian Journal of Fisheries and Aquatic Sciences*, 62(4): 730–737.

Cushing, D.H. (1990). Plankton production and year class strength in fish populations: an update of the match/mismatch hypothesis. *Advances in Marine Biology*, 26: 249–293.

Dahlberg, M.D. (1979). A review of survival rates of fish eggs and larvae in relation to impact assessments. *Marine Fisheries Review*, 41: 1–12.

Doumenge, F. (1968). Hydrologie, biologie et peche en Mediterranee occidentale. *Bull. de la societe Languedocienne de Geographie*, 2(4).

Garavelli R., Gross, A. and Grote, B. (2012). Modeling the dispersal of Cape hake ichthyoplankton. *Journal of Plankton Research*, 34(8): 655–669.

Garcia, S., Kolding, J., Rice, J., Rochet, M.J., Zhou, S., Arimoto, T., et al. (2011). *Selective Fishing and Balanced Harvest in Relation to Fisheries and Ecosystem Sustainability*. Report of a scientific workshop organized by the IUCN-CEM Fisheries Expert Group (FEG) and the European Board of Conservation and Development (EBCD) in Nagoya (Japan), 14–16 October 2010. Available at: http://archimer.ifremer.fr/doc/00026/13697/ (accessed 4 January 2018).

Giménez-Hurtado, E., Arreguín-Sanchez, F. and Lluch-Cota, S.E. (2009). Natural mortality rates during life history stages of the red grouper on Campeche Bank, Mexico. *North American Journal of Fisheries Management*, 29: 216–221.

Herrnkind, W.F., Butler IV, M.J., Hunt, J.H. and Childress, M. (1997). Role of physical refugia: implications from a sponge die-off in a lobster nursery in Florida. *Australian Journal of Marine and Freshwater Research*, 48: 759–769.

Hixon, M.A., Johnson, D.W. and Sogard, S.M. (2014). BOFFFFs: on the importance of conserving old-growth age structure in fishery populations. *ICES Journal of Marine Science*, 71(8): 2171–2185.

Hjort, J. (1914). Fluctuations in the year classes of important food fishes. *Journal du Conseil Permanent International pour l'Exploraton de la Mer*, 164: 73–76.

Kolding, J., Garcia, S.M., Zhou, S. and Heino, M. (2016). Balanced harvest: utopia, failure, or a functional strategy? *ICES Journal of Marine Science*, 73(6): 1616–1622.

Larkin, P.A. (1978). Fisheries management: an essay for ecologists. *Annual Review of Ecology and Systematics*, 9: 57–73.

Law, R., Plank, M.J. and Kolding, J. (2012). On balanced exploitation of marine ecosystems: results from dynamic size spectra. *ICES Journal of Marine Science*, 69(4): 602–614.

Link, J.S. and Demarest, C. (2003). Trawl hangs, baby fish, and closed areas: a win-win scenario. *ICES Journal of Marine Science*, 60: 930–938.

Markle, D.F. and Waiwood, K.G. (1985). Fertilization failure in Gadids: aspects of its measurement. *Journal of Northwest Atlantic Fishery Science*, 6: 87–93.

Martínez-Aguilar, S., Arreguín-Sánchez, F. and Morales-Bojórquez, E. (2005). Natural mortality and life history stage duration of Pacific sardine (*Sardinops caeruleus*) based on gnomonic time divisions. *Fisheries Research*, 71: 103–114.

McKenzie, D. (2002). *Fish Eggs: The Perfect Food? The Starving Ocean*. Available at: www.fisherycrisis.com/fisheggs.html (accessed 4 January 2018).

Middaugh, D.P. and Takita, T. (1983). Tidal and diurnal spawning cues in the Atlantic silverside, *Menidia menidia*. *Environmental Biology of Fishes*, 8(2): 97–104.

Munro, J.L. (1983). Caribbean coral reef fishery resources. *ICLARM Studies and Reviews*, 7.

Myers, R.A. (2001). Stock and recruitment: generalizations about maximum reproductive rate, density dependence, and variability using meta-analytic approaches. *ICES Journal of Marine Science*, 58: 937–951.

Papaconstantinou, C. and Stergiou, K. (1988). On the density-dependent regulation of the 0 group hake (*Merluccius merluccius*, L. 1758) in the Patriakos Gulf, Greece. FAO Fisheries Report, 394: 168–171.

Pauly, D., Christensen, V., Dalsgaard, J., Froese, R. and Torres, F. (1998). Fishing down marine food webs. *Science*, 279: 860–863.

Penttila, J.A. and Gifford, V.M. (1976). Growth and mortality rates for cod from the Georges Bank and Gulf of Maine Areas, ICNAF. *Research Bulletin*, 12: 29–36.

Prager, M.H., O'Brien, J.F. and Saila, S.B. (1987). Using lifetime fecundity to compare management strategies: a case history for striped bass. *North American Journal Fisheries Management*, 7: 403–409.

Puig, R., Canals, M., Company, J.B., Martin, J., Amblas, D., Lastras, G., et al. (2012). Ploughing the deep-sea floor. *Nature*, 489: 286–289.

Ramírez-Rodríguez, M. and Arreguín-Sánchez, F. (2003). Life history stage duration and natural mortality for the pink shrimp *Farfantepenaeus duorarum* (Burkenroad, 1939) in the southern Gulf of Mexico, using the gnomonic model for time division. *Fisheries Research*, 60: 45–51.

Ricker, W.E. (1975). *Computation and Interpretation of Biological Statistics of Fish Populations*. Ottawa: Bulletin Fisheries Research Board of Canada.

Royer, J., Péries, P. and Robin, J.P. (2002). Stock assessments of English Channel loliginid squids: updated depletion methods and new analytical methods. *ICES Journal of Marine Science*, 59: 445–457.

Sale, P.F. (1978). Coexistence of coral reef fishes: a lottery for living space. *Environmental Biology of Fishes*, 3: 85–102.

Sangster, G.I., Lehmann, K. and Breen, M. (1996). Commercial fishing experiments to assess the survival of haddock and whiting after escape from four sizes of diamond mesh cod-ends. *Fisheries Research*, 25: 323–345.

Schmalz, P.J., Luehring, M., Dan Rose, J., Hoenig, J.M. and Treml, M.K. (2016). Visualizing trade-offs between yield and spawners per recruit as an aid to decision making. *North American Journal of Fisheries Management*, 36: 1–10.

Sparholt, H. (1990). Improved estimates of the natural mortality rates of nine commercially important species included in the North Sea multispecies VPA model. *Journal du Conseil Permanent International pour l'Exploraton de la Mer*, 46: 211–223.

Steidinger, K.A. and Walker, L.M. (1984). *Marine Plankton Life Cycle Strategies*. Boca Raton, FL: CRC Press.

Suuronen, P. (2005). Mortality of fish escaping trawl gears. *FAO Fisheries Technical Paper*, 478.

Voss, R., Hinrichsen, H.H. and Wieland, K. (2001). Model-supported estimation of mortality rates in Baltic cod (*Gadus morhua callarias* L.) larvae: the varying impact of 'critical periods'. *BMC Ecology*, 1: 4.

Walters, C. and Kitchell, J.F. (2001). Cultivation/depensation effects on juvenile survival and recruitment: implications for the theory of fishing. *Canadian Journal of Fisheries and Aquatic Sciences*, 58(1): 39–50.

5 Bioeconomics of ocean acidification

Juan Carlos Seijo and Raul Villanueva

Introduction

Ocean acidification is an additional stressor to many fisheries of today, mostly those targeting calcifier species. Responsible assessment and management of these fisheries should then account for the effect on growth and mortality rates of marine species most sensible to changes in ocean pH conditions. This new environmental stressor could have management implications when determining appropriate rates of exploitation aiming at fisheries biological and economic references points.

As carbon dioxide is released into the atmosphere, roughly 25 per cent of anthropogenic emissions are absorbed in the oceans (Canadell et al., 2007). As CO_2 gas dissolves, it combines with seawater to form carbonic acid (H_2CO_3). This weak acid breaks down into hydrogen ions (H^+) and bicarbonate ions (HCO_3^-). As the H^+ ions become more abundant, acidity increases and its pH decreases, a process known as ocean acidification (OA) (Kleypas et al., 1999; Caldeira and Wickett, 2003; Gattuso and Hansson, 2011).

Therefore, through changes in the saturation state values (see Appendix), OA could affect calcifier organisms in several ways. Small changes in pH due to increments in concentrations of CO_2 in oceanic waters can cause negative impacts in calcifier organisms such as molluscs, echinoderms and crustaceans, and ecologically valuable critical habitats such as corals. Impacts may include reductions in individual growth rates and increases in natural mortality (Reynaud et al., 2003; Langdon and Atkinson, 2005; Hoegh-Guldberg et al., 2007; Kurihara et al., 2008; Veron et al., 2009).

The economic impact of OA has only recently begun to be addressed. Most of the economic-related work has simply used the current landing value of the fisheries susceptible to OA and assumes harvest loss in proportion to the decrease of the oceanic pH (Cooley and Doney, 2009; Narita et al., 2012).

Bioeconomic analysis of OA remains a novel approach in the published literature. Punt et al. (2014) analyse the effects of OA on the commercial red king crab fishery in Bristol Bay, Alaska. They assume that the survival rates of the crabs' larval stages (pre-recruits) are a function of different pH conditions. The age structured pre-recruit model is parameterized using results from laboratory analysis. The outputs of the pre-recruit stages are incorporated in a bioeconomic model of the commercial fishery, which forecasts yields and profits up to 100 years in the future based on projected future ocean pH levels. In this work, future pH values were calculated according to the straight line linking the average global predicted ocean pH values between 2000 and 2200 ($pH_{2000} = 8.1$, $pH_{2200} = 7.4$).

Cooley et al. (2015) use a bioeconomic model to assess the impacts of OA on the Atlantic sea scallop (*Placopecten magellanicus*) fishery. Calcium carbonate production and water column temperature are forecast with a biogeochemical model. The recruitment of the scallops, in a population dynamics model, is affected by the calcium carbonate saturation, and the growth rate by the water column temperature and diminishing pH. The socio-economic model calculates the allowable catch and the maximum days at sea by integrating the scallop population model results. Although the spatial approach is incomplete, this research explicitly separates two scallops populations (Georges Bank and the Mid-Atlantic Bight). The integrated assessment ran simulations to 2050 using one of the climate model scenarios (RCP8.5) reported by the Intergovernmental Panel on Climate Change (IPCC).

Seijo et al. (2016) use a bioeconomics model of OA with a decision support framework to deal with the future uncertainty concerning the trend in OA. They assume the growth and natural mortality rates in their age-structured bioeconomic model depend on pH as it varies over time. These pH relationships were developed and calculated based on the results of published meta-analysis performed on the consequences of OA on several species. The possible effects of OA on harvested species with different life cycles are explored by modelling three hypothetical fisheries targeting calcifier species. Each one of the target species represents different life cycles and biological resilience (different initial growth, natural mortality rate and longevity). The work assesses the dynamic effects on biomass and profits of different fishing mortality strategies under alternative OA progress through a 100-year time horizon. The future pH trajectories are forecast using two alternative IPCC scenarios (RCP6.0 and RCP8.5). With net present value as the performance variable, a decision table framework was used to select the optimum fishing management strategies according to decision criteria reflecting different risk attitudes and using different rates of discount. The analysis illustrates how fishery outcomes depend on the extent of ocean acidification and the life cycle of calcifier species. Results also indicate that under uncertainty, there is value in taking precautionary management measures, such as reducing fishing intensity from current fishing mortality at maximum sustainable yield, F_{MSY}, even below F in current maximum economic yield, F_{MEY}, with rates of discount $\delta = [0.02, 0.04]$.

Two additional questions remain to be addressed: (1) how to incorporate analytically the effect of ocean acidification on calcifier species in bioeconomic models in data-limited situations with only catch and effort data; and (2) what are the possible dynamic bioeconomic effects of OA on calcifier species with different renewability capacities.

To address these questions, this chapter presents a bioeconomic biomass dynamic model with OA effects built in the natural growth of biomass function. This model explores the OA effect on fisheries targeting species with different renewability capacity.

A simple bioeconomic model with OA

To develop the implicit form equations for a fishery with the environmental effect of ocean acidification built in, we need to relax the assumptions of constant population carrying capacity, and intrinsic growth rates, and making fishing effort (E) as the control variable, and the calcifier species biomass (X) as the state variable, with a natural growth function:

$$\frac{dX}{dt} = G(X(K(pH), r(pH)))$$

(5.1)

For the fishery, the model has a simple yield function:

$$y = y(E, X(pH))$$

(5.2)

Therefore, the model population growth function is the following:

$$\frac{dX}{dt} = G\left(X(K(pH), r(pH))\right) - y\left(E, X(K(pH), r(pH))\right)$$

(5.3)

We can now proceed to calculate the population equilibrium curve for X.

It should be mentioned that population equilibrium curve (PEC) in the single stock model are obtained by making $\frac{dX}{dt} = 0$, and solving for X, giving the equilibrium stock size for a given level of effort of the sole fleet, and obtain:

$$PEC_X = X(K(pH), r(pH), E)$$

(5.4)

The PECs for the stock implies a long-run curve because it requires effort to be maintained constant a sufficient long period of time to achieve each equilibrium point in the PEC. The period of time required to achieve population equilibrium for each effort level is a function of the species longevity.

Using the PEC, we can derive the sustainable yield (Y) and sustainable revenues curves (SR) by substituting X in the corresponding yield curves to obtain:

$$Y = qEX(K(pH), r(pH), E)$$

(5.5)

The above gives us the basis for finding the fleet effort in bioeconomic equilibrium (E_{BE}) and effort in maximum economic yield (E_{MEY}).

Bioeconomic reference points with OA

Effort in bioeconomic equilibrium for each fleet is obtained by making the resource rent function of the fleet equal to zero and solving for the control variable E. It should be noted that this resource rent function is calculated using a unit cost of effort (c), which includes the opportunity cost of capital invested in the fleet. The implicit form equation for resource rent (π) is:

$$\pi = py\big(E, X\big(K(pH), r(pH)\big)\big) - cE \tag{5.6}$$

Bioeconomic equilibrium level of effort is then obtained by setting Equation 5.4 equal to zero and solving for E. On the other hand, optimum effort (E_{MEY}) for the fleet is obtained by finding the partial derivative with respect to E of fleet sustained resource rent and setting it equal to zero, as indicated in the following equation:

$$\frac{\partial}{\partial E} pqEX\big(K(pH), r(pH), E\big) - cE = 0 \tag{5.7}$$

Effort in maximum sustainable yield (E_{MSY}) with OA effect is calculated by finding the partial derivative of the sustainable yield function with respect to effort, making it equal to zero and solving for E, as follows:

$$\frac{\partial}{\partial E} qEX(K(pH), r(pH), E) = 0 \tag{5.8}$$

The explicit form equations are the following:
The relaxed carrying capacity parameter can be expressed as a function of pH (a proxy of the saturation state Ω) as follows:

$$K_\Omega = Ke^{\lambda_1(\Omega_0 - \Omega_f)} \tag{5.9}$$

Where:

K = carrying capacity parameter without consideration of ocean acidification

K_Ω = carrying capacity with ocean acidification

λ_1 = parameter

Ω_0 = pH at time $t = 0$

Ω_f = pH at time $t = T$

Concerning the population intrinsic growth rate, consideration of changes in ocean acidification can be represented in following equation:

$$r_\Omega = re^{\lambda_2\left(\Omega_0 - \Omega_f\right)}$$

(5.10)

and λ_2 = parameter

The population equilibrium curve (PEC) is calculated by solving for X in the following equations:

$$\frac{dX}{dt} = re^{\lambda_2\left(\Omega_0 - \Omega_f\right)}X\left(1 - \frac{X}{Ke^{\left(\lambda_1\left(\Omega_0 - \Omega_f\right)\right)}}\right) - qEX = 0$$

(5.11)

$$X = \frac{Ke^{\lambda_1\Omega_0}e^{-\lambda_1\Omega_f}\left(r - Eqe^{-\lambda_2\Omega_0}e^{\lambda_2\Omega_f}\right)}{r}$$

(5.12)

Effort in bioeconomic equilibrium with OA

Effort in bioeconomic equilibrium is obtained by simply making the profits function equal to zero and solving for E:

$$\pi = qEp\frac{Ke^{\lambda_1\Omega_0}e^{-\lambda_1\Omega_f}\left(r - Eqe^{-\lambda_2\Omega_0}e^{\lambda_2\Omega_f}\right)}{r} - cE = 0$$

(5.13)

$$E_{BE} = \frac{re^{\lambda_2\Omega_0}e^{-\lambda_2\Omega_f}\left(Kpq - ce^{-\lambda_1\Omega_0}e^{\lambda_1\Omega_f}\right)}{Kpq^2}$$

(5.14)

Effort in maximum economic yield with OA

The bioeconomic reference point of effort in maximum economic yield with ocean acidification, E_{MEY}, is calculated by making $\frac{\partial\pi}{\partial E}$ and solving for E as follows:

$$\frac{\partial}{\partial E}\left(qEp\frac{Ke^{\lambda_1\Omega_0}e^{-\lambda_1\Omega_f}\left(r - Eqe^{-\lambda_2\Omega_0}e^{\lambda_2\Omega_f}\right)}{r} - cE\right) = 0$$

(5.15)

$$E_{MEY} = -\frac{re^{-\lambda_1\Omega_0}e^{\lambda_2\Omega_0}e^{\lambda_1\Omega_f}e^{\lambda_2\Omega_f}\left(c - Kpqe^{\lambda_1\Omega_0}e^{-\lambda_1\Omega_f}\right)}{2Kpq^2}$$

(5.16)

Effort in maximum sustainable yield with OA

Many fisheries of the world still aim to operate in maximum sustainable yield (MSY); therefore, we can also calculate the reference point corresponding effort in MSY, E_{MSY}, with OA by solving for effort E the partial derivative $\frac{\partial Y}{\partial E}$:

$$
\frac{\partial}{\partial E} qE\left(\frac{Ke^{\lambda_1 \Omega_0} e^{-\lambda_1 \Omega_f} (r - Eqe^{-\lambda_2 \Omega_0} e^{\lambda_2 \Omega_f})}{r} \right) = 0 \tag{5.17}
$$

$$
E_{MSY} = \frac{re^{\lambda_2 \Omega_0} e^{-\lambda_2 \Omega_f}}{2q} \tag{5.18}
$$

Reference points in fisheries targeting species with different renewability capacity

Reference points for fisheries targeting species with different renewability capacity are calculated using the parameter set included at the end of this paragraph for alternative states of nature concerning ocean acidification, as reported by the IPCC. Figure 5.1 displays sustainable revenues trajectories resulting from alternative IPCC estimates of long-term scenarios of pH. For alternative states of nature of pH values θ_j, analytically calculated bioeconomic reference points of fishing mortality F in bioeconomic equilibrium (F_{BEE}), maximum sustainable yield (F_{MSY}) and maximum economic yield (F_{MEY}) are also included in Figure 5.2 for fisheries targeting species with different renewability capacity. Species renewability capacity is expressed by their intrinsic population growth rates $r \in [0.2, 0.6]$. Parameters used are the following: $q = 0.00128$, $c = 281{,}000$ (US$/vessel per year), and $p = 10.0$ (US$/kg).

In order to determine catch quotas under the current common MSY criterion, trajectories of backward bending supply curves for alternative states of nature of pH values (θ_j) and their corresponding maximum sustainable yields are presented in Figure 5.2 for the three groups of species with different renewability capacities. As expected, the higher the renewability capacity of the species, the higher the sustainable yield of the fisheries.

For catch quota (TAC_{θ_j}) determination using the bioeconomic reference point of MEY_{θ_j}, Figure 5.3 shows sustainable resource rent trajectories for different levels of sustainable yield and alternative states of nature for pH.

The corresponding TACs generating maximum resource rents (TAC_{θ_1}, TAC_{θ_2} and TAC_{θ_3}) are indicated at the levels at which these rents are maximized (MEY_{θ_1}, MEY_{θ_2} and MEY_{θ_3}).

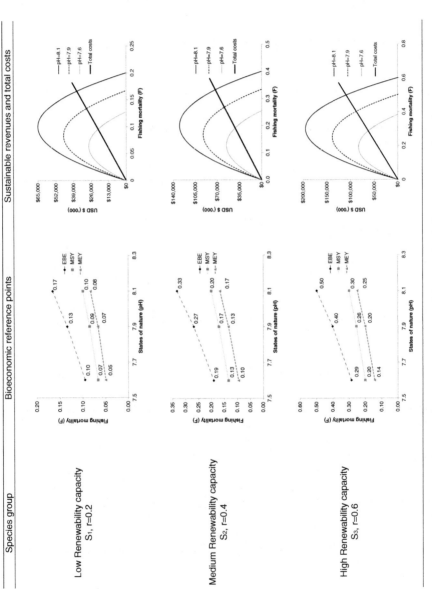

Figure 5.1 Bioeconomic reference points with ocean acidification for different groups of species.

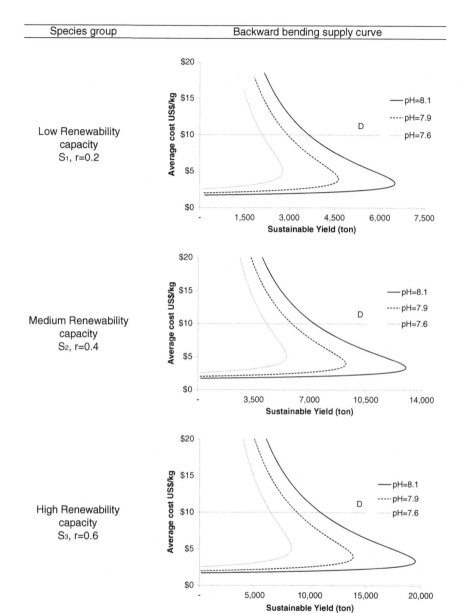

| Species group | Backward bending supply curve |

Low Renewability capacity
S_1, r=0.2

Medium Renewability capacity
S_2, r=0.4

High Renewability capacity
S_3, r=0.6

Figure 5.2 Backward bending supply curves for alternative states of nature of pH values and their corresponding maximum sustainable yields ($MSY_{\theta 1}$, $MSY_{\theta 2}$ and $MSY_{\theta 3}$) for catch quota determination.

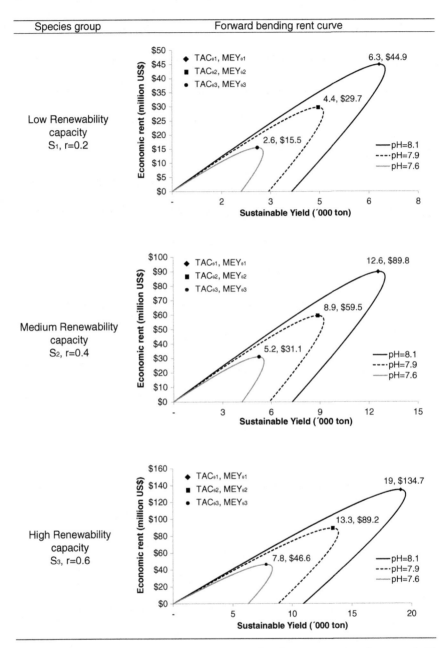

Figure 5.3 Forward bending resource rent curves for alternative states of nature of pH values and their corresponding maximum economic yield ($MEY_{\theta 1}$, $MEY_{\theta 2}$ and $MEY_{\theta 3}$) for catch quota determination.

Decision tables under uncertain future ocean acidification conditions: IPCC scenarios

To answer the second question, within the ocean acidification context and possible effects on fisheries targeting mollusc species, an application of decision theory for systematic choice under uncertainty is suggested, considering different degrees of caution. An approach for doing so is presented in Figure 5.4.

Figure 5.4 shows the bioeconomic dynamics, with possible states of nature of ocean pH values, within a decision theory framework. This decision table uses alternative decision criteria appropriate for situations when there is an absence of mathematical probabilities of occurrence of alternative states of nature. Such an approach is suitable here because there are no estimates of probabilties of occurrence of pH dynamic trajectories towards 2100.

Decision-making under ignorance refers to decision-making when the possible states of nature (in this case, the possible futures of OA) are known, but no information about their probabilities of occurrence is available. This fits with the reality of possible IPCC scenarios of pH for the period 2005–2100 discussed in Seijo et al. (2016). In this situation, fishery decision-makers must choose a fishery management strategy D_i (from a set of alternative strategies of fishing mortality F), with uncertainty about the future changes in pH. This involves taking into account the corresponding consequences in performance variables driven by the cause–effect relationships specified in the fishery model,

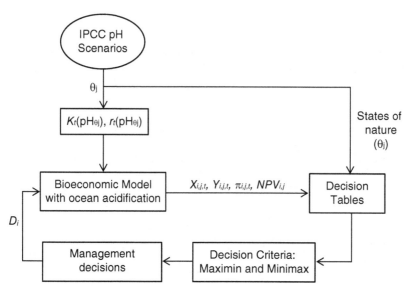

Figure 5.4 Proposed approach for considering the ocean acidification effect on fisheries to aid the selection of policy decisions.

Source: Modified from Seijo et al. (2016).

the estimated bioecologic parameters, and the states of nature θ_j associated with possible IPCC forecasted values of pH.

In decision analysis, it is important to be able to estimate a 'loss of opportunities' function, $L(d,\theta)$, also called a regret matrix (Parmigiani and Inoue, 2009), in which $L(d_i,\theta_j)$ reflects the resulting loss from having selected strategy D_i when the state of nature (i.e. future pH) in the relevant ecosystem turns out to be θ_j. There are, however, different degrees of risk aversion, and therefore decision theory provides alternative criteria for increasing degrees of caution in decision-making (Shotton and Francis, 1997; Seijo et al., 1998). In this case, the degree of caution is associated with the impacts on calcifier species affected by pH reductions.

Decision criteria without mathematical probabilities: maximin and minimax

In the absence of the data required to assign probabilities to possible states of nature, associated to pH concentrations, there are two standard decision criteria reflecting different degrees of precaution concerning selection of fishery management strategies: *maximin* and *minimax* (Seijo et al., 2004; Anderson and Seijo, 2010).

The most cautious decision criteria (highly risk-averse) proposed for decisions under ignorance is the *maximin* rule. For each alternative decision, we define its *security level* as the worst possible outcome with that alternative. It involves choosing the alternative that has the maximum security level, i.e. that *maxi*mizes the *mini*mal (worst) outcome in terms of the fishery performance variable. The *maximin* uses a decision table (pay-off table) showing the resulting values for each combination of an alternative decision and a possible state of nature. Then, the fishery manager selects the maximum of the minimum (thus 'maxi-min') of those values. This criterion proceeds as if nature would

Table 5.1 Application of the maximin decision criterion to ocean acidification effects

Alternative management strategies	Possible states of nature (pH)				Maximin criterion
Decisions	θ_1	θ_2	$\cdots$	θ_j	$Max\left[Min\left(\pi_{D_i\theta_j}\right)\right]$
D_1	$\pi_{1,1}$	$\pi_{1,2}$	$\cdots$	$S\pi_{1,j}$	$Min\left(\pi_{D_1\theta_j}\right)$
D_2	$\pi_{2,1}$	$\pi_{2,2}$	$\cdots$	$\pi_{2,j}$	$Min\left(\pi_{D_2\theta_j}\right)$
$\vdots$	$\vdots$	$\vdots$	$\vdots$	$\vdots$	$\vdots$
D_i	$\pi_{i,1}$	$\pi_{i,2}$	$\cdots$	$\pi_{i,j}$	$Min\left(\pi_{D_i\theta_j}\right)$

select the worst possible scenario of all defined states of nature, which is least favourable for the fishery decision-maker (see Table 5.1).

A second main decision criterion is the minimax regret criterion, as introduced by Savage (1951: 59). The minimax regret criterion involves choosing the option with the lowest maximum regret (i.e. to minimize the maximum regret or loss of opportunities). In this case, the goal would be to minimize the maximum loss of π, across all alternative exploitation rates, given the possible states of nature of ocean pH under consideration. The Minimax regret criterion is cautious but not as pessimistic as the maximin approach. It uses the regret or loss of opportunity matrix to calculate the maximum loss of opportunities of each management strategy and selects the strategy that provides the minimum of the maximum losses associated with possible pH reductions (see Table 5.2). Although the Bayesian method is simple and recognized as an appropriate method for dealing with uncertainty, it inherently has the disadvantage of requiring a prior probability distribution (Medley, 1998).

Results of the decision table analysis presented below indicate that operating the fishery under the risk-averse minimax decision criterion involves setting target fishing mortality at $F_{MEY,\theta2}$ i.e. target reference point that maximizes resource rent if the state of nature θ_2 (pH = 7.9) occurs. The extremely cautious maximin criterion would recommend to operate at $F_{MEY,\theta3}$ which is the F corresponding to state of nature θ_3 (pH = 7.6) (see Tables 5.3–5.8).

In addition to having calculated fishery bioeconomic reference points for alternative ocean acidification scenarios, the dynamic nature of changes in oceanic pH conditions towards acidity may require consideration of a non-equilibrium approach to policy decisions.

Dynamic bioeconomic analysis: a non-equilibrium solution

The dynamic bioeconomic analysis is undertaken by solving numerically (using Euler numerical integration) over time the dynamic differential equations for biomass X and effort E:

$$\frac{dX}{dt} = re^{\lambda_2(\Omega_0 - \Omega_f)} X \left(1 - \frac{X}{Ke^{(\lambda_1(\Omega_0 - \Omega_f))}} \right) - qEX \tag{5.19}$$

$$\frac{dE}{dt} = \emptyset \cdot \pi_t \text{ (Smith, 1969)} \tag{5.20}$$

where the fleet entry-exit dynamics parameter is $\emptyset > 0$.

For the dynamic analysis, the net present value of resource rent is calculated for fisheries targeting three groups of species under the three possible states of nature of ocean acidification θ_j.

Figure 5.5 presents the optimum fishing mortalities $F_{opt,\theta}$ calculated by the dynamic analysis mentioned above, considering alternative ocean acidification states of nature for the three groups of species.

Table 5.9 shows a comparison of static bioeconomic reference points without ocean acidification and the results of applying two risk-averse decision

Table 5.2 Loss of opportunity (regret) matrix for the minimax decision criterion applied to fisheries management under uncertain states of nature of ocean acidification

Alternative management strategies	Possible states of nature (pH)				Minimax criterion
Decisions	θ_1	θ_2	$\cdots$	θ_j	
D_1	$Max\left(\pi_{D,\theta_1}\right) - \pi_{D_1\theta_1}$	$Max\left(\pi_{D,\theta_2}\right) - \pi_{D_1\theta_2}$	$\cdots$	$Max\left(\pi_{D,\theta_j}\right) - \pi_{D_1\theta_j}$	$Min\left\{Max\left[Max\left(\pi_{D,\theta_j}\right) - \pi_{D,\theta_j}\right]\right\}$
D_2	$Max\left(\pi_{D,\theta_1}\right) - \pi_{D_2\theta_1}$	$Max\left(\pi_{D,\theta_2}\right) - \pi_{D_2\theta_2}$	$\cdots$	$Max\left(\pi_{D,\theta_j}\right) - \pi_{D_2\theta_j}$	$Min\left\{Max\left[Max\left(\pi_{D,\theta_j}\right) - \pi_{D,\theta_j}\right]\right\}$
$\cdots$	$\cdots$	$\cdots$			$Max\left[Max\left(\pi_{D,\theta_j}\right) - \pi_{D_2\theta_j}\right]$ $\cdots$
D_i	$Max\left(\pi_{D,\theta_1}\right) - \pi_{D_i\theta_1}$	$Max\left(\pi_{D,\theta_2}\right) - \pi_{D_i\theta_2}$	$\cdots$	$Max\left(\pi_{D,\theta_j}\right) - \pi_{D_i\theta_j}$	$Max\left[Max\left(\pi_{D,\theta_j}\right) - \pi_{D\theta_j}\right]$

Table 5.3 Economic rent π (US$ million) pay-off matrix, maximin criterion, species group with low renewability capacity, $r = 0.2$

Management decision	pH states of nature			$Max\left[Min\left(\pi_{D,\theta_j}\right)\right]$
	$\theta_1 = 8.1$	$\theta_2 = 7.9$	$\theta_3 = 7.6$	
$F_{MSY,\theta1} = 0.10$	43.0	22.5	−3.1	−3.1
$F_{MEY,\theta1} = 0.08$	44.9	28.6	8.4	8.4
$F_{MEY,\theta2} = 0.07$	43.2	29.7	13.0	13.0
$F_{MEY,\theta3} = 0.05$	36.7	27.3	15.5	**15.5**

Table 5.4 Loss of opportunity matrix (regret matrix) calculated to apply the minimax criterion to the species with low renewability capacity, $r = 0.2$

Management decision	pH states of nature			$Min\left\{Max\left[Max\left(\pi_{D,\theta_j}\right) - \pi_{D,\theta_j}\right]\right\}$
	$\theta_1 = 8.1$	$\theta_2 = 7.9$	$\theta_3 = 7.6$	
$F_{MSY,\theta1} = 0.10$	1.9	7.2	18.6	18.6
$F_{MEY,\theta1} = 0.08$	0.0	1.1	7.1	7.1
$F_{MEY,\theta2} = 0.07$	1.7	0.0	2.5	**2.5**
$F_{MEY,\theta3} = 0.05$	8.2	2.4	0.0	8.2

Table 5.5 Economic rent π (US$ million) pay-off matrix, maximin criterion, species group with medium renewability capacity, $r = 0.4$

Management decision	pH states of nature			$Max\left[Min\left(\pi_{D,\theta_j}\right)\right]$
	$\theta_1 = 8.1$	$\theta_2 = 7.9$	$\theta_3 = 7.6$	
$F_{MSY,\theta1} = 0.20$	86.1	45.0	−6.3	−6.3
$F_{MEY,\theta1} = 0.17$	89.8	55.2	12.1	12.1
$F_{MEY,\theta2} = 0.13$	86.4	59.4	26.0	29.0
$F_{MEY,\theta3} = 0.10$	73.4	54.6	31.1	**31.1**

Table 5.6 Loss of opportunity matrix calculated to apply the minimax criterion to the species with medium renewability capacity, $r = 0.4$

Management decision	pH states of nature			$Min\left\{Max\left[Max\left(\pi_{D,\theta_j}\right) - \pi_{D,\theta_j}\right]\right\}$
	$\theta_1 = 8.1$	$\theta_2 = 7.9$	$\theta_3 = 7.6$	
$F_{MSY,\theta1} = 0.20$	3.7	14.4	37.4	37.4
$F_{MEY,\theta1} = 0.17$	0.0	4.2	19.0	19.0
$F_{MEY,\theta2} = 0.13$	3.4	0.0	5.1	**5.1**
$F_{MEY,\theta3} = 0.10$	16.4	4.8	0.0	16.4

Table 5.7 Economic rent π (US$ million) pay-off matrix, maximin criterion, species group with high renewability capacity, $r = 0.6$

Management decision	pH states of nature			$Max\left(\pi_{D,\theta_j}\right) - \pi_{D,\theta_j}$
	$\theta_1 = 8.1$	$\theta_2 = 7.9$	$\theta_3 = 7.6$	
$F_{MSY,\theta1} = 0.30$	129.1	67.5	−9.4	−9.4
$F_{MEY,\theta1} = 0.25$	134.7	84.0	20.9	20.6
$F_{MEY,\theta2} = 0.20$	129.6	89.2	39.0	39.0
$\mathbf{F_{MEY,\theta3} = 0.14}$	110.2	81.8	46.6	**46.6**

Table 5.8 Loss of opportunity matrix calculated to apply the minimax criterion to the species with high renewability capacity, $r = 0.6$

Management decision	pH states of nature			$Min\left\{Max\left[Max\left(\pi_{D,\theta_j}\right) - \pi_{D,\theta_j}\right]\right\}$
	$\theta_1 = 8.1$	$\theta_2 = 7.9$	$\theta_3 = 7.6$	
$F_{MSY,\theta1} = 0.30$	5.6	21.7	56.0	56.0
$F_{MEY,\theta1} = 0.25$	0.0	5.2	25.7	25.7
$\mathbf{F_{MEY,\theta2} = 0.20}$	5.1	0.0	7.6	**7.6**
$F_{MEY,\theta3} = 0.14$	24.5	7.4	0.0	24.5

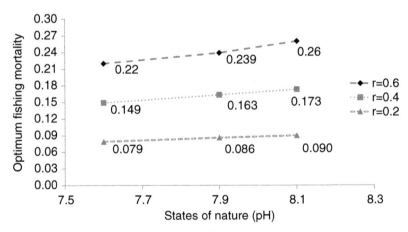

Figure 5.5 Optimum fishing mortalities $F_{opt,\theta}$ under alternative ocean acidification (OA) states of nature θ, obtained from dynamic bioeconomic analysis using a rate of discount of $\delta = 0.02$.

criteria to the calculated $F_{opt,\theta}$ for three fisheries targeting species with different renewability.

For the two decision criteria (minimax and maximin) with OA, the optimum fishing mortality F_{opt} is below F_{MEY} without OA effect. Nevertheless, the reduction could involve decreasing F by only 12 per cent because of the

Table 5.9 Static bioeconomic reference points with and without ocean acidification and the decision criteria selected $F_{OPT,\theta}$ for fisheries targeting species with different renewability

Target species renewability	Reference points without OA		Fishing mortality reference points with alternative decision criteria with OA	
	MSY	MEY	Maximin	Minimax
$r = 0.2$	0.10	0.08	0.079	0.086
$r = 0.4$	0.20	0.17	0.149	0.163
$r = 0.6$	0.30	0.25	0.22	0.239

discounting process over a long period of 100 years needed for the dynamic changes in OA to reach the possible 7.9 and 7.6 pH values, as forecasted by the IPCC. A less cautious but still precautionary approach would be to operate the fishery with fishing mortality at *MEY* instead of *MSY*.

Results also indicate that in fisheries targeting low renewability species (e.g. $r = 0.2$), the long-run effect of ocean acidification could be mitigated by operating the fishery $\sim F_{MEY} = 0.08$, because the two decision criteria under uncertainty caused by ocean acidification undertaken with dynamic bioeconomic analysis are in the range of [0.079, 0.086].

For species with higher intrinsic population growth rate ($r = 0.4$ and $r = 0.6$), the dynamic analysis indicates to operate the fisheries below F_{MEY}.

Discussion and conclusions

This chapter used a modelling and policy decision support approach to examine possible dynamic bioeconomic effects of ocean acidification as an additional stressor on calcifier species such as crustaceans, molluscs and equinoderms. The relationships between the dynamics of pH and the population intrinsic growth rate were determined, considering the possible effects on different calcifier marine organisms (Kroeker et al., 2010, 2013).

Concerning cost functions, the model allows to calculate backward bending harvest cost (US$/ton) for different OA states of nature and management strategies. As stock decreases, because of the negative effect of OA, the cost per ton harvested increases (see Figure 5.2). This figure shows the the corresponding maximum sustainable yield at which the average cost begins to bend backwards.

The bioeconomic simulation experiments developed in this chapter demonstrate that bioeconomic ocean acidification effects on fisheries targeting calcifier species will depend on species life cycle and relative abundance. Three species groups were examined here with different renewability capacities: low ($r = 0.2$), medium ($r = 0.4$) and high ($r = 0.6$).

Simulation results show that OA had greater negative effect over time on the group of species with lowest intrinsic growth rate ($r = 0.2$). The least effect occurs on the group of species with high renewability capacity. Thus, r adds to the resilient capacity of the stock to better respond to OA effect over time. In all these cases, the optimal decisions, as indicated by the minimax regret and maximin criteria, are for the fishery to reduce fishing mortality below the current F_{MSY}. This involves a considerable reduction in two of the cases, but a smaller one for the third species group, for which the effect of ocean acidification is mitigated by species high renewability capacity.

The above results from the dynamic bioeconomic decision analysis indicate that focusing on adaptation to possible effects of OA can be accomplished using, as a precautionary measure, a level of fishing mortality (F) that maximizes the net present value (NPV) of the fishery, with an appropriate decision criteria reflecting the decision-maker's degree of caution. A 2 per cent discount rate was used in this analysis. Seijo et al. (2016) reported the effect on optimun fishing mortality of using different rates of discount, reflecting the marginal productivity of capital, the intertemporal distribution of income and the intertemporal preferences of those associated to the fishery.

While such advances remain in the future, this chapter demonstrates that well-established methods of bioeconomic modelling and decision analysis in data-limited situations can be applied to aid fishery participants in responding to the potential impacts of ocean acidification on fisheries using appropriate precautionary bioeconomic reference points. There are additional complexities to be considered in future research, notably building spatial considerations in fisheries targeting low-mobility resources in areas with significant changes in ocean acidification.

Appendix

The effects of OA on marine calcifier species occurs through dissolution of the saturation state values. The saturation state (known as Ω) of seawater for a mineral is a measure of the thermodynamic potential for the mineral to form or to dissolve. Ω is the product of the concentrations of the reacting ions that form the mineral (Ca_2^+ and CO_3^{2-}), divided by the product of the concentrations of those ions when the mineral is at equilibrium, that is when the mineral is neither forming nor dissolving (Atkinson and Cuet, 2008). Dissolution occurs when $\Omega < 1$ (Doney et al., 2009).

References

Anderson, L.G. and Seijo, J.C. (2010). *Bioeconomics of Fisheries Management*. Hoboken, NJ: Wiley-Blackwell.

Atkinson, M.J. and Cuet, P. (2008). Possible effects of ocean acidification on coral reef biogeochemistry: topics for research. *Marine Ecology Progress Series*, 373: 249–256.

Caldeira, K. and Wickett, M.E. (2003). Anthropogenic carbon and ocean pH. *Nature*, 425: 365.

Canadell, J.G., Le Quéré, D., Raupach, M.R., Field, C.R., Buitenhuis, E.T., Ciais, P., et al. (2007). Contributions to accelerating atmospheric CO_2 growth from economic activity, carbon intensity, and efficiency of natural sinks. *Proceedings of National Academie of Sciences*, 104: 18866–18870.

Cooley, S.R. and Doney, S.C. (2009). Anticipating ocean acidification's economic consequences for commercial fisheries. *Environmental Research Letters*, 4(2): 024007. Available at: http://iopscience.iop.org/174/024007 (accessed 25 January 2018).

Cooley, S.R., Rheuban, J.E., Hart, D.R., Luu, V., Glover, D.M., Hare, J.A., et al. (2015). An integrated assessment model for helping the United States sea scallop (*Placopecten magellanicus*) fishery plan ahead for ocean acidification and warming. *PloS one*, 10(5): e0124145.

Doney, S.C., Fabry, V.J., Feely, R.A. and Kleypas, J.A. (2009). Ocean acidification: the other CO_2 problem. *Annual Review of Marine Science*, 1: 169–192.

Gattuso, J.P. and Hansson, L. (2011). *Ocean Acidification*. Oxford: Oxford University Press.

Hoegh-Guldberg, O., Mumby, P.J., Hooten, A.J., Steneck, R.S., Greenfield, P., Gomez, E., et al. (2007). Coral reefs under rapid climate change and ocean acidification. *Science*, 318: 1737–1742.

Kleypas, J.A., Buddemeier, R.W., Archer, D., Gattuso, J.P., Langdon, C. and Opdyke, B.N. (1999). Geochemical consequences of increased atmospheric carbon dioxide on coral reefs. *Science*, 284: 118–120.

Kroeker, K.J., Kordas, R.L., Crim, R.N. and Singh, G.G. (2010). Meta-analysis reveals negative yet variable effects of ocean acidification on marine organisms. *Ecology Letters*, 13(11): 1419–1434.

Kroeker, K.J., Kordas, R.L., Crim, R.N., Hendriks, I.E., Ramajo, L., Singh, G.S., et al. (2013). Impacts of ocean acidification on marine organisms: quantifying sensitivities and interaction with warming. *Global Change Biology*, 19: 1884–1896.

Kurihara, H., Matsui, M., Furukawa, H., Hayashi, M. and Ishimatsu, A. (2008). Long-term effects of predicted future seawater CO_2 conditions on the survival and growth of the marine shrimp Palaemon pacificus. *Journal of Experimental Marine Biology and Ecology*, 367(1): 41–46.

Langdon, C. and Atkinson, M.J. (2005). Effect of elevated pCO(2) on photosynthesis and calcification of corals and interactions with seasonal change in temperature/irradiance and nutrient enrichment. *Journal of Geophysical Research*, 110: C09S07.

Medley, P.A.H. (1998). A decision theory case study: choosing a season opening for a spiny lobster (*Panulirus argus* L.) fishery. *Fisheries Research*, 36: 159–170.

Narita, D., Rehdanz, K. and Tol, R.S. (2012). Economic costs of ocean acidification: a look into the impacts on global shellfish production. *Climatic Change*, 113(3–4): 1049–1063.

Parmigiani, G. and Inoue, L.Y.T. (2009). *Decision Theory: Principles and Approaches*. London: John Wiley & Sons.

Punt, A.E., Poljak, D., Dalton, M.G. and Foy, R.J. (2014). Evaluating the impact of ocean acidification on fishery yields and profits: the example of red king crab in Bristol Bay. *Ecological Modelling*, 285: 39–53.

Reynaud, S., Leclerq, N., Romaine-Lioud, S., Ferrier-Pagés, C., Jaubert, J. and Gatusso, J.P. (2003). Interacting effects of CO_2 partial pressure and temperature on photosynthesis and calcification in a scleratinian coral. *Global Change Biology*, 9: 1660–1668.

Savage, L.J. (1951). The theory of statistical decision. *Journal of the American Statistical Association*, 46(253): 55–67.

Seijo, J.C., Defeo, O. and Salas, S. (1998). Fisheries bioeconomics: theory, modelling and management. *FAO Fisheries Technical Paper*, 368.

Seijo, J.C., Pérez, E. and Caddy, J.F. (2004). A simple approach for dealing with dynamics and uncertainty in fisheries with heterogeneous resource and effort distribution. *Marine and Freshwater Research*, 55: 249–256.

Seijo, J.C., Villanueva, R. and Charles, A. (2016). Bioeconomics of ocean acidification effects on fisheries targeting calcifier species: a decision theory approach. *Fisheries Research*, 176: 1–14.

Shotton, R. and Francis, R.I.C.C. (1997). Risk in fisheries management: a review. *Canadian Journal of Fisheries and Aquatic Sciences*, 54: 1699–1715.

Smith, V.L. (1969) On models of commercial fishing. *Journal of Political Economy*, 77: 181–198.

Veron, J.E.N., Hoegh-Guldberg, O., Lenton, T.M., Lough, J.M., Obura, D.O., Pearce-Kelly, P., et al. (2009). The coral reef crisis: the critical importance of <350 ppm CO_2. *Marine Pollution Bulletin*, 58(10): 1428–1436.

6 The economics of unwanted by-catch and a landing obligation

Peder Andersen and Lisa Ståhl

Introduction

Unwanted by-catch is a serious problem around the world. Often, by-catch is discarded and results in direct food waste, and indirectly often influences biodiversity, stock abundance and long-term catch. To minimize by-catch problems, various fisheries management rules are applied, such as legal minimum sizes of landed fish, mesh sizes in fishing gears and closed areas. A more dramatic approach is to reduce the discards of unwanted catches by a landing obligation for all caught fish, independent of size and quality. For some years, this has been part of the fishery policy in countries such as Norway and Iceland.

In the European Union's (EU) 2013 reform of the Common Fishery Policy (CFP), a landing obligation (LO) was introduced for the first time (see EU, 2013). This is one of the most significant changes of the Common Fishery Policy since 1983 and may have significant economic consequences for the fishing industry. The political motivations for the LO are partly biological and partly ethical, with little focus on the economic consequences. The basic idea is that an LO will encourage an increased selectivity and support the initiatives to improve marine ecosystems in line with the CFP's goals. The ethical motivation for the LO is to reduce resource waste by reducing the level of previously discarded fish (under LO unwanted by-catch fish) and to use the unavoidable catches for industry or direct consumption purposes. The LO is being implemented in the period from 2015 to 2019, starting with pelagic and industrial species, as well as salmon in the Baltic Sea, and will cover all quota species in all areas by 2019. However, there are some exemptions to the LO, for example related to survivability (EU, 2013).

Despite this significant change in the governance of EU fisheries, there is a lack of theoretical as well as empirical analyses of the consequences of a landing obligation policy. The economics of unwanted by-catch and a landing obligation are closely linked. The literature regarding the economic drivers of discarding is the fundament of understanding the economics of landing obligation. But the knowledge is limited regarding the actual impacts of trying to regulate discarding through a landing obligation. The simple theoretical framework presented in this chapter provides a framework for analysing the consequences of the LO. The empirical analyses of the economic consequences of the landing obligation give some insights into the impacts on the commercial fisheries. The examples look at the short-term impacts (no or limited behavioural changes) and the medium- and long-term impacts when fishing pattern and fleet size can be adjusted. In the final section, some perspectives and potential future research are listed.

Theory

To model the landing obligation problem in the light of the discard literature, the fundament is classical fisheries economics, but extended to consider a broader perspective of the use of marine resources (e.g. see Frost et al., 2015). The following is a simple representation of the maximization problem: the objective is to maximize the welfare (*W*) from the exploitation of a scarce fish resource:

$$\text{Max } W = f(h, \, y, \, z) \tag{6.1}$$

Subject to:

$$\dot{x} = F\left(x\right) - h$$
$$\dot{u} = G\left(u\right) - y$$
$$\dot{v} = K\left(v\right) - z$$

where *h* is the harvest of marketable fish, *y* is the harvest of non-marketable resources (non-target species and year classes), birds and animals, and *z* is an indicator of nature's condition, creating the intellectual well-being of humans knowing that nature is in a 'good' condition (amenity, heritage, etc.). *h*, *y* and *z* can be positively or negatively correlated. The first restriction specifies the change, $\dot{x}$, in the fish stock *x*, the second one specifies the change, $\dot{u}$, in the non-target species *u*, and the third one the change, $\dot{v}$, in the intellectual stocks *v* (i.e. the stocks that influence the pleasure of knowing that the marine environment is in a good condition). *F(x)*, *G(u)* and *K(v)* are the growth functions.

This is a dynamic, complex system, and illustrates the difference between a simple maximization problem and a broader ecosystem-based perspective of the exploitation of the marine system. The discard *y* ('landed unwanted by-catch' under LO) as well as *v* have to be included in *W*. From society's point of view, the objective is to maximize welfare *W*, and in fisheries economics it is often stated that the objective is to maximize the resource rent or sum of resource rent, consumer surplus and producer surplus.

This broader view reflects the reasoning behind, for example, the EU's decision of implementing the landing obligation and the EU Marine Strategy

Framework Directive, which together outline a transparent, legislative framework for an ecosystem-based approach of human activities that supports the sustainable use of marine goods and services. This general welfare approach is the point of departure for a closer look at the consequences for fishermen and how the landing obligation can be modelled in a standard bioeconomic model.

The theoretical framework for analysing the effects of a landing obligation lies within the literature of discarding behaviour (e.g. see Anderson, 1994; Arnason, 1994; Ward, 1994; Boyce, 1996; Vestergaard, 1996; Turner, 1997; Frost et al., 2015; Andersen and Ståhl, 2016). Discarding takes place for various reasons and can be looked upon like by-catch or high-grading (e.g. see Frost et al., 2015). In most fisheries, by-catch cannot be avoided completely. High-grading is the decision to discard low-valued fish to increase profit. Several factors can play a role in a fisherman's decision whether to land certain catches: catchability of target and non-target fish, distributions of species in catch, prices, costs of processing and discarding, distance from harbour to fishing area, stock effects, regulation type, as well as the probability and scale of legal punishment (Frost et al., 2015).

The fisherman's decision process is illustrated in Figure 6.1. As described by Frost et al. (2015), the fisherman faces restrictions by policymakers such as quotas or closed areas (Box 3). With these restrictions in mind, he decides on a fishing effort (Box 1) and obtains a catch – which, dependent on the species and age distribution (Box 2), comprises of target and non-target species and sizes (Box 4). Box 5 shows that with a marketable catch at hand, the fisherman may choose to high-grade and thus discard some of the catch (Box 9). Although not high-grading, he may face restrictions on minimum sizes or have landed amounts above the quota (Box 7), which may contribute to the choice to discard (Box 9). If there are no such restrictions, the catch may be landed (Box 10). Box 6 shows that the fisherman's catch may consist of illegally caught fish, e.g. above-quota catches, but if there is a low probability of legal punishment, the catch may be landed and sold on a black market (Box 8). If the probability of punishment is high, the catch may be discarded (Box 9). These decisions will depend on the net income from legal and illegal catches and the probability of detection and the size of the fine. The potential income from boxes 8, 9, and 10 feeds into the fisherman's profit maximization in box 11 together with the costs of fishing in box 1.

A review of existing literature on discarding behaviour can be found in Frost et al. (2015: 11–16). Natural as well as institutional settings affect incentives to discard, and a range of different types of constraints can be identified (e.g. see FAO, 1996; Nordic Council of Ministers, 2003):

1   Institutional (i.e. management measures defined by managers), for example:

    a   quotas, effort restrictions, individual transferable quotas;
    b   minimum size on fish; and
    c   mesh sizes in fishing gear.

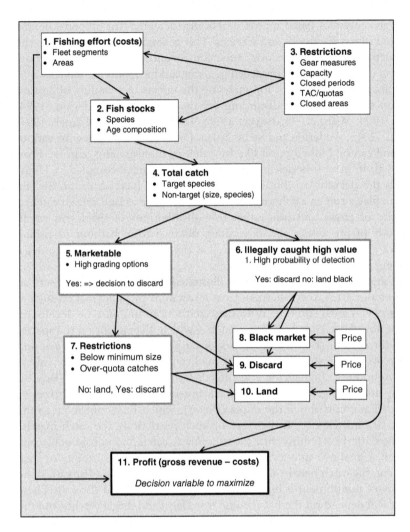

Figure 6.1 Behaviour under restrictions.
Source: Frost et al. (2015).

2 Biological, for example species interaction and characteristics of the fish (gender, poisonous, etc.).
3 Technological, for example gear selectivity (prohibited gear, damages to the fish, etc.).
4 Economical, for example price and costs relationships determined on the market, including high-grading.

As explained in Frost et al. (2015), from an economic perspective, the issue of discarding contains different elements. The first one is the long-run welfare perspective, considering the impact on fish stocks, marine mammals and the quality of the marine environment. A second one is the short-run perspective, including the direct impact on the fishing industry. In that perspective, stock effects are not included. A third perspective is the individual fisherman's view. This is important as this is directly linked to the incentive of the fisherman to cope with discard and a landing obligation. The final perspective is the social costs associated with mitigation of the discarding through a landing obligation. These costs include, among other things, information costs and monitoring and enforcement costs.

It is unlikely to get a full understanding of the incentives to discard, but they include the following elements (e.g. see Frost et al., 2015; see also Figure 6.1):

- species composition in harvest;
- price on fish;
- processing costs on board the vessel;
- catchability rates;
- discard costs;
- penalty for violation of rules;
- probability of being detected;
- management system;
- impact on stock abundance;
- distance to fishing grounds;
- flexibility in fishing activities; and
- selectivity in various fleet segments.

The selectivity issue is crucial as increased selectivity reduces the potential amount of fish to discard or land illegally (e.g. see Pascoe, 1997). Selectivity depends on several factors, including spatial, technical, temporal and market aspects. For example, fishing activities may take place in areas where unwanted catch (e.g. juveniles) is smaller. Switching gear technology can also increase selectivity. Further, fishing activities may take place at times of year where the number of unwanted fish is lower. Where a quota system is in place, measures may be taken to ensure that the quotas match the species composition in the catch. Additionally, reducing effort will reduce the total discard, but most likely at the same time also reduce landings.

As a first step towards a model with the landing obligation restriction, we look at it from the fisherman's point of view. The model is a simple reformulation of Clark (1980) (see also Andersen et al., 2014).

First, we look at the model before discard and the LO restriction are imposed. Harvest (h_i) for a vessel (i) is calculated as the product of a constant catchability coefficient (q), standardized effort of the vessel (E_i) and the fish population biomass (x):

$$h_i = qE_ix \tag{6.2}$$

In this case, harvest is equivalent to landings (*l*). The Clark model does not differentiate between landings and catch, and this plays no role in the profit function. One way to interpret this would be that the net value of discard is zero, or that the cost function includes the cost of handling discard. When biologists make assessment, discard is included in the fishing mortality estimates. A simple way to approach the discard issue is by looking at landings equal harvest minus discards (or unwanted catch). Landings contribute directly to fishing revenue, and discard most likely has an impact on fishing cost. In the following, we assume that discards (*d*) are greater than zero.

Therefore, the following simple observations can be made:

- Effort (*E*) results in total catch, which is the sum of targetable/wanted (landed) and non-targetable/unwanted fish (discard/unwanted by-catch or landed unwanted by-catch), birds, and marine mammals.
- The catchability coefficient (*q*) can vary for different segments of the fish population.
- Biomass (*x*) can be divided into targetable and non-targetable components.

In the simplest case for modelling discards explicitly, catchability can be defined differently for landings and discards:

$$l_i = q_l E_i x \tag{6.3}$$

$$d_i = q_d E_i x \tag{6.4}$$

where $h_i = l_i + d_i$. This approach could be expanded to split the biomass (*x*) into a stock of 'landable' fish and a stock of 'non-landable' fish (in a similar approach to Pascoe, 1997).

The profitability of a vessel can be calculated as in Clark's model:

$$\pi_i = \pi_i\left(x, E_i\right) = pqE_ix - c_i\left(E_i\right) = \left(p_l q_l E_i x + p_d q_d E_i x\right) - c_i\left(E_i\right) \tag{6.5}$$

where the price (*p*) differs for landed and landed-discard quantity. If p_d, the price of discards, equals zero, there is no change in the Clark model if discard fish play no role in the cost function. If we assume that the cost of handling discards is proportional to the amount of discards, we can redefine the cost function by introducing a 'discard' cost function:

$$c_i^d(d_i) = c_d d_i \tag{6.6}$$

Therefore, marginal revenue (*MR*) can be defined as:

$$MR_i = p_l q_l x + (p_d - c_d) q_d x \tag{6.7}$$

Observations:

- If $p_d < c_d$, then the cost of discarding outweighs catching unwanted fish, thus resulting in reduced effort, and also resulting in a higher equilibrium stock level under open access.
- If $p_d > c_d$, then the cost of discarding incentivizes catching unwanted fish, thus resulting in increased effort, and also resulting in a lower equilibrium stock level under open access.

Catchability of unwanted fish can be controlled through the flow of technology investment and effort applied. Therefore, a way to model this is by letting increased costs influence the catchability coefficient for non-target species, described by the function:

$$q_d = q_d\left(c_i\left(E_i\right)\right) \tag{6.8}$$

and

$$\frac{\partial q_d}{\partial c_i} < 0 \tag{6.9}$$

If the cost of new fishing technology implies better selectivity, then less unwanted by-catch fish are caught.

If the cost per vessel goes up, then effort goes down. Moreover, if the cost of effort per vessel goes up, then catchability of discards goes down.

Consider the optimal fishery case where the fishery is regulated by an ITQ system:

$$\max \sum_i^N \pi_i(x, E_i) \tag{6.10}$$

$$F(x) = qx \sum_i^N E_i \tag{6.11}$$

This results in:

$$\left(p - \lambda\right) qx = c_i'\left(E_i\right) = \left(p_l - \lambda_l\right) q_l x + \left(p_d - \lambda_d\right) q_d x \tag{6.12}$$

If $p_d < c_d + \lambda_{d'}$ then the optimal stock with landing obligation ban will be larger than the optimal stock without landing obligation.

Moreover,

- If stock with LO is less than stock at MSY, then the optimal level of landings with discard ban will be greater than landings without discard ban.
- If stock with LO is greater than stock at MSY, then the optimal level of landings with discard ban will be less than the optimal level of landings without discard ban.

The landing obligation changes the equilibrium stock under open access as well as in an optimally regulated fishery. The catchability coefficient plays a significant role, and therefore the incentive to change the catchability coefficient is an important element in the new regulatory system. The model is a simple one-species, two-cohort model, and although most fisheries are much more complicated, the findings illustrate some key features of the introduction of a landing obligation.

In the following, we look at the economic impact of implementing an LO for the Danish fishery, a multispecies fishery regulated by ITQs. This gives some insight into the importance of some of the points mentioned the above.

Case studies: the Danish fishery

Two examples of analyses of the economic impact of implementing of landing obligation will be presented. The first assessment focuses on the short-term impact and under different assumptions about quota uplift, prices of landed unwanted by-catch fish, selectivity, and legal minimum size of marketable fish for human consumption. The second assessment is the medium- and long-term impact of a landing obligation.

Assessment of the short-term economic impact of an LO

The focus in this study is the short-term impact of an LO, as analysed by Ravensbeck et al. (2015). Detailed data for the Danish fishery is used and the importance of various assumptions regarding implementation is considered (see Ravensbeck et al., 2015; Andersen and Ståhl, 2016). The LO covers all quota-regulated species. The analysis uses the fishery's performance in 2013 as a baseline and then imposes the LO under various assumptions. The economic impacts are calculated for an average vessel in each vessel group. Under different assumptions about management regime, costs, prices and behaviour, different scenarios are analysed. Medium- or longer-run changes (e.g. biological impacts due to these changes) are not analysed. Furthermore, full enforcement is assumed. The economic impacts of the LO are calculated as changes against a baseline without an LO. The baseline is the fishery as it was in 2013. The analysis locks the fishery patterns as they were in 2013, and the calculations are carried out as if the full LO is implemented at once on the fishery in 2013. Under the LO, the fishermen thus continue their catch patterns, including where they fish, while facing a new management regime.

Changes are calculated for revenue, variable costs, profitability, wages and gross margin. Revenue is defined as landings value. Variable costs consist of fuel, ice, supplies, landings and sales costs. Profitability is the landings value minus the variable costs. Wages are assumed to be in proportion to the landed value, and thus change with the change in revenue. The gross margin is the landings value minus variable costs and wages. As it is assumed that neither fixed costs nor fishery patterns change in the short run, these are not considered in the analysis.

Overall, without the LO, landings equal catch minus discards. Under the LO, landings equal catches. The analysis considers scenarios with a management regime of quota top-ups and situations without quota top-ups (i.e. landings of previously discarded fish are written off on the quota). Landings above the minimum size, and thus aimed at human consumption, are labelled marketable landings (ML). Under quota top-ups, marketable landings ($ML^{N,Q}$) are simply the old amount of marketable landings (L^O), that is $ML^{N,Q} = L^O$, since the quota has simply been increased with the former amount of discard. Without quota top-ups, marketable landings (ML^N) are reduced by the amount of previously discarded fish, $ML^N = L^O(1 - dp)$, where dp is the discard percentage.

The analysis then explores what happens when assumptions change with regard to handling costs and minimum sizes. Furthermore, the analysis includes behavioural changes resulting in changes in quota utilization and in an improved selectivity. This is done while keeping the fishery patterns as they were in 2013 and under regimes of either quota top-ups or quota write-offs.

By assumption, vessels' behaviour is driven by the species they have quotas for. Therefore, only landings data on quota species are directly included in the analysis, and changes in landings of these species drive the economic results. Landings of non-quota species change in proportion to changes in effort, and are thus indirectly included in the analysis. Changes in the amount of fish landed, be it quota or non-quota species, are assumed not to change prices obtained at harbour or at fishmeal and oil factories.

Neither stock effects, technology changes, complex behavioural changes, such as change of fishing area or quota purchases, imperfect enforcement nor choke species issues are considered in the analysis. Choke species are species for which quotas are fished before those of the target species, and therefore the fishery has to stop. This could, for example, be cod caught while targeting Norway lobster. Further, only demersal species, and no pelagic or industrial species, are considered in the analysis. Downstream effects are assessed by an input/output model, while long-term effects are assessed descriptively.

Data

The analysis made use of publicly available data for 2013 on Danish landings and quotas obtained through the AgriFish Agency and economic data obtained through Statistics Denmark. The year 2013 was chosen since this was the most recent year with final economic data in the database. The discard ratios per species based on vessel type and area have been estimated by DTU Aqua (see Ravensbeck et al., 2015).

Because of data limitations, only demersal species are considered. Demersal fisheries do indeed face issues regarding selectivity (e.g. minimum sizes), thus being impacted to a large degree by the landing obligation.

The landed unwanted by-catch fish (previously discarded), that is fish below the minimum size for consumption, is assumed to supply the fishmeal and oil industry, obtaining a price of DKK2/kg (Marine Ingredients, 2015). The price of transportation to the fishmeal and oil plant has been estimated at DKK1/kg by COWI (2015). Thus, unwanted by-catch fish obtain a sales price of DKK1/kg.

Vessel data in the database are at the level of length or gear group. Only non-specialized vessels at commercial activity levels[1] are included. Specialized fisheries target mussels, for example, and are managed by licenses and not individual transferrable quotas (ITQs) as the rest of the Danish fishery. The analysis is thereby carried out for 19 segments, and for the North Sea fleet, Baltic Sea fleet and Skagerrak/Kattegat fleet, as well as the Danish fleet as a whole.

To provide an overview, Table 6.1 shows the economic performance of the fishery as it was in 2013 by fishing area and in total. As explained in the methodology section, the economic impacts are calculated as changes compared to this baseline situation.

The North Sea accounts for the largest share of revenue and costs. Kattegat/Skagerrak has almost twice the revenue of the Baltic Sea, but has the lowest costs, reflecting the high-value species such as Norway lobster caught in Kattegat/Skagerrak.

Table 6.1 Economic performance of the Danish fishery in 2013

	DKK1,000[1]			
	Baltic Sea	*Kattegat/Skagerrak*	*North Sea*	*Total*
Revenue	278,135	493,440	1,745,283	2,516,858
Variable costs	84,373	58,182	442,961	585,515
Wages	61,155	42,651	366,602	470,408
Gross margin	132,607	392,607	935,720	1,460,935

Source: Ravensbeck et al. (2015).

Note: (1) €1 = DKK7.5.

Scenarios

To illustrate the impacts of the LO under possible management regimes and fisher behaviour, the analysis is carried out for several different scenarios. The economic impact is calculated as changes from a baseline scenario: the fishery in 2013 without the landing obligation (scenario 0).

As can be seen in Table 6.2, scenarios with quota top-ups are labelled A-scenarios, and scenarios without are labelled B-scenarios. A-scenarios thus entail the crowding out of more valuable consumption landings by previously discarded fish that now take up part of the quota.

Scenarios A1 and B1 consider the imposition of the LO directly on the fishery as it was in 2013, without and with quota uplifts, respectively. Scenarios A2 and B2 are like A1 and B1, although with an additional cost of handling and landing previously discarded fish that need to be brought into harbour. A1, A2, B1 and B2 thus illustrate the situations in which no further management change takes place except the LO itself.

Scenarios A3 and B3 are like A1 and B1, although with increased minimum sizes of cod and Norway lobster in some areas. This means that a quantity of previously discarded cod and Norway lobster are now above the new minimum size but below the old minimum size. As these particular landings are assumed to no longer be below the minimum consumption size, and thus to no longer fetch the price of fish for meal and oil purposes, it is assumed that they fetch the price of consumption fish in the lowest price bracket. As the lowest price bracket contains the lowest-quality fish, and thus the smallest fish, it is deemed plausible that because of their small size, they would fetch a price of this level. It is assumed that these new quantities of fish supplied to the consumption market do not affect consumption prices in the short run. These scenarios thus illustrate the effect of the LO combined with a potential management measure and hypothetical market response to reduce potential economic adversity of the new policy.

Without the discard ban, underutilized quotas are observed across species and areas. It is likely that a discard ban without quota uplifts will result in an increased quota utilization. Such an increased utilization, and thus higher landings revenue, will reduce the negative economic consequences in face of the LO. Therefore, an additional scenario without quota uplifts, A4, incorporates increased quota utilization. This scenario thus illustrates the imposition of the LO with no further management changes, but where behavioural changes initiated by fishers themselves can reduce negative economic impacts.

Additionally, two scenarios called C1 and C2 resemble scenarios A1 and A2 but assume a behavioural change that reduces discard rates by 25 per cent. Scenario C2 is only calculated for the Danish fleet as a whole. These scenarios thus exemplify situations without additional management measures in which fishermen themselves find ways to reduce landings of previously discarded fish. This could, for example, take place by changing fishing time and place. Table 6.2 provides an overview of the scenarios.

Table 6.2 Scenarios

Scenario	Description	Explanation
0	Basis scenario: the Danish fishery in 2013 is used as basis for comparison.	2013 situation with discard for different segments and fishing areas.
	Landing obligation is implemented. The price obtained for fish previously discarded is DKK1/kg[1]	
A1	2013 situation without quota uplift, and therefore a reduction of landings and effort **(effort reduction)**.	Reduction of catch value, the landings of previously discarded fish/unwanted by-catch fish replace some of the wanted catch. Effort reduction (reduction in variable costs) in proportion to the reduction in catch.
A2	As scenario A1 and additional costs of handling former discard onboard **(A1 + handling costs)**.	Increased variable costs caused by costs of handling a more mixed catch. This can be viewed as a 'worst-case scenario'.
A3	No quota uplift, and therefore effort reduction, but a part of landed unwanted by-catch fish can now be sold for consumption **(A1 + new minimum sizes)**.	2013 situation, no quota uplift, but where the part of landed unwanted by-catch fish that was previously between the old and new minimum sizes will be sold for consumption (lowest price class).
A4	No quota uplift, and therefore effort reduction, but with improved quota utilization (≤ TAC) **(A1 + improved quota utilization)**.	2013 situation, no quota uplift, but the quota utilization increases when the previously discarded fish is included in the quota.
B1	2013 situation with quota uplift and no reduction in effort **(quota uplift)**.	Landings = previous landings + estimated discard (after LO: landed unwanted by-catch fish).
B2	Quota uplift, no effort changes, but additional costs of handling former discard on board **(B1 + handling costs)**.	Increased variable costs caused by costs of handling a more mixed catch.
B3	Quota uplift and a part of former discard can now be sold for consumption purposes **(B1 + new minimum sizes)**.	2013 situation, with quota uplift, but where the part of former discard that was previously between the old and new minimum sizes can be sold for consumption purposes (lowest price class).
C1	2013 situation with behavioural changes **(A1 + behavioural changes)**.	C1 is like A1, but a change in behaviour is assumed, which reduces unwanted catches (former discard) by 25 per cent.
C2	2013 situation, with quota uplift and behavioural changes **(B1 + behavioural changes)**.	C2 is like B1, but a change in behaviour is assumed, which reduces unwanted catches (former discard) by 25 per cent (C2 is only calculated for the total fishery).

Source: Based on Ravensbeck et al. (2015).

Note: (1) €1 = DKK7.5.

Results of the short-term analysis

Overall, fleet segments with higher discard rates are the ones most affected by the LO (i.e. small and medium-sized trawlers). The results show a clear divide with respect to the effect of quota write-offs or quota top-ups on economic performance, as seen in the A- and B-scenarios, respectively. Quota uplifts allow fishermen to maintain their previous revenue while obtaining additional revenue from the sale of below minimum size fish to the fishmeal and oil industry. An LO with quota top-ups may therefore benefit the fishermen. If, on the other hand, the LO was to be implemented by writing off previously discarded fish on the quota, these will crowd out more valuable target fish and revenue, and profitability losses are observed.

A reduction of the minimum sizes of cod and Norway lobster also reduces losses compared to a situation of quota write-offs with no additional management measure. Further, a behavioural change of increased quota utilization, where possible, can reduce the economic losses for some segments. A (technically imposed) behavioural change reducing discard percentages by 25 per cent can also alleviate negative effects. New minimum sizes improve earnings and profitability in the B-scenarios compared to the baseline, as well as compared to the LO, with no further measures.

Norway lobster, cod and plaice in Kattegat, the Baltic Sea and Skagerrak, respectively, affect results the most as these are highly valuable catches, but at the same time have high discard rates for some segments and in some areas.

Further, the assessment of activity impacts on the fishery and downstream industry shows that the LO could increase activity if implemented with quota uplifts, while it would decrease activity if implemented without.

Table 6.3 presents the overall results for the whole Danish fleet. The scenarios are listed to the left and downwards. Economic impacts are presented in either DKK1,000 or in percentages compared to the baseline (i.e. the economic situation in 2013), and are listed horizontally for each scenario. Landings of previously discarded fish as well as changes in marketable landings (i.e. landings for human consumption) are also presented.

As seen in the A-scenarios in Table 6.3, implementing the LO without quota uplifts forces fishers to reduce effort. Here, the more valuable marketable landings are crowded out by less valuable landings of previously discarded fish now being sold to the fishmeal and oil industry at a lower price. The LO implemented with no further management measures decreases effort, and thus revenue and gross margin, by 7 and 9 per cent, respectively. When taking into account the increased handling and landing costs, the revenue and gross margin decrease by 7 and 10 per cent, respectively, compared to the baseline. New minimum sizes as well as increased quota utilization reduce economic losses. New minimum sizes in A3 reduce both revenue and gross margin by 4 per cent, while increased quota utilization decreases revenue and gross margin by 3 and 4 per cent, respectively. In these scenarios, the ratio between marketable and more valuable landings and previously discarded fish is increased compared to A1 and A2.

Scenarios with quota top-ups (B-scenarios) illustrate that increasing quotas with the previously discarded amounts benefits fishers in tackling the LO. The economic impact is almost neutral in scenarios B1 and B2, with increases in revenue of 0.4 per cent. Gross margins increase by 0.6 per cent in B1, whereas taking into account increased handling costs in B2 reduces gross margin by 1 per cent. It can even bring about a slight increase in revenue and gross margin if minimum sizes are reduced by 3 and 4 per cent, respectively. Behavioural changes reducing discard rates by 25 per cent will help reduce losses compared to A1 and A2, while the effect is almost neutral compared to B1 and B2. The effects seen for the whole Danish fleet, however, cover significant differences between fishing areas and fleets (see Andersen and Ståhl, 2016).

Conclusions on short-term impacts

Overall, implementing the LO without quota uplifts (A-scenarios) will cause reduced revenues and profitability in the Danish fisheries. In that case, the fisherman has to replace target fish with previously discarded fish on the same quota. It will take fewer trips to fill the quota. Effort and therefore also variable costs are reduced. However, in the analysis, it is assumed that non-target fish sell for a lower price than target fish for human consumption, and thereby revenue is reduced. If it is assumed that handling and sorting non-target fish carry an additional cost, revenue and profitability decrease further. However, if the minimum sizes on cod and Norway lobster are reduced, and assuming that part of the previously undersized and therefore discarded catch could be sold at the lowest consumption price since they would be eligible for consumption instead of fishmeal and oil, this would increase revenue and reduce the overall losses from the LO. Additionally, another scenario without quota top-ups but higher quota utilization analyses the effects of increasing utilization in order for the fishermen to better exploit the opportunities in their quotas. This would reduce losses from the LO. The effect of this, of course, depends on the level of quota utilization at the starting point. In the absence of new minimum sizes or increased quota utilization, a technically imposed behavioural change reducing discard rates by 25 per cent alleviates losses.

If implementing the LO without quota uplifts, but in combination with reduced minimum sizes or by fishermen increasing their quota utilization, losses can be reduced considerably, in some places by more than 50 per cent.

Increasing the quotas with the previously discarded amounts alleviates many of the potential losses, and does under certain assumptions bring about economic gains for the fisheries. The latter especially refers to scenarios of reduced minimum sizes where previously discarded cod and Norway lobster can now be sold at consumption prices.

The areas most affected by the LO are the Baltic Sea and Kattegat/Skagerrak, while the fisheries in the North Sea are less impacted. By vessel group, small and medium-sized trawlers are the ones most affected by the LO. Here, the

Table 6.3 The Danish fleet

| Scenarios | DKK1,000[1] or % | | | | Tons | |
| | Changes in | | | | | |
	Δ revenue	Δ gross margin	Δ revenue	Δ gross margin	Δ unwanted by-catch landings	Δ marketable landings
A1: Effort reduction (no quota adjustment)	−168,815	−127,792	−7%	−9%	−3,896	−8,541
A2: A1 + handling costs	−168,815	−147,554	−7%	−10%	−3,896	−8,541
A3: A1 + new minimum sizes	−92,719	−65,272	−4%	−4%	−5,891	−6,328
A4: A1 + increased quota utilization	−69,356	−58,270	−3%	−4%	−1,689	−2,469
B1: Corresponding quota uplifts	10,769	8,435	0.4%	0.6%	0	0
B2: B1 + handling costs	10,769	−20,490	0.4%	−1%	0	0
B3: B1 + new minimum sizes	73,349	64,997	3%	4%	−4,084	6,685
C1: A1 + behavioural changes (25 per cent less unwanted by-catch)	−126,613	−95,845	−5%	−7%	−5,614	−6,406
C2: B1 + behavioural changes (25 per cent less unwanted by-catch)	6,822	5,209	0.3%	0.4%	−3,947	0

Source: Ravensbeck et al. (2015).

Note: (1) €1 = DKK7.5.

decrease in revenue is, on average, 20 per cent, while the decrease in gross margin is between 30 and 50 per cent. Trawlers overall are indeed the group most affected, experiencing revenue decreases of between 17 and 28 per cent, and decreases in gross margin of between 27 and 48 per cent.

Because of high discard rates and highly valuable target catches for consumption, the fisheries for Norway lobster and cod in Kattegat, as well as cod and plaice in the Baltic Sea and Skagerrak, are affected the most by the LO.

Assessment of the medium- and long-term economic impact of an LO

The following sections go through the analysis of medium- and long-term impacts of the LO, as analysed by Hoff and Frost (2017). The medium- and long-term analysis is based on a linear programming model (e.g. see Andersen et al., 2010; Hoff and Frost, 2017). The data used in the analysis by Hoff and Frost (2017) is as for the short-term analyses, but extended to the years 2012–2014 and to 34 fleet segments, and includes 20 species. Each vessel maximizes profit by trading quotas and by reallocating fishing effort. The incentives for the Danish fishery to adjust to policy changes are strongly influenced by the Danish ITQ system, which covers almost the entire Danish fishery.

The medium-term analysis is defined by a fishery that adjusts its fishing pattern through quota trading while the number of vessels is fixed within each fleet segment. In the long-term scenarios, the fixed number of vessels assumption is removed.

Scenarios

The scenarios (see Table 6.4) illustrate the impacts of the LO for three alternative assumptions regarding price of landed unwanted by-catch (used in the fishmeal and oil industry), high landing cost, and lower legal minimum size for human consumption. The economic impacts for the various scenarios with and without quota uplift are calculated as changes from a baseline scenario without the landing obligation. The LP model gives estimates for the medium-term case and the long-term case based on data for the fishery for the years 2012–2015. The impact of the LO is the differences between the estimates without and with LO.

In the analyses, the medium term with LO with a positive price for landed previously discard fish (ML1) is compared to the medium term without LO (ML0) and extended to the case with high landing costs (ML3) and a lower legal minimum fish size for human consumption (ML4). In all the medium-term analyses, the number of vessels is kept constant, but fishing effort across vessels and between months and fishing areas is allocated to maximize economic profit for the whole fleet.

The analyses of the long term are done as for the medium term, except that the number of vessels is adjusted to maximize long-term economic profit for the whole fleet. The long term with LO with a positive price for landed previous discard fish (L1) is compared to the long term without LO (L0) and

Table 6.4 Scenarios in the analysis of the long-term consequences of the landing obligation[1]

Scenario	Description	Explanation
K0	Basis short term: the Danish fishery in 2015.	2015 situation where the LO is not implemented. Quotas are those for 2015, while days at sea, catch per unit of effort and landing patterns are based on averages for 2012–2014.
ML0	Basis medium term: the Danish fishery in 2015 optimized with regard to days at sea.	As K0, but where it is asked how the economic situation in 2015 could have been if days at sea were distributed in an economically optimal way between fleet segments, months and fishing areas. The number of vessels are kept constant.
L0	Basis long term: the Danish fishery in 2015 optimized with regard to days at sea and number of vessels.	As ML0, but where the number of vessels are adjusted to the optimal number.

Landing obligation is implemented. The price obtained for fish previously discarded is DKK1.5/kg[2]

ML1	Landing obligation – medium term	As ML0, but where landing costs for previously discarded fish/unwanted by-catch fish is DKK0 and sales price for these fish is DKK1.5/kg.
L1	Landing obligation – long term	As ML1, but where the number of vessels in each segment is adjusted so that the economic performance of the total fleet is maximized.
ML3	Handling costs – medium term	As ML1, but with a landing cost of DKK2.5/kg for fish below the reference size.
L3	Handling costs – long term	As ML3, but where the number of vessels is adjusted to maximize the economic performance of the total fleet.
ML4	New minimum sizes – medium term	As ML1, but where the quantity of previously discarded fish/unwanted by-catch fish that is now between the old and the new minimum size can be sold for human consumption.
L4	New minimum sizes – long term	As L1, but where the quantity of previously discarded fish/unwanted by-catch fish that is now between the old and the new minimum size can be sold for human consumption.

Source: Hoff and Frost (2017).

Notes: (1) In Hoff and Frost (2017), a scenario 2 (ML2 and L2) is included, and covers an EU rule of maximum by-catches and no LO. (2) €1 = DKK7.5.

extended to the case with high landing costs (L3) and a lower legal minimum fish size for human consumption (L4). In all the long-term analyses, the number of vessels can be adjusted, and fishing effort across vessels and between months and fishing areas is allocated to maximize economic profit for the whole fleet.

Results and conclusions on the medium and long-term analysis

The overall picture for the scenarios without quota uplift is that total revenue, the profit and fishing effort will be reduced (see Tables 6.5 and 6.6). The fishery is restricted by the total allowable quota (TAC), and with no quota uplift, the fishing effort is reduced in all scenarios. The best case is where a larger part of the former discard can be landed for human consumption due to a lower minimum size. In this case, there is only a marginal reduction in profit. In the analyses, it is assumed that there are no price effects of the increased supply. Furthermore, it is assumed in the calculation that the stocks are constant, although there might be some increase in stocks due to a reduction in fishing mortality as catches are reduced compared to the management regime with no LO.

The picture is very different when the management regime allows for quota uplift (see Tables 6.7 and 6.8). In the analyses, it is assumed that the landing TAC is equal to the former catch TAC plus the (estimated) historical discard. If we assume no enforcement problems related to discard and that all catches are landed and reported, stock levels will be as under the regime without LO. In all scenarios, the consequences of quota uplifts are an increase in total revenue, profit and fishing effort. The positive effects are, as expected, largest in the long-term scenarios due to the adjustments of fleet size and changes of the fleet structure, which will increase the efficiency.

Discussion and conclusion

A fishery management system with landing obligation demands an extended version of the 'standard' fisheries economic models. At the same time, empirical analyses of the impact of an LO-based fisheries management system become more complicated. Furthermore, economic advice regarding an efficient management system will include focus on the incentives to fish more selectively and on illegal discard. The landing obligation will also have environmental impacts, as birds, seals and, more generally, ecosystem services will be affected as discards of fish will be reduced significantly.

If the landing obligation is rigorously introduced, then fishers will be restricted by choke species as the catch composition most likely will not fit the relative quotas between different species very well. This problem will differ across fleet segments if the allocation system is sticky or the ITQ system is restricted. For these reasons, the EU Common Fishery Policy, with the relative quota stability as a core element, will be put under pressure as only some of

Table 6.5 Key figures for medium-term scenarios without quota uplift

Scenarios	DKK billion[1] (%)		1,000 tons		1,000 days
	Total revenue	Gross margin	Marketable landings	Unwanted by-catch landings	Fishing effort/days at sea
ML0: Basis, no LO	4.0	2.0	903.2	23.0	74.6
Changes					
ML1: LO, fishmeal price	−0.3 (−5.4)	−0.1 (−2.9)	−9.3 (−1.0)	−10.0 (−43.7)	−8.8 (−11.8)
ML3: LO, ML1 + high handling costs	−0.3 (−6.8)	−0.1 (−3.9)	−12.9 (−1.4)	−10.6 (−46.1)	−10.1 (−13.5)
ML4: LO, ML1 + new minimum sizes	−0.2 (−3.1)	−0.0 (−0.1)	−13.6 (−1.5)	−10.0 (−43.6)	−9.7 (−13.1)

Source: Hoff and Frost (2017).

Note: Changes in absolute numbers from the basis scenario have been calculated based on absolute numbers for the scenarios in Hoff and Frost (2017). Numbers in parenthesis are percentage changes as presented in Hoff and Frost (2017) in relation to ML0. Gross margin = revenue − wages − variable costs.

Note: (1) €1 = DKK7.5.

Table 6.6 Key figures for long-term scenarios without quota uplift

Scenarios	DKK billion[1] (%)		1,000 tons		1,000 days
	Total revenue	Gross margin	Marketable landings	Unwanted by-catch landings	Fishing effort/days at sea
L0: Basis, no LO	4.1	2.1	1019.1	23.9	73.9
Changes					
L1: LO, fishmeal price	−0.3 (−6.1)	−0.1 (−3.6)	−29.3 (−2.9)	−11.6 (−48.4)	−9.3 (−12.6)
L3: LO, L1 + high handling costs	−0.3 (−7.2)	−0.1 (−4.6)	−30.2 (−3.0)	−12.0 (−50.3)	−10.0 (−13.5)
L4: LO, L1 + new minimum sizes	−0.2 (−3.6)	−0.0 (−0.1)	−31.7 (−3.1)	−11.5 (−48.4)	−10.4 (−14.0)

Source: Hoff and Frost (2017).

Note: Changes in absolute numbers from the basis scenario have been calculated based on absolute numbers for the scenarios in Hoff and Frost (2017). Numbers in parenthesis are percentage changes as presented in Hoff and Frost (2017) in relation to L0. Gross margin = revenue − wages − variable costs.

Note: (1) €1 = DKK7.5.

Table 6.7 Key figures for medium-term scenarios with quota uplift

Scenarios	DKK billion[1] (%)		1,000 tons		1,000 days
	Total revenue	Gross margin	Marketable landings	Unwanted by-catch landings	Fishing effort/days at sea
ML0: Basis, no LO	4.0	2.0	903.3	23.0	74.6
Changes					
ML1: LO, fishmeal price	0.1 (2.5)	0.0 (1.5)	2.1 (0.2)	−4.3 (−18.8)	3.4 (4.6)
ML3: LO, ML1 + high handling costs	0.0 (0.7)	0.0 (0.2)	−0.6 (−0.1)	−5.1 (−22.1)	2.5 (3.4)
ML4: LO, ML1 + new minimum sizes	0.3 (7.6)	0.1 (7.0)	−0.8 (−0.1)	−4.3 (−19.0)	1.6 (2.1)

Source: Hoff and Frost (2017).

Note: Changes in absolute numbers from the basis scenario have been calculated based on absolute numbers for the scenarios in Hoff and Frost (2017). Numbers in parenthesis are percentage changes as presented in Hoff and Frost (2017) in relation to ML0. Gross margin = revenue − wages − variable costs.

Note: (1) €1 = DKK7.5.

Table 6.8 Key figures for long-term scenarios with quota uplift

Scenarios	DKK billion[1] (%)		1,000 tons		1,000 days
	Total revenue	Gross margin	Marketable landings	Unwanted by-catch landings	Fishing effort/days at sea
L0: Basis, no LO	4.1	2.1	1,019.1	24.0	73.9
Changes					
L1: LO, fishmeal price	0.1 (2.7)	0.0 (1.7)	6.2 (0.6)	−6.2 (−25.7)	2.9 (3.9)
L3: LO, L1 + high handling costs	0.0 (1.4)	0.0 (0.5)	5.3 (0.5)	−6.7 (−27.6)	2.7 (3.7)
L4: LO, L1 + new minimum sizes	0.3 (7.4)	0.1 (7.3)	−3.1 (−0.3)	−6.5 (−26.8)	1.4 (1.9)

Source: Hoff and Frost (2017).

Note: Changes in absolute numbers from the basis scenario have been calculated based on absolute numbers for the scenarios in Hoff and Frost (2017). Numbers in parenthesis are percentage changes as presented in Hoff and Frost (2017) in relation to L0. Gross margin = revenue − wages − variable costs.

Note: (1) €1 = DKK7.5.

the EU member states use an ITQ system and there is no general quota trading system across member states in place.

Models and data are important for doing applied economic analyses of a landing obligation. Empirical analyses using such models could help in providing answers for a number of fisheries, analysing and evaluating what is useful and what might happen. Such analyses could include changing behaviour with regard to selectivity, substitution, economic viability of fleets, learning across fleets and fisheries, and investment decisions and disinvestment. The empirical part of the chapter gives a few examples of such analyses.

Future work on the landing obligation is part of the EU project Discardless (www.discardless.eu), with focus on impacts of stock effects and biodiversity, technology changes and selectivity, complex behavioural changes, as well as imperfect control and enforcement of the landing obligation.

Acknowledgements

Thanks to referees and conference participants for valuable comments and suggestions. Part of this project has been funded by the European Union Horizon 2020 Research and Innovation Programme under Grant Agreement. No. 633680 (Discardless Project).

Note

1 The Department of Food and Resource Economics classify commercially active vessels according to earnings. In 2012, the minimum earnings for being categorized as a commercial vessel were DKK270,000 (US$1 = approximately DKK6.70).

References

Andersen, P. and Ståhl, L. (2016). The economics of a landing obligation: short term impacts for the Danish fishery of implementing the EU landing obligation. *IFRO Report*, No. 253. Department of Food and Resource Economics, University of Copenhagen.

Andersen, P., Andersen, L. and Frost, H. (2010). ITQs in Denmark and resource rent gains. *Marine Resource Economics*, 25: 11–22.

Andersen, P., Andersen, J. and Mardle, S. (2014). What's going to happen with the CFP reform discard policy? *IIFET 2014 Australia Conference Proceedings*.

Anderson, L.G. (1994). An economic analysis of highgrading in ITQ fisheries regulation programs. *Marine Resource Economics*, 9: 209–226.

Arnason, R. (1994). On catch discarding in fisheries. *Marine Resource Economics*, 9: 189–207.

Boyce, J.R. (1996). An economic analysis of the fisheries bycatch problem. *Journal of Environmental Economics and Management*, 31: 314–336.

Clark, C.W. (1980). Towards a predictive model for the economic regulation of commercial fisheries. *Canadian Journal of Fisheries and Aquatic Science*, 37: 1111–1129.

COWI (2015). Merværdipotentialet i fisk landet som følge af indførelsen af landings-forpligtelsen. *NaturErhvervstyrelsen 2015* (in Danish). Available at: http://eur-lex.europa.eu/legal-content/EN/TXT/PDF/?uri=CELEX:32013R1380&from=EN (accessed 5 January 2018).

EU (European Union) (2013). Regulation (EU) no 1380/2013 of the European Parliament and of the Council of 11 December 2013 on the Common Fisheries Policy. *Official Journal of the European Union*, L354: 22–61. Available at: http://eurlex.europa.eu/legal-content/EN/TXT/PDF/?uri=CELEX:32013R1380&from= EN (accessed 5 January 2018).

FAO (Food Agriculture Organization) (1996). Report of the technical consultation on reduction of wastage in fisheries. Tokyo, Japan, 28 October–1 November 1996. *FAO Fisheries Report*, No. 547. Rome: FAO.

Frost, H., Hoff, A. and Andersen, P. (2015). Report on the available economic data related to discard, on bio-economic fishery models, on the current knowledge on discard incentives, perception, attitudes and resulting fisher behaviour and on knowledge gaps for all case studies fisheries. *Discardless Deliverable*, 2.1. Available at: www.discardless.eu/media/results/DiscardLess_Deliverable_-_D2-1_14Sept2015. pdf (accessed 5 January 2018).

Hoff, A. and Frost, H. (2017). *Langsigtede erhvervsøkonomiske konsekvenser af discardforbuddet* [*Long-Term Economic Impact of the Discard Ban*]. IFRO Report, No. 256. Department of Food and Resource Economics, University of Copenhagen (in Danish).

Marine Ingredients (2015). Personal communication at a meeting with the Director, 18 March 2015.

Nordic Council of Ministers (2003). Report from a workshop on discarding in Nordic Fisheries. Ed.: John Willy Valdemarsen, Fangstseksjonen, Havforskningsinstituttet, Bergen, Sophienberg Slot, København, 18–20 November 2002. TemaNord 2003: 537. Nordic Council of Ministers, Copenhagen.

Pascoe, S. (1997). Bycatch management and the economics of discarding. *FAO Fisheries Technical Paper 370*. Rome: FAO.

Ravensbeck, L., Ståhl, L., Andersen, J.L. and Andersen, P. (2015). Analyse af de erhvervsøkonomiske konsekvenser af discardforbuddet. *IFRO Rapport 242* (in Danish). Available at: http://curis.ku.dk/ws/files/143083454/IFRO_Rapport_242.pdf (accessed 5 January 2018).

Turner, M.A. (1997). Quota induced discarding in heterogeneous fisheries. *Journal of Environmental Economics and Management*, 33: 186–195.

Vestergaard, N. (1996). Discard behaviour highgrading and regulation: the case of the Greenland shrimp fishery. *Marine Resource Economics*, 11: 247–266.

Ward, J.M. (1994). The bioeconomic implications of bycatch reduction devise as a stock conservation management measure. *Marine Resource Economics*, 9(3): 227–240.

7 A simple application of bioeconomics to fisheries subsidies

U. Rashid Sumaila and Anna Schuhbauer

Introduction

The practice by governments of providing financial support, whether directly or indirectly, to the fishing sector is known as fisheries subsidies. Since a back-of-the-envelope calculation by the Food and Agricultural Organization of the United Nations (FAO) revealed that the total amount of fisheries subsidies paid by maritime countries globally could be over US$50 billion annually in the early 1990s, eliminating harmful fisheries subsidies has become a central issue in the quest to achieve sustainable fisheries worldwide. It is, however, worth noting that the issue of fisheries subsidies and its effects on overfishing is not new. Adam Smith (1970) himself expressed concerns about fisheries subsidies in his famous book *On the Wealth of Nations*:

> The [subsidy] to the white-herring fishery is a tonnage bounty; and is proportioned to the [weight] of the ship, not to her diligence or success in the fishery; and it has, I am afraid, been too common for vessels to fit out for the sole purpose of catching, not the fish, but the bounty.
>
> (Smith, 1970: 520)

Even though the initial FAO estimate of fisheries subsidies of US$54 billion per year has triggered the debate on the appropriateness of governments providing subsidies to their fishing sector, the actual estimate itself has come to be seen as an overestimate. More recent detailed studies put the amount of subsidies provide by maritime countries at between US$15 billion and US$27 billion (Milazzo, 1998; Sumaila et al., 2010). This is still a substantial amount given that the total gross revenue from the world's fisheries was estimated at between US$80 billion and US$85 billion (FAO, 2010).

There is a strong connection between fisheries governance, sustainable development, and how subsidies serve as a stumbling block for meeting sustainability goals (e.g. Clark et al., 2005; von Moltke, 2012). The crucial issue is that subsidies that motivate fishers to exert more fishing pressure in the face of ineffective management make the attainment of sustainability and conservation goals difficult, if not impossible, to achieve. These types of subsidies that can lead to overcapacity and overfishing are called variously in the literature 'harmful', 'bad' or 'capacity-enhancing' (for further explanations of these types of subsidies, see Milazzo, 1998; Sumaila et al., 2010).

Despite the significant amount of effort devoted to identifying and measuring fisheries subsidies and to analysing their potential and actual impacts on environmental and economic sustainability over the past decades (e.g. Milazzo, 1998; Heymans et al., 2011), there has been little progress in formulating an international regime for the regulation of fisheries subsidies. The negotiation for the improved discipline on fisheries subsidies at the World Trade Organization (WTO) has stalled in recent years, and considerable challenges remain before a meaningful agreement can be attained.

We present latest research results that show that as little as 16 per cent of the total global fisheries subsidies are given to the world's small-scale fisheries sector, even though they land an estimated 50 per cent of total global fish landings and employ about 90 per cent of fishing vessels (FAO, 2016; Pauly and Zeller, 2016). Hence, fisheries subsidies actually undermine the competitiveness of this vitally important fishing sector in terms of supporting the livelihoods of the world's economically vulnerable coastal communities (Charles, 2006).

Also, we present a simple application of bioeconomics to fisheries subsidies with the goal of explaining why we should care that our governments give away taxpayers' money as fisheries subsidies, especially subsidies that stimulate overcapacity and overfishing. We use a very simple bioeconomic model to show why certain subsidies stimulate overfishing, and provide the latest estimates of fisheries subsidies in the literature, as well as showing that the amount of taxpayer dollars given to the fishing sector are large. We also show that a significant majority of the subsidies provided are likely to stimulate overcapacity and overfishing, especially in situations where fisheries management is ineffective.

The basic bioeconomic model with subsidies

In the most basic sense, a bioeconomic model has two components, the biological and the economic. The former simply defines the rate of change of the fish biomass (Equation 7.1), while the latter defines the net benefit or profit generated from fishing (Equation 7.2):

$$\text{net annual change of biomass} = \text{growth} + \text{recruitment} - \text{natural mortality} - \text{catch} \tag{7.1}$$

$$\text{net benefit} = \text{benefit} - \text{cost} \tag{7.2}$$

Let X denote the biomass of fish; R, H, E, p and c represent net benefit, catch, fishing effort, price of fish and unit cost of fishing per unit of effort, respectively, then we have:

$$R = pH - cE \tag{7.3}$$

Under open access, the fishery reduces the biomass or stock level, X, until $R = 0$. If we substitute the famous Schaefer catch equation, expressed as $H = qEX$ (where q is the catchability coefficient), into Equation 7.3 and set the equation to zero, we obtain the open-access equilibrium where the following condition holds:

$$X = \frac{c}{pq}; \frac{dX}{dc} > 0, \frac{dX}{dp} < 0, \frac{dX}{dq} < 0 \tag{7.4}$$

Equation 7.4 is simple and yet very powerful. It says that under open access (or to generalize, under ineffective fisheries management), from the perspective of the fish (i.e. preferring a higher biomass), high cost of fishing, low prices and low technology are all good things. On the other hand, if your goal is to profit from fishing, then the reverse is true: therein lies one of the sources of tension and conflict between economics and ecology.

If government subsidies are provided that artificially reduce the cost of fishing (Equation 7.5), increase the price of fish (Equation 7.6) and/or improve the catchability coefficient (Equation 7.7), this would result in lower fish biomass:

$$X' = \frac{(c - s)}{pq} \tag{7.5}$$

$$X'' = \frac{c}{(p + s)q} \tag{7.6}$$

$$X''' = \frac{c}{pq(1 + zs)} \tag{7.7}$$

In the above equations, s denotes the amount of subsidy provided while z is a scaler that determines the fraction by which a unit of subsidy improves the catchability coefficient. A subsidy that reduces the cost of fishing, increases the price for fish or increases the catchability coefficient under open access or ineffective management would reduce fish biomass. This is the reason why many fisheries scientists, economists and managers argue for the elimination of cost-reducing, price-increasing and catchability-enhancing subsidies when a stock is already fully or over-exploited.

In the next sections, we present the latest estimates of the quantity and types of subsidies provided by governments around the world, and how much of these are provided to small-scale and large-scale fisheries, respectively.

Fisheries subsidies types and amounts

A number of categories, types and typologies of subsidies have been proposed in the literature (Milazzo, 1998; APEC, 2000; OECD, 2000; Charles, 2006) using various combinations of the following criteria: policy objectives; programme descriptions; scope, coverage and duration; monetary values; sources of funding; administering authority; subsidy recipients; and mechanisms of transfer (Westlund, 2004).

Using the potential impact of subsidy programmes on the sustainability of fishery resources, Khan et al. (2006) and Sumaila and Pauly (2006) classify subsidies as 'good' or 'beneficial', 'bad' or 'capacity enhancing', and 'ugly' or 'ambiguous'. We provide below more details about these types of subsidies, as defined by the cited articles.

Beneficial subsidies are programmes that lead to investment in the fishery resources, including enhancement of fish stocks through conservation and effective surveillance and enforcement of management measures:

- *Fisheries management programmes and services*: Programmes ensuring that fishery resources are appropriately managed and that regulations are enforced. These programmes include monitoring and surveillance, stock assessment and resource surveys, and habitat and stock enhancement (e.g. hatcheries).
- *Fishery research and development*: Programmes aimed at improving fishing methods, processing and other technological improvements to enhance the resource base and promote its sustainable exploitation.
- *Marine protected areas*: Programmes for the establishment and management of areas where commercial fishing is prohibited, with the aim of replenishing the enclosed and surrounding fish stocks.

Capacity-enhancing subsidies are programmes that lead to disinvestments in natural capital assets such that the fishing capacity develops to a point where resource over-exploitation makes it impossible to achieve optimal long-term yield (i.e. maximum economic yield, MEY, or maximum sustainable yield, MSY). These programmes include all forms of capital investments by the government that reduce cost of fishing or enhance revenue. It might be noted here that in small-scale fisheries (SSF), it has been argued that some of these subsidies may be crucial to increase product value (e.g. 'provide land-based infrastructures' such as ice plants) or save lives (e.g. 'fishery development projects and support services').

- *Fuel subsidies*: Programmes that enable fishers to purchase fuel below the national average price applied to purchases for other uses. These programmes include fuel price support, rebates and fuel tax exemptions.
- *Boat construction, renewal and modernization programmes*: Programmes where fishers receive public funds for purchase, construction, renewal and modernization of fishing vessels, including lending programmes and loan guarantees that enable fishers to receive loans at a below market rate.

- *Fishing port construction and maintenance*: Programmes where public funds are used to provide land-based infrastructures and services to fishers. Examples include landing sites, harbour maintenance and discounted moorage for fishing vessels.
- *Price and marketing support*: Programmes of market interventions such as value addition and price support to enhance the revenue generated from the fisheries (see comment regarding SSF above).
- *Fishery development projects and support services*: Programmes geared for fisheries enterprises development, including the provision of institutional support and services such as crew and vessel insurance, duty-free imports of inputs and other economic incentive programmes.
- *Foreign access fee*: Bilateral or multilateral fishing agreements where public funds are used to secure fishing rights in foreign exclusive economic zones for the domestic distant water fleet. Acquisition of such fishing rights are commonly achieved through cash payments or provision of fishing technologies or favourable market access, and when the costs of fishing right acquisitions are not recouped from the fishing industry, they are considered subsidies.

Ambiguous subsidies are programmes whose impacts are undetermined and may depend heavily on the conditions under which they are granted:

- *Fisher assistance programmes*: Payments to fishers to stop fishing temporarily or to ensure income during seasons of reduced catches. This type of subsidy can be capacity-enhancing since it increases revenue, or possibly beneficial as it may reduce fishing pressure by enabling fishers to cease fishing and allow the recovery of exploited fish stocks.
- *Vessel buy-backs*: Programmes where public funds are used to promote decommissioning of fishing vessels and retirement of fishing licences. In principal, such programmes would reduce fishing pressure and allow stock recovery; however, if these programmes are anticipated by fishers, they can be capacity-enhancing by encouraging fishers to increase their fishing capacity prior to the buy-backs (Clark et al., 2005).
- *Rural fishing community development programmes*: Programmes geared towards development of rural fishing communities with objectives of poverty alleviation and food security. Subsidy support programmes such as these are unsustainable without sufficient fisheries management, and promote a large excess of rural labour that may lead to Malthusian overfishing (Pauly, 1997).

Determining the amount of subsidies paid by maritime countries to their fishing sector is difficult because of the lack of access to reliable and consistent information on fisheries subsidies programmes. Also, there is little consistency in definition, data source or methodology across the estimates in many maritime countries. As a result, there has been a diverse range of estimates of the magnitude of government subsidies to the sector.

The first global estimate of fisheries subsidies was provided by the FAO (1993), which was calculated simply by deducting the estimated total costs from the total revenue generated by global fisheries to arrive at global estimated annual fisheries subsidies of US$54 billion. The next was an in-depth study by Milazzo (1998), which found that annual fisheries subsidies were in the range of US$11 billion to US$20 billion per year, which was nearly 20 per cent of the landed value of gross revenues of global fisheries. At the regional level, a study by a major international accounting firm conducted for the Asia-Pacific Economic Cooperation estimated subsidies given by its members at US$8.9 billion (APEC, 2000), while the OECD estimated annual fisheries subsidies of US$6.4 billion (OECD, 2005, 2006b) for its member countries. The WWF, using subsidies reported by APEC, OECD and WTO members, found that officially reported subsidies were US$13 billion per year in 2001, and concluded that the actual global yearly total was at least US$15 billion, and very possibly higher (WWF, 2001).

Following their earlier publications (e.g. Khan et al., 2006; Sumaila and Pauly, 2006), Sumaila et al. (2010) estimated global total subsidies to be between US$25 billion and US$29 billion a year. Using the classification of subsidies described above, the authors concluded that US$16 billion, or about 60 per cent of the global subsidies, can be classified as 'harmful', with another US$3 billion categorized as 'ambiguous' subsidies. These estimates show that the developed countries jointly accounted for nearly 70 per cent of the global fisheries subsidies and 65 per cent of the 'capacity-enhancing' ones.

Although there are large differences among the various estimates of fisheries subsidies, all studies conclude that the scale of fisheries subsidies is considerable, given that the total value of global fisheries (i.e. landed values of the marine fisheries catches) has recently been estimated to be around US$100 billion per year (Swartz et al., 2013).

The newest global estimate of subsidies is US$35 billion in 2009, which is similar to two of the latest estimates once inflation is taken into account. The composition of this total is illustrated in Figure 7.1, showing that fuel subsidies represent the largest subsidy category. Capacity-enhancing subsidies are still larger than beneficial and ambiguous subsidies combined, representing 57 per cent of the total US$35 billion (see Figure 7.1).

About 65 per cent of total subsidies go to developed country fisheries in comparison to developing countries (see Figure 7.2). Since most of the world's small-scale fishers are in the developing world, small-scale fishers generally receive relatively less subsidies per person compared to large-scale fishers. In the next section, we present more details on the distribution of subsidies to small- compared to large-scale fisheries.

Similar to what had been found in previous studies, Asia dominates subsidies provided to marine fisheries, both in total and also when looking specifically into the capacity-enhancing category (see Figure 7.3). This result should probably not be too surprising since Asia catches more than 50 per cent of the global marine fish catch.

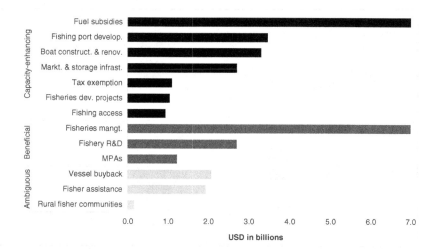

Figure 7.1 Composition of the subsidy estimates by sectors. This shows that fuel subsidies contribute the greatest part of the total subsidy (22 per cent of the total), followed by subsidies for management (20 per cent of the total) and ports and harbours (10 per cent of the total). Subsidies contributed by developed countries (65 per cent of the total) are far greater than those contributed by developing countries (35 per cent of the total).

Source: Sumaila et al. (2016).

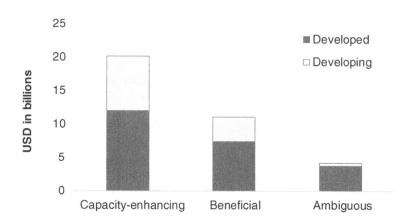

Figure 7.2 Global fisheries subsidy estimates by categories. This shows that capacity-enhancing subsidies are far greater than ambiguous and beneficial subsidies, in both developing and developed countries.

Source: Sumaila et al. (2016).

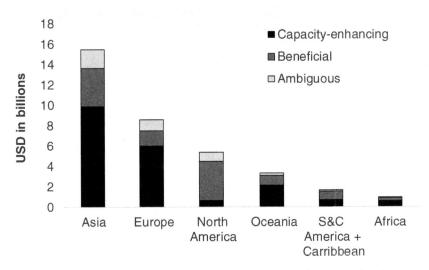

Figure 7.3 Subsidy estimates by major geographic region. This shows that Asia is
by far the greatest subsidizing region (43 per cent of total), followed by
Europe (25 per cent of total) and North America (16 per cent of total).
For all regions, the amount of capacity-enhancing subsidies is higher than
other categories, except in North and South America, which have higher
beneficial subsidies.

Source: Sumaila et al. (2016).

Allocation of subsidies to small- and large-scale fisheries

The material presented in this section is based on recent work reported in
Schuhbauer (2017) and Schuhbauer et al. (2017). Our objective is to understand the role that fisheries subsidies play in small- compared to large-scale
fisheries globally, in particular as it relates to their ability to be economically
viable (Schuhbauer et al., 2017). Most current studies focus on the large-
scale fishing sector, and the impact these subsidies have specifically on small-
scale fisheries (SSF) are unknown. Small-scale fisheries around the world
are facing similar problems and threats, some of which are: low economic
performance; inability for small-scale fishing communities to retain most of
the benefits from their fisheries; relatively high incidence of poverty and
undernourishment in certain SSF communities; and pressure from globaliza-
tion and industrialization, as well as climate change. Identifying the impacts
that fisheries subsidies might have on these fisheries will help improve the
understanding of their vulnerabilities and prepare them to withstand some of
the threats they face.

Small-scale fisheries are defined in many ways using a variety of criteria.
Characteristics used to split a country or a region's fishery into large- and

small-scale are often relative (i.e. small-scale in one region might be considered large-scale in another). Hence, there is no single universally agreed definition of small-scale fisheries (for an attempt, see Sumaila et al., 2001; Guyader et al., 2013; Natale et al., 2015). Despite SSF being such a contextual term, there is also some common ground found in these fisheries. SSF are often perceived to be fisheries that use low technologically advanced gears, and whose products are usually for the fisher's own household consumption and/or sold locally (Charles, 2001; FAO and World Fish Center, 2008; McConney and Charles, 2009; Pomeroy and Andrew, 2011). Often, small-scale fisheries tend to be tied to their local communities, reflecting their traditional and cultural values (FAO and World Fish Center, 2008; Pomeroy and Andrew, 2011). For the purposes of this study, however, we use each country's own definition of SSF. In cases where no national definitions were found for the small-scale or artisanal fishing sector, we adopt the definition proposed by the *Sea Around Us*: SSF operate in domestic waters, within their country's exclusive economic zone (EEZ), maximum 50 km off the coast or 200 m depth, and include both commercial and non-commercial fisheries (Pauly and Zeller, 2015, 2016).

The starting point for the analysis reported in Schuhbauer (2017) and Schuhbauer et al. (2017) is the country-level fisheries subsidies database reported in (Sumaila et al., 2010, 2016). Of the 146 maritime countries that are included in the database, subsidies in 81 countries were analysed, selected based on data availability and the total amount of subsidies they provide globally. In all, these countries gave 98 per cent of the estimated US$35 billion annual global fisheries subsidies in 2009.

A simple approach is applied to divide national subsidies amounts into those received by small-scale and large-scale fisheries (illustrated in Figure 7.4). First, we identify and record the quantitative data available about the amount of subsidies given to small- and large-scale fisheries, respectively (Group 1). Where there are no quantitative data, we ask whether qualitative information is available about the split, and if the answer is yes (Group 2), then we use the available qualitative data to allocate subsidies to the two sectors (e.g. subsidies to deep-sea trawler fleets are allocated to LSF while subsidies provided to artisanal, non-motorized vessels are allocated to SSF). For the subsidies that we do not have any qualitative data on (Group 3), we allocate according to catch, i.e. if the catch taken by SSF is 30 per cent of the total, we allocate 30 per cent of the total subsidy to SSF (see Figure 7.4).

Out of the estimated US$35 billion, Schuhbauer (2017) and Schuhbauer et al. (2017) estimate that about US$5.6 billion (i.e. 15.8 per cent of total) go to the small-scale sector. Furthermore, the majority of overall fisheries subsidies that go to large-scale fishers are capacity-enhancing subsidies (see Figure 7.5).

Looking at subsidies provided per fish worker or fisher, we find that at a global scale, a fisher employed in LSF receives around four times more support

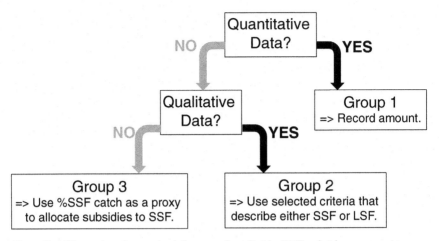

Figure 7.4 Illustrating the methodology used to divide 2009 subsidy amounts into small- and large-scale fisheries.

Source: Schuhbauer (2017) and Schuhbauer et al. (2017).

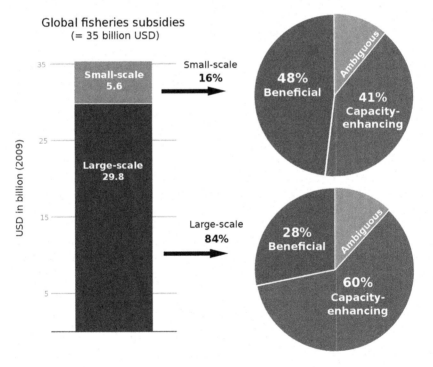

Figure 7.5 Global fisheries subsidies divided into large- and small-scale fisheries and split into three subsidy categories: beneficial, capacity-enhancing and ambiguous.

Source: Schuhbauer (2017) and Schuhbauer et al. (2017).

Table 7.1 Subsidies in US$ million from 2009 and subsidy intensity (subsidy amount / number of fishers), information on direct employment (# of fishers)

Region	SSF subsidies (US$ × 10⁶)	LSF subsidies (US$ × 10⁶)	SSF subsidies (per cent)	SSF subsidy intensity (US$ per fisher)	LSF subsidy intensity (US$ per fisher)	Ratio SSF/ LSF intensity
Africa	291	600	33	129	717	5.5
Asia	3,023	12,490	19	194	418	2.5
Oceania	141	3,178	4	212	68,988	325★
South America & Caribbean	526	1,164	31	188	1,058	5.6
Europe	600	7,971	7	3,682	12,654	3.4
North America	1,023	4,362	19	2,279	12,219	5.4
Total	5,605	29,767	16	256	1,028	4.0

Source: Teh and Sumaila (2013).

Note: ★ The value for Oceania is an outlier probably due to an underestimation of large-scale fishers active in that region because of the presence of large-scale foreign pelagic vessels active in its waters.

through subsidies than a fisher employed in SSF (see Table 7.1). Regionally, it is interesting to note that while Africa provides the largest percentage of subsidies to SSF, overall it provides the smallest amount of total fisheries subsidies compared to all other regions (see Table 7.1).

Example: Mexican fisheries subsidies

Schuhbauer et al. (2017) estimate that approximately 30 per cent of all fisheries subsidies go to the small-scale sector. To arrive at this number, data on Mexican fisheries subsidies were collected from different reports and publications and updated where possible using fisheries reports, National Commission of Aquaculture and Fishing (CONAPESCA) annual reports, peer-reviewed articles, Organisation for Economic Co-operation and Development (OECD) reports, and grey literature (OECD, 2006a; Lara and Guevara-Sangines, 2012; Ramírez-Rodríguez and Almendárez-Hernández, 2013; Sumaila et al., 2016).

As shown in Figure 7.6, the large-scale sector receives most capacity-enhancing fisheries subsidies, not only in Mexico, but also globally. Figure 7.7 shows annual subsidies provided from 2000 to 2012 to Mexican fisheries divided into those provided to small- and large-scale fisheries. While the amount of subsidies provided to Mexican fisheries has increased, the percentage provided to the small-scale sector decreased from almost 40 per cent in 2000 to only 12 per cent in 2012. On average, from 2000 to 2012, this analysis suggests that large-scale fisheries have received over 70 per cent of all fisheries subsidies. While SSF employ more people, and take about half of the total fisheries catches, they receive only a small fraction of total subsidies.

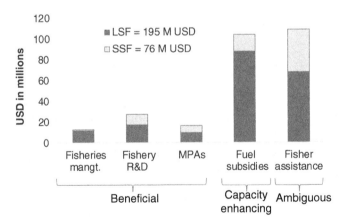

Figure 7.6 Mexican fisheries subsidies divided into large- and small-scale fisheries by subsidy types.

Source: Schuhbauer (2017) and Schuhbauer et al. (2017).

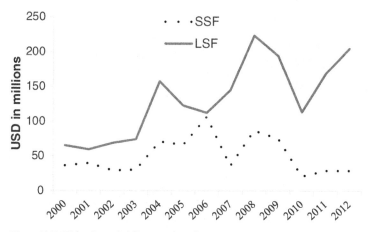

Figure 7.7 Fisheries subsidies presented in constant 2015 US$ million of Mexican small-scale fisheries (SSF) and large-scale fisheries (LSF) from 2000 to 2012.

Source: Schuhbauer (2017) and Schuhbauer et al. (2017).

Concluding remarks

To conclude, a few observations are in order. First, it is clear from the literature and the current contribution that bad (harmful) subsidies are the big problem, consuming close to 60 per cent of the estimated US$35 billion total subsidies. And what is more, large-scale industrial fisheries receive a higher proportion of these bad subsidies.

Second, only a small fraction of fisheries subsidies goes to small-scale fishers, thereby affecting their ability to be economically viability. This is bound to undermine the lofty United Nations Sustainable Development Goals (SDGs) of eliminating poverty (SDG1) and hunger (SDG3), and reducing inequality (SDG10).

Third, it is worth noting that even in the case of 'beneficial' subsidies, the use of public funds that could go elsewhere in society needs to be examined. For instance, we must look at whether managing fisheries and creating MPAs, as two kinds of good subsidies, is better than building hospitals or roads. These results strengthen the need for the global community to work relentlessly, in particular to eliminate harmful subsidies.

References

APEC (Asia-Pacific Economic Cooperation) (2000). *Study into the Nature and Extent of Subsidies in the Fisheries Sector of APEC Member Economies*. Singapore: APEC Committee on Trade and Investment. PricewaterhouseCoopers and Asia Pacific Economic Cooperation Secretariat.

Charles, A. (2001). *Sustainable Fishery Systems*. Oxford: Wiley-Blackwell.

Charles, A. (2006). Subsidies in fisheries: an analysis of social impacts within an integrated sustainable development framework. AGR/FI(2004)6. OECD. Also published as: Social impacts of government financial support of fisheries. In: OECD (ed.), *Financial Support to Fisheries: Implications for Sustainable Development*. Paris: OECD, pp. 225–260.

Clark, C.W., Munro, G.R. and Sumaila, U.R. (2005). Subsidies, buybacks, and sustainable fisheries. *Journal of Environmental Economics and Management*, 50: 47–58.

FAO (Food and Agriculture Organization) (1993). *The State of World Fisheries and Aquaculture 1992*. Rome: FAO.

FAO (Food and Agriculture Organization) (2010). *The State of World Fisheries and Aquaculture (SOFIA)*. Rome: FAO.

FAO (Food and Agriculture Organization) (2016). *The State of World Fisheries and Aquaculture 2016: Contributing to Food Security and Nutrition for All*. Rome: FAO.

FAO (Food and Agriculture Organization) and World Fish Center (2008). *Small-Scale Capture Fisheries: A Global Overview with Emphasis on Developing Countries: A Preliminary Report of The Big Numbers Project*, World Fish Center Working Papers.

Guyader, O., Berthou, P., Koutsikopoulos, C., Alban, F., Demanèche, S., Gaspar, M.B., et al. (2013). Small scale fisheries in Europe: a comparative analysis based on a selection of case studies. *Fisheries Research*, 140: 1–13.

Heymans, J.J., Mackinson, S., Sumaila, U.R., Dyck, A. and Little, A. (2011). The impact of subsidies on the ecological sustainability and future profits from North Sea fisheries. *PLoS One*, 6(5): e20239, DOI: 10.1371/journal.pone.0020239.

Khan, A., Sumaila, U.R., Watson, R., Munro, G. and Pauly, D. (2006). The nature and magnitude of global non-fuel fisheries subsidies. *Catching More Bait: A Bottom-Up Re-Estimation of Global Fisheries Subsidies*, 14(6): 5–37.

Lara, J. and Guevara-Sangines, A. (2012). *Apoyos al sector pesquero en Mexico 2005–2011*. Mexico City: WWF.

McConney, P. and Charles, A. (2009). Managing small-scale fisheries: moving towards people-centered perspectives. In: R.Q. Grafton, R. Hilborn, D. Squires, M. Tait and M. Williams (eds), *Handbook of Marine Fisheries Conservation and Management*. New York: Oxford University Press, pp. 532–545.

Milazzo, M. (1998). *Subsidies in World Fisheries: A Reexamination*. Washington, DC: World Bank.

Natale, F., Carvalho, N. and Paulrud, A. (2015). Defining small-scale fisheries in the EU on the basis of their operational range of activity: the Swedish fleet as a case study. *Fisheries Research*, 164: 286–292.

OECD (Organisation for Economic Co-operation and Development) (2000). *Transition to Responsible Fisheries*. Paris: OECD.

OECD (Organisation for Economic Co-operation and Development) (2005). *Review of Fisheries in OECD Countries: Country Statistic 2001–2003*. Paris: OECD.

OECD (Organisation for Economic Co-operation and Development) (2006a). *Agriculture and Fisheries Policies in Mexico: Recent Achievements, Continuing the Reform Agenda*. Paris: OECD.

OECD (Organisation for Economic Co-operation and Development) (2006b). *Financial Support to Fisheries: Implications for Sustainable Development*. Paris: OECD.

Pauly, D. (1997). Small-scale fisheries in the tropics: marginality, marginalization, and some implications for fisheries management. In: E.K. Pikitch, D.D. Hupert and M.P. Sissenwine (eds), *Global Trends: Fisheries Management*. American Fisheries Society Symposium 20, London: Chapman & Hall, pp. 40–49.

Pauly, D. and Zeller, D. (2015). *Sea Around Us Concepts, Design and Data*. Vancouver: University of British Columbia. Available at: www.seaaroundus.org (accessed 25 January 2018).

Pauly, D. and Zeller, D. (2016). Catch reconstructions reveal that global marine fisheries catches are higher than reported and declining. *Nature Communications*, 7: 10244.

Pomeroy, R. and Andrew, N.L. (eds) (2011). *Small-Scale Fisheries Management Frameworks and Approaches for the Developing World*. Oxford: CABI.

Ramírez-Rodríguez, M. and Almendárez-Hernández, L.C. (2013). Subsidies in the jumbo squid fishery in the Gulf of California, Mexico. *Marine Policy*, 40: 117–123.

Schuhbauer, A. (2017). *The Economic Viability of Small-Scale Fisheries*. PhD Dissertation, University of British Columbia.

Schuhbauer, A., Chuenpagdee, R., Cheung, W.W.L., Greer, K. and Sumaila, U.R. (2017). How subsidies affect the economic viability of small-scale fisheries. *Marine Policy*, 82: 114–121.

Smith, A. (1970). *Wealth of Nations*. London: Hayes Barton Press.

Sumaila, U.R. and Pauly, D. (2006). Catching more bait: a bottom-up re-estimation of global fisheries subsidies. *Fisheries Centre Research Reports*, 14.

Sumaila, U.R., Liu, Y. and Tyedmers, P. (2001). Small versus large-scale fishing operations in the North Atlantic. *Fisheries Impacts on North Atlantic Ecosystems: Evaluations and Policy Exploration*, 9(5): 28–35.

Sumaila, U.R., Khan, A.S., Dyck, A.J., Watson, R., Munro, G., Tydemers, P., et al. (2010). A bottom-up re-estimation of global fisheries subsidies. *Journal of Bioeconomics*, 12: 201–225.

Sumaila, U.R., Lam, V., Le Manach, F., Swartz, W. and Pauly, D. (2016). Global fisheries subsidies: an updated estimate. *Marine Policy*, 69: 189–193.

Swartz, W., Sumaila, U.R. and Watson, R. (2013). Global ex-vessel fish price database revisited: a new approach for estimating 'missing' prices. *Environmental and Resource Economics*, 56: 467–480.

Teh, L.C.L. and Sumaila, U.R. (2013). Contribution of marine fisheries to worldwide employment. *Fish and Fisheries*, 14(1): 77–78.

von Moltke, A. (2012). *Fisheries Subsidies, Sustainable Development and the WTO*. London: Routledge.

Westlund, L. (2004). *Guide for Identifying, Assessing and Reporting on Subsidies in the Fisheries Sector*, No. 438. Rome: FAO.

WWF (World Wildlife Fund) (2001). *Hard Facts, Hidden Problems: A Review of Current Data on Fishing Subsidies*. Washington, DC: World Wildlife Fund.

8 Eco-labelling and eco-certification of fisheries

Benefits, challenges and the future

Kevern L. Cochrane

Introduction

Achieving sustainability in fisheries remains a challenge for most countries around the world. The most recent information from the FAO was that in 2013, an estimated 31.4 per cent of fish stocks were being overfished, compared with only 10 per cent overfished stocks in 1990 (FAO, 2016). The FAO estimates are generally based on the bigger and more socio-economically important fisheries, for which there is usually sufficient information available to estimate stock status. The FAO numbers do not consider the many smaller, typically unmanaged stocks around the world, and are therefore probably underestimates of the actual number of over-exploited stocks.

The goal of fisheries management can be summarized as to address 'the multiple needs and desires of societies, without jeopardizing the options for future generations to benefit from the full range of goods and services provided by marine ecosystem' (FAO, 2003a: 14). The standard and most common management measures fall into the category of rules and regulations or 'command and control' measures supported by monitoring and enforcement systems to punish those who violate the rules and regulations. These measures include, for example, catch quotas, effort restrictions, gear regulations, and time and area closures. They have an essential role to play, and are likely to remain the foundation of fisheries management for the foreseeable future. There is, however, considerable benefit in complementing command and control measures with positive incentives that encourage behaviour that contributes to sustainable and responsible fishing while still leaving room for individual or group decisions and choices (FAO, 2005). Eco-labelling and certification in fisheries are designed as positive, market-based incentives that reward fishers and the fishing sector for sustainable fishing. Certification and eco-labelling provide information to the buyers (Wessells et al., 2001), who can be in the form of, for example, retailers, processors or the general public. Eco-labelling schemes, individually and collectively, help to create a demand from buyers for fish and other seafood products that the buyers can be sure come from well-managed and sustainably harvested stocks. Demand for eco-labelled products can be expected to result in higher prices paid in some markets for labelled products and to preferential access to some markets (Wessells et al., 2001).

Eco-labelling refers to the practice of labelling products, in this instance products derived from capture fisheries, with labels that provide information to the buyer that assures them that the product they are considering buying comes from a well-managed and sustainable fishery. Certification is much wider in scope and may or may not lead to explicit labelling of the certified product. It can be defined as a 'Procedure by which a third party gives written or equivalent assurance that a product, process or service conforms to specified requirements' (FAO, 2009a: 4), and can include, for example, certification that a product comes from legally harvested source, confirmation of the country of origin, that the product meets specified food safety requirements, or that it meets particular environmental or social standards. In this chapter, certification is used to refer specifically to the certification that products meet specified ecological standards, and that it will generally be a prerequisite for issuing an eco-label.

The concept of eco-labelling was promoted at the 1992 United Nations Conference on Environment and Development (the Rio Conference), and paragraph 4.21 of Agenda 21, which was endorsed by the participating governments, called upon governments to 'encourage expansion of environmental labelling and other environmentally related product information programmes designed to assist consumers to make informed choices'. The first major development in eco-labelling in fisheries occurred in 1996, when the non-governmental organization (NGO) WWF and the industrial giant Unilever, which produced fish products under brands including Iglo, Birds Eye UK and Gorton's, announced their intention to create the Marine Stewardship Council (MSC) for assessing and certifying sustainable fisheries and labelling products from certified fisheries. The purpose of the Council was to 'recognise and reward responsible management of seafood resources and drive behaviour change among buyers'.[1]

Reactions to the growing interest in eco-labelling and the early initiative by WWF and Unilever were mixed. At an FAO technical consultation in 1998 to discuss whether guidelines should be developed for eco-labelling schemes, attended by 45 member countries of the FAO, there were divergent opinions. Some of the views expressed by countries were as follows (FAO, 1998):

- It was generally agreed that biological and conservation considerations would be essential criteria for eco-labelling; some countries called for the inclusion of social and economic criteria as well, but at the same time many countries argued that social and economic objectives in a fishery were to be decided by the countries themselves, and could not be prescribed by private eco-labelling schemes.
- Some countries queried whether eco-labelling would lead to net gains or would just increase the transaction costs of fisheries, and also called for assessment of the impact of eco-labelling on domestic food security.
- There was concern from many countries, especially developing countries, that eco-labelling could lead to barriers to trade and reduce market opportunities.

Notwithstanding the growth in eco-labelling in the global seafood markets, some of these concerns persist today, as will be shown in sections of this chapter. The FAO Committee on Fisheries (COFI) considered the report of this consultation at its meeting in 1999, but there was no consensus on whether or not the FAO should become involved in the issue through developing technical guidelines (FAO, 1999), and the FAO effectively dropped the issue from its priorities for the next four to five years. However, at the COFI meeting in 2003, 'The increasing role of labelling and traceability of fishery products in international fish trade was highlighted and many countries requested FAO to further work on this topic' (FAO, 2003b: 6). Many countries expressed similar concerns to those raised in 1998, but the COFI agreed that the FAO should develop guidelines on eco-labelling, and after many meetings to review and revise various drafts of the guidelines, a final version was adopted by the COFI in 2005, and subsequently updated in 2009 (FAO, 2009a). In the opinion of this author, this change in 2003 did not mean that the concerns of many countries had been reduced, but rather that by then, most countries recognized that eco-labelling was growing as a private initiative, without requiring government approval, and that it was better for governments to become more involved in the process and to influence it to the benefit of their national fisheries as much as they were able.

The growth in eco-labelling in the fisheries and seafood sector that had started in the 1990s continued after that, to the extent that by 2012, producers, processors, retailers and others in the seafood industry were complaining about the confusion they were experiencing with the number of eco-labelling schemes that had been established and the difficulties they were experiencing in being able to identify which of these schemes were credible. This was making decision-making more difficult and increasing their costs, thereby also making seafood more expensive for consumers. In an effort to reduce this confusion, many stakeholders in the seafood industry agreed to establish an organization, the Global Sustainable Seafood Initiative (GSSI) to 'provide clarity on seafood certification and ensure consumer confidence in certified seafood'.[2] The role and impact of the GSSI is discussed later in this chapter.

The standards for certification

The process of certification and eco-labelling should include: (1) the setting of the standards that have to be met in order for a fishery or equivalent to be allowed to use the label; (2) certification by certifying bodies that are independent of the eco-labelling scheme and are accredited as being competent to carry out an assessment against the standards; and (3) the assessment and certification that a fishery meets the required standards. The requirements for certification have to include verification that the chain of custody is able to guarantee that a labelled product put on the market has come from the certified fishery, which requires that the product can be tracked and traced along the full chain from capture to processing, distribution and marketing (FAO, 2009a).

The standards required can vary between schemes, which gave rise to the decision by FAO member countries to develop a set of guidelines for eco-labelling that specify minimum standards that any eco-labelling scheme should be required to meet in order to be considered credible. The revised version of the guidelines (FAO, 2009a) has been widely accepted as the definitive global standard. The standards that the GSSI uses for assessing eco-labelling and certification schemes are based on the FAO guidelines and, for example, two of the bigger eco-labelling schemes in fisheries, MSC and Friend of the Sea, report that their standards are consistent with the FAO guidelines[3, 4]. The FAO guidelines stipulate that any eco-labelling scheme must be consistent with the 1982 United Nations Convention on the Law of the Sea, the Agreement for the Implementation of the Provisions of the United Nations Convention on the Law of the Sea of 10 December 1982 relating to the Conservation and Management of Straddling Fish Stocks and Highly Migratory Fish Stocks (the 1995 UN Fish Stocks Agreement), the FAO Code of Conduct for Responsible Fisheries and the World Trade Organization (WTO) rules, as well as with other relevant international instruments.

The FAO guidelines specify a set of 'minimum substantive requirements' that an eco-labelling scheme should require a fishery to meet in order to qualify for certification and labelling. Those requirements consist of three categories: the management system applied to the fishery, the status of the stock being considered for certification, and the impacts of the fishery on the ecosystem. The guidelines also specify requirements for the procedural and institutional aspects of the fishery, which encompass, as explained in the first paragraph of this section, the setting of standards of sustainable fisheries, guidelines for accreditation of certification bodies, and guidelines for the certification, including of the fishery and the chain of custody.

Successes of certification

A growing number of certified fisheries

There are many programmes and schemes covering capture fisheries and aquaculture that aim to provide information to consumers on the ecological or environmental sustainability of seafood. These include eco-labelling and certification schemes as well as rating lists that inform consumers on whether specific species come from sustainable sources or not (e.g. the Monterey Bay Aquarium Seafood Watch and the WWF South African Sustainable Seafood Initiative, SASSI). FAO (2014a) lists 25 eco-labelling schemes, labels issued by retailers and consumer guides for fishery products. This chapter, however, is focused on eco-labelling programmes, of which, based on available knowledge, there are seven that currently label products from capture fisheries or plan to do so in the near future (see Table 8.1). The biggest of these, by a considerable margin, is the MSC, which at the end of 2016 reported that there were 306 fisheries certified by the MSC, covering more than 30 different countries. The MSC reports that its certified fisheries produce about 9.5 million tonnes of seafood annually, accounting for nearly 10 per cent of the global annual catch.[5] The MSC estimates that in 2015 and 2016, consumers spent approximately US$4.6 billion on MSC-certified seafood (MSC, 2016a). The second largest scheme is Friend of the Sea, with 88 certified fisheries from 32 different countries (see Table 8.1).

The increasing interest in eco-labelling can be seen from the growth in the number of fisheries being certified by the MSC. The first fishery to be certified was the Western Australian lobster fishery in March 2001, followed by the Alaskan salmon fishery in September of the same year. The first fishery from a developing country to be certified by the MSC was the Mexican Baja California rock lobster fishery in 2004. By 2008, there were 100 fisheries with MSC certification, which had increased to 256 fisheries by March 2015, and more than 300 fisheries by the end of 2016.[6] During this period, there was also growth in the number of schemes, as shown in Table 8.1, that, together with the growth experienced by the MSC, demonstrate the rapid acceptance and development of eco-labelling in capture fisheries.

Impacts on prices and markets

The theory behind certification and eco-labelling is that by informing consumers that a product comes from a sustainable fishery, that product should command a higher price, preferred access to some markets, or both. There have been many studies to assess whether these expectations have been met in specific fisheries. Those studies have produced somewhat mixed results.

Some of the earlier studies into the existence of price premiums for eco-labelled seafood reported that there was, at that time, no evidence of the benefits from eco-labelling to either sustainability or prices obtained. Washington (2008) referred to 'the price premium myth', and reported that stakeholders in seafood value chains in Alaska, the Netherlands and New Zealand had reported that there had been no evidence of price premiums. An OECD High Seas Task Force report recommended studies to establish the effect of these schemes on the market and resource sustainability, as well the economic costs (OECD High Seas Task

Table 8.1 Certification and eco-labelling programmes for capture fisheries

Scheme	Geographical coverage	No. of certified fisheries
Marine Stewardship Council	> 30 countries	306
Friend of the Sea	32 countries	88
Alaska Responsible Fisheries Management	Alaska	7
Iceland Responsible Fisheries	Iceland	4
Marine Eco-Label Japan	Japan	24
Naturland	Germany + Tanzania	3
G.U.L.F. Certification	USA Gulf of Mexico	Still under development

Note: Information as available from programme websites in November 2016.

Force, 2006). Several years later, Stemle at al. (2015) summarized the results of studies on UK markets as indicating a willingness by consumers to pay premiums of between 10 and 15 per cent for eco-labelled products derived from, for example, Alaska pollock, cod, haddock and salmon. The investigation by Asche et al. (2015) demonstrated considerable variation in the premiums, however, depending on the outlet. They estimated negative (but statistically not significant) price premiums for MSC-labelled salmon products sold in Marks & Spencer and Tesco, while a premium of 57 per cent was charged in the Asda outlet. The authors concluded that high premiums were paid in 'low-end' retail chains but not in 'high-end' chains. The outlets sampled were all in the city of Glasgow, but the authors assumed that these reflected pricing by the chains across the UK. Interestingly, the study estimated that salmon products labelled as organic enjoyed a more or less uniform premium of 25 per cent in all seven chains. Sogn-Grundvåg et al. (2013) also found evidence of similar, more specific consumer preferences in the UK cod and haddock markets, where they estimated price premiums for products labelled as being line-caught (as opposed to coming from trawl or gill net fisheries) of 18 per cent for cod and 10 per cent for haddock, compared to a premium of 10 per cent for MSC-labelled products. Results from an experimental auction of salmon products in Japan found that in the absence of information on the status of fish stocks and the rationale for eco-labelling, consumers were not prepared to pay a price premium for eco-labelled products (Uchida et al., 2014). However, the results indicated that if consumers were provided with this information, there was a price premium of approximately 20 per cent. The authors of that paper concluded that with greater awareness creation among consumers, there is considerable potential for obtaining price premiums in the Japanese market.

It is difficult to compare the results from an investigation into the value of MSC certification for the entire South African trawl fishery for hake (see Table 8.2) to the specific estimates of price premiums in other fisheries, but a study on that fishery estimated that if the current MSC certification was lost or surrendered, the total net present value of the fishery over the following five years would be reduced by 37.6 per cent, equal at that time to US$392.7 million. This example is discussed further below, in terms of implications of the MSC label for market access.

While Table 8.2 provides good evidence for price premiums, albeit from a limited number of species and geographical range, the distribution of those benefits along the value chain is less clear. The impacts of MSC labelling on prices obtained at the dockside in three fisheries were examined in a study by Stemle et al. (2015). Their assessments yielded mixed results. The authors concluded that MSC certification was associated with a significant increase in the prices at the dockside for chum and pink salmon (Alaska) and flathead flounder (Japan), but that there was no significant difference in the prices for certified chinook and coho salmon and halibut (all from Alaska fisheries) compared to uncertified fisheries, and that certification was associated with a lower price for Alaska sockeye salmon. The authors suggested that the contrasting results between different salmon species could have been a result of differences in the market. There had

Table 8.2 Estimates of price premiums paid for eco-labelled seafood products

Species/product	Market	Estimated price premium	Reference
Frozen processed Alaskan cod products	Supermarkets in London (UK)	14.2%	Roheim et al. (2011)
223 different salmon products	Glasgow (UK) branches of seven leading supermarket chains	(1) MSC label – ranges from 0 to 56.6% (2) Labelled as organic – approx. 25%	Asche et al. (2015)
Chilled and pre-packed line-caught cod and haddock	Seven leading supermarket chains in the UK	(1) MSC label – 10% (2) Certified as being line-caught – 18% (cod) and 10% (haddock)	Sogn-Grundvåg et al. (2013)
Frozen cod fillets	Retail stores across Sweden	Approx. 10%	Blomquist et al. (2015)
Salmon products	Japan (results obtained in controlled experiment)	No significant difference	Uchida et al. (2014)
Trawl-caught hake from South Africa	Entire market	37.6% of current total retail value	Lallemand et al. (2016)

Note: All labels are from the MSC unless otherwise indicated.

been growing demand for pink and chum salmon on the European markets, where there is considerable demand for MSC products, while Chinook and coho salmon are sold mainly in North America, where there has been a lower demand for MSC-certified products. The authors suggested that the decrease in prices of sockeye salmon after MSC certification could have been caused by other factors, such as the relatively high variability in quality of the species and changes in demand that were not related to MSC certification (Stemle et al., 2015). Another investigation into whether the fishers received a price premium on eco-labelled catches was undertaken on the Swedish Eastern Baltic cod fishery (Blomquist et al., 2015). Those authors concluded that while there was a price premium in the retail markets, there was no evidence that the producers received a premium.

The second economic expectation from eco-labelling is that it could provide preferential access for eco-labelled products to specific markets. There is less information on specific examples in which this potential benefit has been found to occur, but one example is the demonstrated impact of MSC certification on the Kyoto Danish Seine Fishery Federation in Japan (Wakamatsu, 2014). The fishery is a multispecies fishery targeting, among other species, snow crab (*Chionoecetes opilio*) and flathead flounder (*Hippoglossoides dubius*). The authors noted that other studies had found that there were no price premiums for eco-labelled seafood products in Japan, and opted therefore for investigating whether there was any decoupling of markets for certified and uncertified products. They concluded that MSC certification had an impact on the flathead flounder fishery and that the wholesalers differentiated between the MSC certified products and others to the benefit of those with MSC certification. As an example, after certification, the labelled fishery was approached by one of the country's bigger retailers that was interested in buying and retailing its eco-labelled products. The author noted that at the time of writing, seafood eco-labelling was still known by only a few consumers in Japan, but the positive impacts of labelling that his study had shown provided an incentive for its expansion.

A second example can be found in the South African trawl fishery for hakes *Merluccius paradoxus* and *Merluccius capensis*, referred to earlier. Approximately 70 per cent of the annual catch from the fishery is exported, and historically much of that was exported to Spain with little value addition. The study reports that this changed in 2008 with the global financial crisis, which resulted in lower prices and demand for hake in Spain (Lallemand et al., 2016). This could have had a serious negative impact on the South African trawl fishery, but, according to the study, the fact that the fishery had obtained MSC certification in 2004 (recertified in 2010 and 2015) enabled the exporters to access the Northern European markets, with the added benefit that these markets prefer value-added fillet products, which has allowed for additional local job creation in processing. These value-added developments are included in the estimated value of the MSC certification shown in Table 8.2.

The examples described in this section demonstrate that, in some cases at least, the expected economic benefits of eco-labelling in the form of price premiums and preferential market access are being achieved. The research by, for example, Uchida et al. (2014) and Lallemand et al. (2016) indicates that there is also considerable scope for expanding the opportunities presented by these benefits. Roheim et al. (2011), however, point out that there are still important questions to be asked about these benefits. One of those is whether the price premiums obtained are sufficient to cover costs of a sustainable fishery and certification, to which should also be added the value of improved market access where appropriate. Lallemand et al. (2016) concluded that the answer was a decisive yes for South African hake, but this author is unaware of other comparable investigations, and Roheim et al. (2011) called it an open question. The answer to that question is likely to be different for different fisheries, depending on their size, markets and other characteristics. A second important and still largely unanswered question, touched on in the examples above, is whether the economic benefits of eco-labelling reach the fishers and producers in general. As Roheim et al. (2011) point out, which is also apparent in the information presented in this chapter, the best evidence of the general benefits comes from the ongoing growth in the number of fisheries seeking and being awarded eco-labels. This must indicate a considerable measure of confidence that it is worthwhile.

Challenges for certification

As was described in the introduction to this chapter, there have been concerns about the desirability and possible negative impacts of eco-labelling and certification in fisheries since the subject started to emerge in the 1990s. Some of the more important potential challenges and problems that have been raised include (Wessells et al., 2001; De Young *et al.*, 2008):

- concerns about insufficient transparency and stakeholder participation in developing certification and labelling standards;
- the risks of requirements for eco-labelling leading to trade imbalances and barriers to trade, particularly for developing countries;
- developing countries and small-scale fisheries and suppliers being placed at a disadvantage because of the high costs of certification;
- eco-labelling could require the addition of new, effective institutional frameworks to ensure compliance with the specified standards across a whole fishery;
- early concerns about the absence of international standards and guidelines (subsequently addressed by the FAO and GSSI, discussed later in this chapter);
- whether the benefits of price premiums for certified products would reach the fishers; and
- concerns from countries that the requirements of certification schemes could impinge on the sovereignty of governments and their national management authorities.

Notwithstanding the ongoing growth in eco-labelling of fisheries and seafood products, many of these concerns remain. At the 2014 meeting of the FAO

Sub-Committee on Fish Trade, some countries expressed a number of reservations, echoing several of those in the list above, including: the potential for eco-labelling schemes to lead to trade barriers, generate higher costs, the need for improvements in the FAO guidelines on eco-labelling, and the need for technical assistance to be provided to developing countries to enable them to meet the emerging requirements of certification for market access (FAO, 2014b).

Most of the above problems are of greatest concern to developing countries, and they are real. The information available from the MSC at the time of writing this chapter recorded that over 300 fisheries had been certified, but only 18 of those were from developing countries, with a further eight in the process of full assessment at the time.[7] Acknowledging the problem, the MSC Global Impacts Report (MSC, 2016b: 9) reported that 'With the exception of the South African hake trawl and the Juan Fernández rock lobster fishery, there are no certified fisheries around the African continent nor along the Pacific South American coast, and very few in South East Asia'. The discrepancy between developed and developing country fisheries is less marked in Friend of the Sea, the second largest fisheries eco-labelling scheme (see Table 8.2), which records 41 fisheries from developing countries among the total of 82 fisheries listed as being certified.[8] The fisheries in developing countries that have been certified cover a wide range of countries and species and fishery types (see Table 8.3).

The constraints that are faced by developing countries were examined in some detail in a recent study that focused on the MSC, far and away the largest scheme at present. Drawing on the experience of the nine co-authors of the paper reporting on the study, input from the MSC Developing World Working Group and a review of the literature, the study identified the following factors (summarized here) perceived to be constraints to certification for developing countries (Stratoudakis et al., 2016):

- no obvious benefits arising from MSC certification;
- low leadership in a fishery to drive improvements in practice;*
- lack of or insufficient information on MSC and its processes;
- management authority and stakeholders do not have sufficient capacity or expertise for assessing, managing and monitoring fishery;*
- insufficient or unreliable information on catch, effort, stock status, etc.;*
- enforcement is weak or non-existent;*
- fishery may be stable and sustainable, but this is difficult to substantiate with available information;
- fishery may not act on stock or ecosystem in isolation, and therefore its ability to meet the certification standards is impacted by other fleets beyond its control;
- inadequate or non-existent regulation of access;*
- stock boundaries and movements are poorly understood, stock straddles national boundaries (relevant also to previous point);* and
- there are subsidies in the fishery that contravene certification requirements.*

Table 8.3 Some examples of developing country fisheries that were listed on the websites of the specified schemes as being certified at the time of writing this chapter

Country and fishery	Certification scheme	Country and fishery	Certification scheme
Tanzania – Nile perch (freshwater)	Naturland	Argentina – anchovy	MSC
Peru – purse seine – *Scomber japonicus peruanus*	Friend of the Sea	Chile – mussel	MSC
Indonesia – trammel nets – *Penaeus monodon, P. semisulcatus, P. indicus*	Friend of the Sea	Mexico (Baja California) – red rock lobster	MSC
Madagascar – bottom trawlers – *Penaeus monodon, P. semisulcatus*	Friend of the Sea	South Africa – trawl fisheries – hakes (two species)	MSC
Nigeria – otter trawls – *Penaeus monodon*	Friend of the Sea	Suriname – Atlantic seabob shrimp	MSC
Sri Lanka – handline – *Thunnus albacares, Xiphias gladius*	Friend of the Sea	Vietnam – Ben Tre clam fishery	MSC
Brazil – pole and line – *Katsuwonus pelamis, Thunnus albacores, T. alalunga*	Friend of the Sea	Fiji – longline – albacore tuna	MSC
Maldives – handline fleet – *Thunnus albacares*	Friend of the Sea		MSC

Note: Species names are as provided on the sites.

Factors marked with an asterisk (*) are those considered to be basic constraints in managing a fishery, the third category of constraints discussed below. The Caribbean spiny lobster fishery operating in the Sian Ka'an and Banco Chinchorro Biosphere on the Atlantic coastline of Mexico provides an interesting example of the first problem: that the benefits from certification may not always be sufficient to justify the costs. The fishery has an annual catch of approximately 280 tonnes, which is caught by free divers. Most of the catch is sold within the region to supply the tourist trade centred on Cancun, and the remaining small fraction is sold elsewhere in Mexico and the USA. The fishery was certified by the MSC in July 2012 and the certificate was valid until July 2017. The most recent surveillance audit was undertaken in May 2015 and recommended that the certification should remain valid. However, in 2016, the cooperative representing the fishery voluntarily withdrew its fishery from the MSC programme, and from 1 June 2016 could no longer apply the MSC logo to their products. According to a report on IntraFish, those involved in the fishery would have preferred to have retained the certification, but with the small size of the annual catch they did not have the funds to pay for its continuation and did not see that the situation would improve in the future.[9] They informed the MSC that they intended to maintain the standards required by the MSC in order to maintain the sustainability of the fishery. It may also be significant that in 2009, a group of key stakeholders in the fishery, including six fishing cooperatives, adopted a collective label to identify spiny lobster from the Sian Ka'an and Banco Chinchorro Biosphere. The label, 'Chakay de la Reservas de la Biósfera de Banco Chinchorro y Sian Ka'an', is intended to identify that the product comes from that area and that the fishery for lobster in the area operates within the regulations and in a sustainable way. The hope and expectation of the stakeholders was that the label would lead to improved access to markets and a price premium through being able to sell directly to the final markets without the need for intermediaries (Ley-Cooper and Quintanar-Guadarrama, 2010). Given that most of the products from the fishery are sold locally, it would be useful to determine the relative effectiveness in terms of economic benefits of the Chakay and MSC labels.

Returning to the full list of constraints, in the opinion of this author, it needs to be divided into three distinct categories. The first of those is the question of whether there will be meaningful benefits that result from certification (whatever the scheme) for a fishery. The examples provided in the third section of this chapter demonstrate that some fisheries have derived considerable benefit from certification in the form of price premiums, access to markets, or both, but that others have not. Clearly, the answer to this question will depend entirely on the nature of the fishery and its products (e.g. value per unit of catch, average annual size of catch, value addition) and the nature of the market, whether it gives preference to eco-labelled products, and, if so, whether it is already saturated or could absorb additional supplies.

The second set of constraints in the list are those that reflect the genuine difficulties of meeting MSC standards even though a fishery may be being sustainably managed and implemented. Those are constraints to certification itself, and responsibility for addressing those constraints should lie with the certification schemes and markets, working collaboratively with impacted fisheries. The third group, each of which is marked with an asterisk (*) in the list above, is very different, and those problems are not so much related to certification as they are constraints to managing a fishery in a sustainable way, whether or not certification is being sought. Given that eco-labelling and certification are, by design, intended to identify fisheries that are being implemented in a biological and sustainable way, fisheries that suffer from any of those are, a priori, unsuitable for certification. In terms of the UN Law of the Sea, the countries themselves must take responsibility for addressing those problems, although it would clearly be in the general interest of eco-labelling schemes, developed country importers and development assistance programmes to assist them to do so.

The list from Stratoudakis et al. (2016), in particular the constraints marked above with an asterisk (*), demonstrate a fundamental problem and underlying reason for the threat that eco-labelling could pose for developing countries. That is, the difficulties that many developing countries are encountering in implementation of sustainable fisheries. The boundary between developing and developed country fisheries is not clear-cut, and there are many fisheries in developing countries that are well managed, and equally many fisheries in developed countries that are not well managed, but on average developing countries tend to perform worse than developed countries (e.g. see Pitcher et al., 2009; Melnychuka et al., 2016). In their recent review of fisheries management effectiveness, Melnychuka et al. (2016) concluded that, in general, the wealthier countries performed better than less wealthy countries because they are able to invest more in ensuring effective management. They found that three of the most important factors associated with effective management were: (1) the per capita gross domestic product of the country; (2) high catches in the country's exclusive economic zone (implying countries give greater attention to their fisheries if they are of high value); and (3) the ratio of investment in research, management and enforcement to the landed value of the fishery catches.

Those findings highlight the basic constraints that are being faced by many developing countries and small-scale fisheries: insufficient management resources and capacity to meet the standards required for sustainable management. Eco-labelling is intended to certify that 'the fish has been harvested in compliance with conservation and sustainability standards. The logo or statement is intended to make provision for informed decisions of purchasers whose choice can be relied upon to promote and stimulate the sustainable use of fishery resources', and that a scheme should be consistent with international law regulating and guiding fisheries including the FAO Code of Conduct for Responsible Fisheries (FAO, 2009a: paras 21 and 2.1). Where markets are seeking eco-labelled seafood, countries and fisheries that fail to meet those requirements cannot blame the eco-labelling schemes for the difficulties they may experience accessing those markets.

On the other hand, the eco-labelling schemes must share at least some responsibility for the other constraints in the list that deal with challenges directly linked to seeking certification and being recognized (those not marked with an asterisk). Those constraints related to poor information on the MSC and its processes, difficulties in substantiating that a fishery is sustainable even when it is, and the problem of how to handle fisheries that are, on their own, making serious efforts to achieve sustainability but are confounded by sharing resources and ecosystems with other fisheries that are not doing so. While they were identified specifically in relation to the MSC, it is a reasonable assumption that they also apply to all or at least most other schemes too. If the full potential for eco-labelling to provide incentives for fisheries to ensure that they are managed in a sustainable way is to be achieved, those obstacles need to be addressed. Cochrane et al. (2011) described the problems being experienced in attempts to manage many low-value small-scale fisheries and the less intensive approaches that were being used to ensure sustainability. They differentiated between three categories of fisheries management. At one end of the range is primary fisheries management, in which limited capacity restricts the goal to managing primarily for sustainability and to minimize the risks of crossing undesirable thresholds. At the other end is tertiary management typical of modern, large-scale commercial fisheries, which entails science-based and adaptive management that has the capacity to strive for optimal benefits. An important question for eco-labelling and certification schemes is whether their standards would recognize and accept effective primary management, or if they are skewed to favour only tertiary management.

The study by Stratoudakis et al. (2016) also presented some of the approaches considered or under consideration by the MSC aimed at making the scheme better suited and more available to developing countries. They are (summarized and reordered from the original):

- Adapt the language of the MSC standards to developing country fisheries and provide more guidance to developing country and small-scale fisheries interested in eco-labelling.
- Initiate a special fund to provide support for MSC assessments of developing country fisheries and encourage partnerships with commercial seafood stakeholders that would increase the market incentives.
- Increase stakeholder and public awareness of eco-labelling.
- Increase the number of assessors in developing countries with the skill and mandate to undertake MSC assessments.
- Encourage discrete small-scale fisheries to work together with others in seeking group certification.
- Find more champions to pursue certification in these fisheries.
- Expand and facilitate partnerships for fisheries improvement programmes (FIPs). FIPs are projects involving a range of stakeholders that work towards improving management with, in the context of eco-labelling, a view to assisting the fishery to meet the required standards.*

- The use of 'credible' FIPs that are underway as a means of obtaining some market benefits, for example granting of 'partial market recognition' to fisheries engaged in credible FIPs.*
- Providing assistance in strengthening capacity in the MSC certification process and standards and in fisheries management.*

The distinction between solutions in this list that address fundamental management shortcomings and those that specifically address eco-labelling issues is not always as clear as it was in the list of constraints, but those solutions that could help to address the fundamental shortcomings being experienced by many developing countries are marked with an asterisk (*). Those activities could assist in improving currently poorly or inadequately managed fisheries, helping to shift them towards sustainable practices. The other solutions appear more suitable for developing country fisheries that are already sustainable and well-managed but do not or cannot obtain certification for one or more of the constraints in the earlier list directly linked to certification itself and being recognized. Fisheries falling into this second category are almost certainly a minority among developing country fisheries. These fisheries would benefit from secure access to the most lucrative markets, and in some instances, such as the South African hake fishery, eco-labelling facilitates this. It is therefore important to ensure good awareness of the goals and value of eco-labelling among all stakeholders in such fisheries so that they can assess the potential for their fishery and pursue labelling when appropriate. This should include increasing the awareness of consumers in developing countries so as to increase local interest in and demand for fish and fish products from fisheries that have been certified as being sustainable.

A frequently expressed concern on the impacts of eco-labelling on developing countries is the potential impact of eco-labelling on food security. The possible impact of eco-labelling on domestic food security was raised at the first FAO Technical Consultation on eco-labelling in 1998 (FAO, 1998). On the same theme, Stratoudakis et al. (2016) referred to criticisms about unintended and unexpected changes in the 'political economy' as a result of certification. These could be particularly damaging in cases where there are high levels of poverty and vulnerable people rely heavily on local fish as a source of protein. A shift from selling locally to those consumers to selling to distant markets at higher prices could have significant, undesirable impacts on the local consumers. The concerns are justified, especially in the light of the increasing proportion of fish and fish products that enter into international trade. The FAO (2016) reported that the quantity of these products involved in international trade increased by more than 245 per cent between 1976 and 2014. The live weight equivalent of fish exported in 2014 represented approximately 36 per cent of total fish production in 2014.

It is, in the opinion of this author, incorrect, however, to blame eco-labelling for this trend and for the likely negative impacts on domestic poverty and food security in many cases. Eco-labelling is not the driver of increasing international trade, but a consequence of a desire by stakeholders in a fishery or at national level to meet the required standards for sustainability to be able to export products to markets that require those standards to be met, presumably hoping for higher prices and profits as a result. Eco-labelling, where relevant, is simply a tool to assist in achieving that objective. As was pointed out at the FAO (1998) consultation, 'social and economic objectives in a fishery were a matter of national policy and that any private eco-labelling system could not prescribe management policy to States or infringe upon their sovereign rights' (para. 14). The imperative is therefore on governments, together with stakeholders, to consider the social and economic consequences of diverting fishery products from local markets to distant markets, and to take whatever actions may be required to identify positive and negative impacts and to minimize the latter. Stratoudakis et al. (2016) recommended that when eco-labelling is being considered, it is necessary to understand the social and economic impacts that could result, for example negative impacts on food security, including contribution of fish to protein and micronutrient intake, compared to the possible economic benefits from selling elsewhere at higher prices. There is no single solution that will fit all cases, and the ideal arrangement, resulting in the optimal benefits, will depend on the specific context and objectives, and will therefore differ from case to case.

Proliferation of schemes and confusion in markets

As a result of growing interest in certification, there is currently a large number of initiatives providing some form of labelling or guidance on sustainable seafood, including eco-labels, certification schemes and rating lists. The FAO (2014a) lists 25 such initiatives, but the total number could be as many as 75 (H. Wisse, GSSI, personal communication). The proliferation of schemes has resulted in uncertainty about the quality and comparability of different schemes. This problem was raised at the 11th session of the FAO Sub-Committee on Fish Trade (COFI-FT) in 2008, where member countries requested the FAO Secretariat to investigate the extent to which private eco-labelling schemes were using the FAO guidelines on eco-labelling, and whether the claims by some schemes that their standards were consistent with the guidelines could be validated (FAO, 2008). However, at the 28th session of the full Committee on Fisheries, countries were divided on whether the FAO should be involved in assessing private eco-labelling schemes, and the FAO Legal Counsel advised the COFI that the FAO, as an international organization, should be cautious about undertaking such an evaluation of private entities (FAO, 2009b). Nevertheless, the FAO Secretariat was subsequently asked to develop a framework that could be applied to evaluate the extent to which public and private eco-labelling schemes conformed to the FAO guidelines. A draft framework was submitted to the 30th session of the COFI in 2012, but countries could not agree on its adoption (FAO, 2012).

At much the same time, a consortium made up of private sector members of the seafood supply chain, NGOs and the Deutsche Gesellschaft für

Internationale Zusammenarbeit (GIZ) got together and, in February 2013, established the Global Sustainable Seafood Initiative (GSSI). The mission of the GSSI is 'to ensure confidence in the supply and promotion of certified seafood as well as to promote improvement in the seafood certification schemes'. It aims to do this primarily by taking on the task that the FAO, as an international, intergovernmental organization, was unable to do, which is to assess the performance of seafood certification schemes as a means of reducing the confusion about standards and comparability of the many schemes, and thereby reduce costs and eliminate redundancy in the use of schemes.[10]

As of February 2017, 34 companies from around the world and across the seafood industry are funding partners of the GSSI. They cover companies engaged in harvesting, processing, food services and retailers, including big names (nature of company and location of headquarters in brackets) such as ANOVA Seafood (fish supplier to retail and food services, the Netherlands), Bumble Bee Seafoods (seafood producer, USA), Deepwater Group (provision of leadership and support to deepwater fisheries, New Zealand), Iglo, Nomad Foods (frozen food brand, UK), Metro Group (retailer, Germany), Cabomar (fishing and seafood production, Spain), Sainsbury's (retailer, UK), as well as seven affiliated partners, including FAO, WWF, New England Aquarium and the Centro de Desarrollo y Pesca Sustentable (CeDePesca, Latin America and the Caribbean).[11]

The impact of the GSSI will lie in preferential selection of eco-labelling and certification schemes that have met the benchmark standards and been recognized by the GSSI. To this end, the GSSI partners have all made the commitment that:

> As strong supporters of GSSI we, the below retailers, brand manufacturers, traders and food service companies, commit to include the outcomes of the GSSI Benchmark Tool in our daily operations by recognizing all GSSI recognized certification schemes as acceptable when sourcing certified seafood. We encourage companies across the seafood sector worldwide to join our commitment.[12]

The identities and distribution of the partners making this commitment demonstrate the importance to the seafood industry of bringing clarity and transparency to the process and standards of eco-labelling and certification of fisheries and seafoods.

After its launch, the GSSI developed its global benchmark tool that set out the standards that an eco-labelling tool must meet to achieve recognition by the GSSI. The tool was developed in a transparent and participatory process, and is based on the FAO Code of Conduct and the FAO eco-labelling guidelines for capture fisheries and the guidelines for certification schemes for aquaculture. The minimum requirement for GSSI recognition is for a scheme to meet the essential components, but a scheme can also be evaluated against additional supplementary components, which provide additional information that can advise stakeholders on differences between the schemes. The inclusion of supplementary components was, in many respects, a compromise between two partially conflicting concerns. On the one hand, there was a desire, particularly among the conservation NGOs, to provide some differentiation between schemes to avoid schemes settling for the minimum required standards (essential components) and not having an incentive to continue trying to improve their standards. On the other hand, the seafood companies, in particular, wanted to avoid a system that ranked, or could be used to rank, the different schemes as they were concerned that this would lead to a monopoly, with the top-ranked scheme attracting all the business. The system of supplementary components achieves a balance between these two desires in that it helps to identify schemes that are going further than the minimum, and in what aspects of certification, but could not easily be translated into a simple ranking system. The GSSI expects that this overall approach will: (1) allow fishing industries (producers) to select only one scheme that best meets their needs, instead of having to apply for certification by several schemes in order to access different buyers; (2) provide simpler, consistent and comparable information on schemes that will help the buyers of seafood to decide which schemes to buy from; and (3) generate open and verified information on schemes available for all stakeholders, including NGOs.[13]

As with a fishery applying to a scheme for certification, undergoing GSSI benchmarking is entirely voluntary, and a labelling and certification scheme must apply to be benchmarked. At the time of writing, two schemes had undergone benchmarking and received recognition: the Alaska Responsible Fisheries Management (RFM) Certification Program (recognized on 13 July 2016) and the Iceland Responsible Fisheries Management (IRFM) Certification Programme (recognized on 8 November 2016). The MSC is currently undergoing benchmarking.[14]

Conclusions and the future

The continued growth in the number of fisheries applying for and receiving certification and eco-labelling demonstrates that such recognition has, or at least is perceived to have, sufficient benefit to justify the costs and any remedial actions that may be required for compliance. With the limited information available, it is still difficult to determine which groups are driving the demand for certified seafood products, whether it is the consumers, retailers, conservation NGOs or others. The history of eco-labelling, starting with the partnership between the WWF and Unilever to form the MSC, suggests that retailers and NGOs are playing important roles, with the former aiming at their own branding and gaining an advantage over the competition, and the latter aiming to provide incentives for responsible and sustainable fishing practices. The price premiums being paid by consumers, as discussed in the third section, indicates that consumers are also playing some role, and at least some consumers in some markets are helping to fuel the demand for eco-labels.

Eco-labelling is not a global panacea, however, for either achieving the economic goals of higher prices or access to all markets or the ecological goals of promoting sustainable fishing. At present, somewhere close to 10 per cent of the global annual landed catch is taken by certified fisheries, which means that approximately 90 per cent is not. It is widely recognized that the demand for eco-labelled products occurs mainly in Europe, particularly Northern Europe, and to a lesser extent North America, with signs of growing demand in some other developed countries and regions such as Japan, New Zealand and Australia. Fishing nations and fisheries from other areas and supplying local demand or exporting to other areas would seem to have little to gain from an eco-label at present. A further important consideration for a fishery trying to decide whether or not to apply for an eco-label is the benefits that will be obtained compared to the costs. Smaller fisheries are less likely to see a net benefit than larger fisheries of a similar type. The South African hake fishery provides an example of clear advantages gained from an eco-label, while the Mexican lobster fishery is an important reminder that such net advantages cannot be taken for granted. Two characteristics that may help to explain the differences in relative benefits are scale of annual catches (over 100,000 tonnes for the hake fishery and 280 tonnes for the spiny lobster fishery) and markets (particularly Europe for the former, and locally in Mexico for the latter).

Another important question for strategic planning in a country or fishery is how much longer the growth in demand for eco-labelling and eco-labelled products observed in the first nearly two decades of the twenty-first century is going to continue, and by how much. That is not easy to determine and could be affected by a number of factors outside the realm of just the sea-to-plate network for seafood. An important factor, again well illustrated by changes in the markets for South African hake because of the recent global economic crisis, is future economic growth globally and in countries that are currently big consumers of seafood. A serious economic downturn could quickly reduce demand for higher-priced, labelled seafood. However, if it is assumed that there will be no major and sustained economic shocks, it seems likely that demand will continue to grow at a fairly rapid pace in the coming decade or more as a result of increasing environmental awareness and awareness of the existence and goals of eco-labelling in the currently fringe countries (in terms of demand for eco-labelled products) such as Japan, Australia and possibly China too. There is also considerable scope for expanding the incidence of eco-labelling in developing countries, where eco-labelling could also potentially have particularly positive benefits on sustainability of fisheries (Bush et al., 2013). For that to be achieved, however, the existing constraints to eco-labelling will have to be resolved, including those to the certification and labelling approaches themselves, but also to the bigger and more difficult challenges of achieving sustainable fisheries.

The distribution of certified fisheries clearly demonstrates that the impact and benefits of eco-labelling up to now have been strongly skewed in favour of developed countries, thereby demonstrating the fear of developing countries from the start that they could be disadvantaged by the growth of eco-labelling was well-founded. There are, however, two basic reasons for this skewness, and the most important reason, that many fisheries in developing countries are still not being effectively managed for sustainability, places the responsibility for the problem more to the countries themselves than to the schemes. Nevertheless, there are also clearly still biases and weaknesses in both the assumptions and current implementation of eco-labelling that hinder wider application in many developing country fisheries, and in some particularly small-scale fisheries in developed countries. Cost will often be a strong deterrent, as in the case of the Sian Ka'an and Banco Chinchorro Biosphere lobster fishery. Again, in addressing this reality, it is necessary to recognize two primary categories of fishery: those that would benefit from eco-labelling sufficiently to justify striving for certification, and those that would not. The ones that would not can broadly be classified as fisheries dealing with fish and products that are of relatively low economic value, including those destined for markets in which factors such as food security, poverty and price preclude the option to pay a premium for sustainability. Certification of social and labour issues could potentially have a role to play in such cases, but eco-labelling will usually not be a useful tool for encouraging sustainable practices and other incentives, and tools will need to be used.

The second category is those fisheries that would gain net benefits from being certified and labelled but need assistance to improve their performance to meet the standards required for certification, as well as those that are being implemented and managed sustainably but are not being recognized because the methods used and information available for the fishery is not being recognized because of biases and other shortcomings in the certification process and standards. The optimal course of action will be fundamentally different depending on to which of these two categories a fishery belongs. It could be a valuable exercise for countries, aided by expert advisors familiar with responsible fisheries management and eco-labelling, but independent of any eco-labelling scheme, to undertake impartial assessments of the status and needs of the different fisheries in the country. The assessment should identify those fisheries that are unsustainable and in need of intervention and improvement, and the top priority needs and opportunities for each to improve. In cases where eco-labelling would be a valuable tool, the options from Stratoudakis et al. (2016) described in the second section of this chapter could be considered, such as finding private sector partners who would also benefit from certification to assist in improving the fishery, identifying champions, seeking donors to implement an FIP, and others. In cases where eco-labelling would be of no or only marginal benefit, government, stakeholder and donor interest should focus on the other solutions considered to be more appropriate to that specific case.

In conclusion, eco-labelling and certification has had a marked impact on many fisheries, leading to the economic and sustainability benefits that theory had predicted. It is likely to continue to expand for the foreseeable future, with opportunities lying in increasing awareness of the environmental value of eco-labelling and certification in those countries that have the wealth to make environmentally responsible choices but currently have limited knowledge of or access to eco-labelled products, such as Japan, Australia, New Zealand and others. For this full potential to be realised, eco-labelling schemes need to ensure that well-managed fisheries from developing countries also have equitable and cost-effective access to eco-labelling. For most fisheries, particularly small-scale fisheries and fisheries of low or moderate value in developing countries, eco-labelling is unlikely to be a useful tool and incentive in helping them to achieve sustainability and improved benefits for their stakeholders. Such fisheries and the governments, development agencies and development and conservation NGOs should not be distracted by the high interest in eco-labelling, and should focus instead on measures and incentives that are more appropriate and more likely to be effective.

Notes

1 See www.msc.org/about-us/our-history (accessed 24 January 2017).
2 See www.ourgssi.org/about-2/gssi-story/ (accessed 26 January 2017).
3 See www.msc.org/about-us/credibility/how-we-meet-best-practice (accessed 26 January 2017).
4 See www.friendofthesea.org/about-us.asp?ID=2 (accessed 26 January 2017).
5 See www.msc.org/global-impacts/key-facts-about-msc (accessed 27 January 2017).
6 See www.msc.org/about-us/our-history/2010-2015-new-horizons (accessed 27 January 2017).
7 See www.msc.org/about-us/credibility/working-with-developing-countries/fisheries-involved-in-the-developing-world-programme (accessed 6 February 2017).
8 See www.friendofthesea.org/fisheries.asp?ID=71 (accessed 6 February 2017).
9 See www.intrafish.com/news/762451/citing-lack-of-funds-lobster-fishery-leaves-msc (accessed 13 February 2017).
10 See www.ourgssi.org/about-2/gssi-headlines/ (accessed 9 February 2017).
11 A full list of partners can be found at www.ourgssi.org/partnership/partners/ (accessed 10 February 2017).
12 See www.ourgssi.org/about-2/gssi-headlines/ (accessed 9 February 2017).
13 See www.ourgssi.org/about-2/gssi-story (accessed 10 February 2017).
14 See www.ourgssi.org/ (accessed 10 February 2017).

References

Asche, F., Larsen, T.A., Smith, M.D., Sogn-Grundvåg, G. and Young, J.A. (2015). Pricing of eco-labels with retailer heterogeneity. *Food Policy*, 53: 82–93.

Blomquist, J., Bartolino, V. and Waldo, S. (2015). Price premiums for providing eco-labelled seafood: evidence from MSC-certified cod in Sweden. *Journal of Agricultural Economics*, 66: 690–704.

Bush, S.R., Toonen, H., Oosterveer, P. and Mol, A.P.J. (2013). The 'devil's triangle' of MSC certification: balancing credibility, accessibility and continuous improvement. *Marine Policy*, 37: 288–293.

Cochrane, K.L., Andrew, N.L. and Parma, A.M. (2011). Primary fisheries management: a minimum requirement for provision of sustainable human benefits in small-scale fisheries. *Fish and Fisheries*, 12(3): 275–288.

De Young, C., Charles, A. and Hjort, A. (2008). *Human Dimensions of the Ecosystem Approach to Fisheries: An Overview of Context, Concepts, Tools and Methods*. FAO Fisheries Technical Paper, No. 489. Rome: FAO.

FAO (Food and Agriculture Organization) (1998). *Report of the Technical Consultation on the Feasibility of Developing Non-Discriminatory Technical Guidelines for Eco-Labelling of Products from Marine Capture Fisheries*. Rome, Italy, 21–23 October 1998. FAO Fisheries Report No. 594. Rome: FAO. Available at: www.fao.org/docrep/005/x0881t/x0881t00.htm (accessed 25 January 2017).

FAO (Food and Agriculture Organization) (1999). *Report of the Twenty-Third Session of the Committee on Fisheries*. Rome, Italy, 15–19 February 1999. FAO Fisheries Report No. 595. Rome: FAO. Available at: www.fao.org/docrep/meeting/X2930E.htm#REP (accessed 25 January 2017).

FAO (Food and Agriculture Organization) (2003a). *The Ecosystem Approach to Fisheries*. FAO Technical Guidelines for Responsible Fisheries, No. 4, Suppl. 2. Rome: FAO.

FAO (Food and Agriculture Organization) (2003b). *Report of the Twenty-Fifth Session of the Committee on Fisheries*. Rome, Italy, 24–28 February 2003. FAO Fisheries Report No. 702. Rome: FAO.

FAO (Food and Agriculture Organization) (2005). *Putting into Practice the Ecosystem Approach to Fisheries*. Rome: FAO.

FAO (Food and Agriculture Organization) (2008). *Report of the Eleventh Session of the Sub-Committee on Fish Trade*. Bremen, Germany, 2–6 June 2008. FAO Fisheries and Aquaculture Report No. 872. Rome: FAO.

FAO (Food and Agriculture Organization) (2009a). *Guidelines for the Ecolabelling of Fish and Fishery Products from Marine Capture Fisheries. Revision 1*. Rome: FAO.

FAO (Food and Agriculture Organization) (2009b). *Report of the Twenty-Eighth Session of the Committee on Fisheries*. Rome, Italy, 2–6 March 2009. FAO Fisheries and Aquaculture Report 902. Rome: FAO.

FAO (Food and Agriculture Organization) (2012). *Report of the Thirtieth Session of the Committee on Fisheries*. Rome, Italy, 9–13 July 2012. FAO Fisheries and Aquaculture Report No. 1012. Rome: FAO.

FAO (Food and Agriculture Organization) (2014a). Evidence on utilization of the FAO draft evaluation framework and the economic impact from ecolabelling on returns to the fisheries sector. COFI/XIV/2014/Inf.9. Unpublished report submitted to the Fourteenth Session of the COFI Sub-Committee on Fish Trade, Bergen, Norway, 24–28 February 2014.

FAO (Food and Agriculture Organization) (2014b). *Report of the Fourteenth Session of the Sub-Committee on Fish Trade*. Bergen, Norway, 24–28 February 2014. FAO Fisheries and Aquaculture Report 1070. Rome: FAO.

FAO (Food and Agriculture Organization) (2016). *The State of World Fisheries and Aquaculture 2016: Contributing to Food Security and Nutrition for All*. Rome: FAO.

Lallemand, P., Bergh, M., Hansen, M. and Purves, M. (2016). Estimating the economic benefits of MSC certification for the South African hake trawl fishery. *Fisheries Research*, 182: 98–115.

Ley-Cooper, K. and Quintanar-Guadarrama, E. (2010). Chakay: marca colectiva con identidad de origen de las cooperativas de Quintana Roo. CONABIO. *Biodiversitas*, 90: 10–15.

Melnychuka, M.C., Peterson, E., Elliott, M. and Hilborn, R. (2016). Fisheries management impacts on target species status. *Proceedings of the National Academy of Sciences of the USA*. Early edition. Available at: www.pnas.org/cgi/doi/10.1073/pnas.1609915114 (accessed 8 February 2017).

MSC (Marine Stewardship Council) (2016a). *From Sustainable Fishers to Seafood Lovers: Annual Report 2015–2016*. Available at: www.msc.org/documents/msc-brochures/annual-report-archive/annual-report-2015-16-english (accessed 27 January 2017).

MSC (Marine Stewardship Council) (2016b). *Marine Stewardship Council: Global Impacts Report 2016*. London: MSC.

OECD High Seas Task Force (2006). *Closing the Net: Stopping Illegal Fishing on the High Seas*. New York: Governments of Australia, Canada, Chile, Namibia, New Zealand, and the United Kingdom, WWF, IUCN and the Earth Institute at Columbia University.

Pitcher T.J., Kalikoski, D., Short, K., Varkey, D. and Pramoda, G. (2009). An evaluation of progress in implementing ecosystem-based management of fisheries in 33 countries. *Marine Policy*, 33: 223–232.

Roheim, C.A., Asche, F. and Insignares, J. (2011). The elusive price premium for ecolabelled products: evidence from seafood in the UK market. *Journal of Agricultural Economics*, 62(3): 655–668.

Sogn-Grundvåg, G., Larsen, T.A. and Young, J.A. (2013). The value of line-caught and other attributes: an exploration of price premiums for chilled fish in UK supermarkets. *Marine Policy*, 38: 41–44.

Stemle, A., Uchida, H. and Roheim, C.A. (2015). Have dockside prices improved after MSC certification? Analysis of multiple fisheries. *Fisheries Research*, 182: 116–123.

Stratoudakis, Y., McConney, P., Duncan, J., Ghofard, A., Gitonga, N., Mohamed, K.S., et al. (2016). Fisheries certification in the developing world: locks and keys or square pegs in round holes? *Fisheries Research*, 182: 39–49.

Uchida, H., Roheim, C.A., Wakamatsu, H. and Anderson, C.M. (2014). Do Japanese consumers care about sustainable fisheries? Evidence from an auction of ecolabelled seafood. *Australian Journal of Agricultural and Resource Economics*, 58: 263–280.

United Nations Sustainable Development (1992). *Agenda 21*, United Nations Conference on Environment and Development Rio de Janeiro, Brazil, 3–14 June. Available at: https://sustainabledevelopment.un.org/content/documents/Agenda21.pdf (accessed 23 January 2018).

Wakamatsu, H. (2014). The impact of MSC certification on a Japanese certified fishery. *Marine Resource Economics*, 29(1): 55–67.

Washington, S. (2008). Ecolabels and marine capture fisheries: current practice and emerging issues. *GLOBEFISH Research Programme*, 91.

Wessells, C.R., Cochrane, K., Deere, C., Wallis, P. and Willmann, R. (2001). *Product Certification and Ecolabelling for Fisheries Sustainability*. FAO Fisheries Technical Paper No. 422. Rome: FAO.

9 The implementation of ecosystem-based fisheries management

A precautionary pathway with needed bioeconomic analysis

Lee G. Anderson

Introduction

Ecosystem-based fisheries management (EBFM) has been the 'next step' in fisheries management for over a decade (Ecosystems Principles Advisory Panel, 1999; Hilborn, 2004; Pikitch et al., 2004; Frid et al., 2006; Christie et al., 2007; Sanchirico et al., 2008; Link, 2010; Hilborn, 2011; Cowan et al., 2012). Recently, two reports have been published, and each suggests how to proactively make steps towards EBFM implementation. While both are in the context of fisheries management in the US, the analyses are generally applicable. The first report, *Building Effective Ecosystem Plans*, is a report from the Lenfest Fishery Ecosystem Task[1] (Essington et al., 2016):

> The Task Force believes that operationalizing EBFM – putting principles into practice - requires a systematic framework. A framework creates a scaffold on which to hang our knowledge of a fishery system. A framework illustrates the pathways through which managers can identify a coherent set of actions to increase and sustain the multiple benefits people derive from fisheries.
>
> (Essington et al., 2016: 10)

Further they believe that the work on a framework can begin 'using existing tools and processes' (Essington et al., 2016: 58).

Specifically, they propose that management agencies use a new generation of fishery ecosystem plans (FEPs) to develop and implement a structured, deliberate and transparent process for operationalizing EBFM. The report contains a detailed analysis of the origin of FEPs, and suggestions for how the new generation of FEPs should be designed, constructed and implemented. It stresses that the process should be designed to accomplish critical tasks that are needed to operationalize EBFM such as:

> setting and prioritizing overarching goals for the fishery system based on a transparent, stakeholder-driven process; setting performance measures, considering a wide range of alternative actions, and explicitly confronting

the trade-offs inherent in selecting an alternative; specifying an internally consistent set of policies that achieve fishery system goals across multiple fisheries; and adopting adaptive management.

(Essington et al., 2016: 10)

The second report, *NOAA Fisheries Ecosystem-Based Fisheries Management Road Map*, is a policy guidance document prepared by the National Ocean and Atmospheric Agency, which oversees national fisheries policy in the United States (NMFS, 2016). Its purpose is to encourage and help the Regional Fisheries Management Councils to implement EBFM. The road map states that the implementation of EBFM should be based on the following guiding principles: implement ecosystem-level planning; advance our understanding of ecosystem processes; prioritize vulnerabilities and risks to ecosystems and their components; explore and address trade-offs within an ecosystem; incorporate ecosystem considerations into management advice; and maintain resilient ecosystems (NMFS, 2016: 2).

The purpose here is not to review these reports, nor to compare and contrast them. It should be said, however, that the documents do have important similarities, and both provide excellent background and advice for those considering EBFM, especially on the development of FEPs. Rather, after noting that both suggest an orderly process using an FEP to organize and structure the move from single-species management to EBFM, the purpose here is to describe a specific procedure or pathway to follow while building and implementing an FEP. By necessity, the discussion will be limited by space constraints, but it should be clear at the outset in order to achieve the desired benefits that the procedure must achieve the critical tasks identified in the Lenfest study, and also must consider and integrate the six principles of the NOAA road map.

In the Lenfest report, EBFM is defined as:

> a holistic, place-based framework that seeks to sustain fisheries and other services that humans want and need by maintaining healthy, productive and resilient fishery systems . . . where fishery systems consist of linked biophysical and human subsystems with interacting ecological, economic, social, and cultural components.
>
> (Essington et al., 2016: 2, 6)

In the NOAA road map, EBFM is defined as:

> a systematic approach to fisheries management in a geographically specified area that contributes to the resilience and sustainability of the ecosystem; recognizes the physical, biological, economic, and social interactions among the affected fishery-related components of the ecosystem, including humans; and seeks to optimize benefits among a diverse set of societal goals.
>
> (NMFS, 2016: 5)

Combined, these definitions capture current thinking on EBFM, with its focus on systems and the interconnections between physical, biological, economic and social sectors in the fish production process. However, as a long-time student of fisheries management and as an active participant in the fisheries management process, to me there is something lacking because the definitions fail to consider that the bottom line in fisheries management is setting limits on the amounts of fish that may be harvested.

There is, of course, a lot more to the actual practices of fisheries management. A more complete definition is: Fisheries management is the integrated process of information gathering, analysis, planning, decision-making, allocation of resources, and formulation and enforcement of fishery regulations by which the fisheries management authority controls the present and future behaviours of the interested parties in the fishery, so as to optimize the use of fishery resources as a source of human livelihood, food and recreation while ensuring the continued productivity of the living resources.

And even when the focus is only on setting harvest levels, it is also necessary to include specifications on how, when, where and by whom the harvesting will occur. Further, when implementing EBFM, it will of course be necessary to consider all of the elements of the broader definition, but nonetheless putting focus on the basic task of setting catch limits in a broad ecosystem context will help meet the goals and objectives of the task force and the road map.

More specifically, I suggest using the accepted paradigm for single-species management as part of the 'structured and deliberate' framework for operationalizing EBFM. This follows directly from the finding of the Lenfest report that operationalizing EBFM can be accomplished using existing tools and processes (Essington et al., 2016: 58). The concepts in the received single-species paradigm are well known and accepted, and productive first steps towards EBFM can be taken by expanding the paradigm using current methodology and data.

The discussion will proceed as follows. The next section will describe the basic elements of the single-species paradigm, and the third section will start the discussion of how each element can be expanded to be applicable to EBFM. The final section will provide a summary with emphasis on changes on the economic analysis that will be necessary to expand the paradigm.

The precautionary paradigm of single-species fisheries management

There is an accepted paradigm for single-stock management that follows from the FAO's precautionary approach to fisheries management (FAO, 1996, 2009), and it is used as the basis for current fisheries management policies throughout the world. The analysis of this chapter will be based on the US National Standards for Fishery Conservation and Management (Magnuson-Stevens Act, 2017). This paradigm, which will be called the precautionary paradigm here, provides a detailed protocol that is used to implement single-species fisheries management. I suggest that this paradigm provides a very workable template for developing an analogous protocol for implementing EBFM. The success of this endeavour will depend in large degree on the practicality of increasing the dimensionality of current process, and this will be a recurring theme of what is to follow. In the US as well as many other fishing nations, it will also likely require some changes in fisheries laws or regulations. At the very least, thinking about possible EBFM implementation in this manner may illuminate other issues that do not follow directly from increasing the dimensionality of the single-species precautionary paradigm, and this in itself will be a contribution.

According to the precautionary paradigm, the basic function of fisheries management is the determination of the annual allowable harvest level of the specified stock. The allowable harvest level is based on a predetermined control rule that specifies a relationship between harvest level and stock size such that it will determine a harvest path that will cause the stock to achieve or maintain a predetermined target stock size.

The selection of the target stock and the control rule are conceptually policy rather than scientific decisions, although they should be based on solid biological and socio-economic information. The overall goal in setting the target stock and the control rule is to optimize the net benefits from the stream of harvests to current and future participants and users. Of course, as mentioned above, harvest policy must also be concerned with the where, when, how and by whom questions that are very important in determining the value of the stream of harvests over time. The where and the when can affect economic efficiency and have important biological effects. The how and by whom can also affect efficiency and have biological effects, but importantly they also have distributional effects

The success of meeting the target stock size will depend up the validity of the stock assessments, the process used to determine the operational harvest paths, and the success of the regulation process in keeping actual harvests equal to desired harvests and in controlling side effects of harvest, such as by-catch and habitat modification, on the overall productivity of the ecosystem.

The material here will describe in graphical terms the main concepts of the precautionary paradigm, giving special attention to those nuances that will require considerable attention when it is adapted to EBFM. The discussion will be, by necessity, somewhat superficial. The goal is to present the basics so that the process can be understood. The interested reader may want to dig deeper into the technical and legal details by reviewing the references. Of special importance will be the search for analogous concepts that capture the necessary complexities, including ways to address trade-offs. The main topics of discussion will be: target stock size, limit stock size, the control rule, limit harvest level, target harvest level and the limit/target buffer, and the concepts of overfished and overfishing.

Target stock size

To begin the discussion, consider Figure 9.1, which shows the relationship between sustainable yield and stock size, both measured in terms of biomass, for a hypothetical stock. Graphs such as, or analogous to, this are a common result from stock assessment work for modern-day fisheries. The sustainable yield for any stock size on the horizontal axis is the long-term average annual amount that can harvested from that stock size without causing it to change. The natural biomass growth of the stock through recruitment and growth of individuals will compensate for the biomass removed by harvest, and the stock size will remain the same. Note that the sustainable yield reaches a maximum at X_{msy}.

The population dynamics of stock size can be explained in simple terms using this graph. At any stock size, if the level of harvest is below the curve, the stock will tend to grow because catch is less than stock growth, and if the harvest is above the curve, the stock will tend to decrease because catch is greater than growth. The success of any management system depends upon the ability to control the difference between harvest and stock growth.

But the sustainable yield curve can be used for more general purposes. If the goal of fisheries management is to maximize the long-term benefits to current and future users, and if benefits are commensurate with biomass yield, then the overall goal of fisheries management should be to achieve and maintain a stock size of X_{msy}. This becomes the target stock size, and it provides the basis for setting annual harvest levels. Quite simply, annual harvest levels should be set such that, given the population dynamics considering natural growth and other sources of mortality, the stock will move towards or maintain X_{msy}.

The main point at this juncture is that given a target stock size, there is a basis for setting annual harvests. The exact manner in which the harvest levels are determined is called the control rule, and it is the next topic to be discussed. But a critical point as the discussion turns to EBFM is how the target stock should be determined if net benefits are not strictly, and perhaps not even remotely, commensurate with biomass yield. This has been a topic of debate between economists and biologists for decades (see Anderson and Seijo, 2010: Chapter 2). Economists argue that the net value of harvest, as measured by

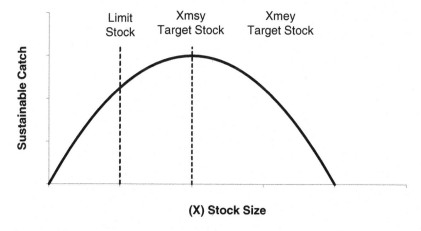

Figure 9.1 Target and limit stock sizes with reference to the sustainable catch curve.

the revenue from the harvest minus the cost of obtaining it, is a better measure of benefits. Rather than maximizing the physical yield, it makes sense to maximize the net value of harvest. This is referred to as the maximum economic yield (MEY). The debate is relevant because the stock size that maximizes sustainable yield will not be the stock size that maximizes the net value. However, fisheries law in the US and most other countries supports the use of biomass yield as a metric of success in fisheries management, and specifies that X_{msy} should be the target stock. Australia is one exception. It has established a policy that the target stock size should be the one where the net present value (NPV) of efficiently harvesting the sustainable yield it produces is maximized (Australian Government, 2007). This stock size is referred to as X_{mey}, and while its exact location will depend on the situation, it is most often larger than X_{msy}, as pictured in Figure 9.1. Although the yield is lower than at X_{msy}, the net returns are higher partly because the larger stock means that harvest can be taken more efficiently.

If one of the concerns of EBFM is making wise choices with respect to the trade-offs between the harvests of different species that will be inevitable in EBFM, a metric other than the biomass harvest will be necessary. A ton of harvest from species 1 is not comparable with a ton of harvest from species 2. It seems apparent that in order to move ahead with EBFM implementation, it will be necessary to follow the lead of Australia and adopt some measure of the net value of output as the metric of success.

Of course, there are many issues of operationalizing the measurement of net value of harvest, including the choice of the discount rate if NPV is to be considered. Also, the net value and the stock size where it is maximized will change with changes in technology, prices and costs. Also, it is necessary to consider the full range of outputs, including commercial, recreational and artisanal harvests, as well as other so-called ecosystem services. While net value of output, even broadly defined, may not be a perfect metric, it will be more useful than measures of biomass for the comparison of outputs of different species that will be required in the trade-off decisions that will be necessary in EBFM.

The bottom line is that even in the single-species case, an argument could be made for the use of almost any viable sustainable stock size as the target stock size, depending upon the amount and distribution of benefits (broadly defined) that can be derived from the sustainable harvest. The same is true of selecting targets in EBFM. The proper metric to use when selecting biological targets will be an important part of developing a proper EBFM process.

Limit stock size

A second biological reference point is the limit stock size. If the target stock size is what managers are shooting for, the limit stock size is a level they do not want to go below. Rather than a policy choice, the limit stock size should be determined on biological criteria. Under US law, the limit stock size is known as the minimum stock size threshold (MSST), and it is defined as the level of biomass below which the capacity to produce MSY (the growth rate at the legally mandated target stock size) on a continuing basis is jeopardized (Magnuson-Stevens Act, 2017). When a stock falls below the limit stock size, the stock is said to be overfished.

Another important biological reference point is the estimation of current stock size, X_c. If the goal of fisheries management is to achieve the target stock size, it is important to know how the current stock size relates to the target stock.

As a sidelight, it should not be forgotten that the process of doing the assessment work necessary to derive these curves is a very complicated, expensive process involving fishery dependent and independent data collection and skilled biometricians. It is frequently the case that there is not enough information to draw curves such as this, and it is necessary to use biological proxies as biological reference points.[2] Even when there are sufficient data, it must be remembered that the curves and the biological reference points are only estimates based on the existing information. Changes in the estimates of natural mortality (which is not uncommon) and changes in fishing technology, which affect age-specific mortality, can change both the general height of the sustainable yield curve and the stock level where sustainable harvest is maximized. In some sense, while there are target and limit stock sizes, the job of achieving the former while avoiding the latter is difficult because the location of both are uncertain and changeable.

Control rules

A second main concept of the precautionary paradigm is a predetermined control rule that specifies the harvest path that will cause the stock to grow to or be maintained at the target stock size. A control rule is a relationship between the current stock size and the desired harvest. For discussion purposes, three different control rules relationships are superimposed on the sustainable growth curve in Figure 9.2. Each point on the curves represents a combination of stock size and a harvest level. The harvest level is the mandated catch limit for that stock size. The f_{msy} control rule sets a catch level by applying the fishing mortality rate that will yield MSY when stock size is at X_{msy}. Continuous use of this control rule will cause the stock to grow to X_{msy}, although the time it takes to get there will vary from case to case. The 10-year control rule is based on using a constant fishing mortality rate that will cause the stock to grow from the current size to the target X_{msy} in 10 years. The flat curve is the constant harvest control rule that sets a fixed harvest level regardless of the current stock size. Advocates argue for this type of control rule on the grounds that industry can plan better if they know what they will be allowed to take each year. The time it takes to get to the target stock size depends upon how high the constant harvest is set.

The biological underpinning of the control rules is that at all points to the left of the target stock size, the selected harvest is less than the sustainable growth, and so stock size will grow. How fast the stock will grow depends in

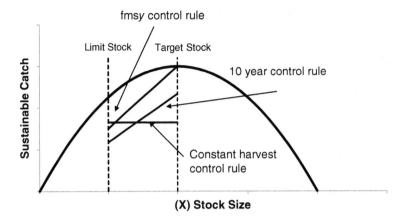

Figure 9.2 Control rules specify a relationship between allowable harvest and stock size.

part on the distance between the sustainable growth curve and the control rule. Of the two positively sloped control rule curves, the lower one will require a shorter time to get to the target stock, but faster growth comes at the expense of higher forgone harvests.

There is technically an infinite number of control rules that will cause a stock to grow from its current size to the target stock size, and the choice of which one to use is a policy decision. Some argue for the control rule that achieves the target stock in the shortest possible time, but in some sense it can also be viewed as an investment problem. How much should society forgo in current harvests in order to achieve the benefits of the higher possible future sustainable harvests when the stock is rebuilt? Without going into the details, economists would argue for that harvest path that maximizes the net present value of harvests over the growth period.

There are pros and cons to the different control rules, most of them having to do with issues of comparing harvest values at different points in time, which could also mean differences in which entities actually do the harvesting and reap the rewards for doing so. Suffice it to say that the choice of control rules can be a thorny problem, even in the relative simplicity of single-species management. As will be seen below, these problems will multiply when the dimensions increase and the discussion is about the setting of the growth rates of several stocks simultaneously and the comparison is not just about the weights of current and future harvest of one species, but it is the comparison of the harvests of different valued species in different time periods, to say nothing of the different entities that will be doing the harvesting.

It will be useful to provide a little more detail about the mindset of the managers who actually make decisions for single species using this paradigm. While they are shooting for a target stock size using the chosen control, given the uncertainty in determining the difference between the current and the target stock size, and in the predictability of the results of the control rule, they do not expect to be exactly at the target stock size at all times. In fact, if when looking, a past record that showed estimates of current stock size that are always relatively close to the target stock size and always a safe distance away from the limit stock size, managers will be congratulating themselves on a job well done. Not to make too light of it, but when working with the known lack of data, uncertainty, and stochasticity, when shooting for a target stock, 'close counts', errors of 20 per cent or more are common and are of little concern. This type of attitude will be necessary when the dimensions of the game increase with EBFM.

It is useful to explain the use of the adjective 'predetermined' with respect to target and limit stocks and the control rule. The point is that these are not meant to be ad hoc decisions or, in the case of limit stock size, a decision to be made when stocks are in trouble. These are to be well considered decisions taking into account the best scientific information and balanced input from the relevant stakeholders and based on established policies. The lesson for this discussion is that when making the move to expand the dimensionality of the single-species model to establish EBFM, a major part of the work will be to make sure that the analysis of the biological reference points is predetermined in the sense that, to the extent possible, the science and policy effects have been fully considered.

The emphasis on predetermined notwithstanding, it is also important to note the tension between flexibility and predetermined control rules. While target and limit stock sizes and control rules are predetermined so as to avoid making decisions in haste and to avoid short-term political pressure, in a stochastic world with scarce, expensive and uncertain data it may be necessary to make midterm corrections if for no other reason than to avoid getting caught up in red tape or being painted into a regulatory corner. Prudent flexibility is necessary for success, and it will be even more necessary when introducing EBFM because of the necessity to address the many trade-offs.

Limit and target harvest and the limit/target buffer

The harvest level that is specified by the control rule is known as the *limit* harvest level. Technically, this is the highest catch level that can be taken while keeping stock size growing properly. However, given the uncertainty involved in data collection and model specification, etc., there is some chance that the actual safe harvest level is lower. Also, given the practical ability of monitoring and enforcing harvest levels, even under the best of circumstances, it is possible that the actual harvest will be higher than that which is specified. This is compounded by the natural stochasticity of the population dynamics of harvested stocks. In other words, there is reason to believe that using the harvest level that is derived from the control rule as the basis for actual regulation can potentially lead to problems. Prudence and a precautionary approach have led to the concept of target harvest level. To use a simple analogy, in order to avoid overshooting the limit harvest level, a lower target harvest level is set, which is used as the basis for setting the actual regulations and controls on fishing and industry participants. The difference between the limit harvest level and the target harvest level is often referred to as the buffer. It is a buffer to reduce the risk of overfishing.

The policy in the US on these issues has just been updated, and current policy specifies that the Councils develop a 'risk policy' to determine the size of the buffer (Magnuson-Stevens Act, 2017):[3]

> The Council's risk policy could be based on an acceptable probability (at least 50 percent) that catch equal to the stock's *target harvest level* will not result in overfishing, but other appropriate methods can be used. When determining the risk policy, Councils could consider the economic, social, and ecological trade-offs between being more or less risk averse. The Council's choice of a risk policy cannot result in a *target harvest level* that exceeds the *limit harvest level*.

The term overfishing means that actual harvest exceeds the limit harvest.

The previous version of the policy mandated a policy based on an acceptable probability (at least 50 per cent) that catch equal to the 'target harvest limit will not result in overfishing'. There was no mention of using economic, social or ecological trade-offs. From an economic point of view, this is a vast improvement for the single-species paradigm, which will make the move to EBFM more practical. The previous policy, which demanded an arbitrary selection of an acceptable risk factor, gives the appearance of rigor but is not a complete analysis. Economists would argue that some form of cost–benefit analysis be used. That is, it should be necessary to compare possible losses in future production from overfishing to the known immediate losses of foregoing current harvests in order to reduce the chances of overfishing. In the short time since the policy has changed, there have been no reports of councils changing their risk policy, but any future changes should be considered when implementing EBFM. When the concept of target catch levels is transferred to EBFM, the increased dimensionality will make setting these buffers even more critical, and it will be even more important to ensure that a balanced rigorous analysis is used to set them, taking into account the expected benefits and costs. This will require developing rigorous methodologies and the necessary databases.

Overfished and overfishing

There are two other important concepts in the single-species precautionary paradigm dealing with the status of the stock: overfished and overfishing. A stock is considered overfished when it falls below the limit stock size. In such an event, there are specified predetermined procedures that must be taken to correct the problem. Exactly what must be done is a policy choice that can vary from stock to stock, depending upon characteristics of the stock (such as reproductive capacity) and of the stock structure (such as age class distribution and the difference between the existing stock size and the limit stock size). Most often, a modified, more conservative harvest control rule is used, but in extreme cases a fishing moratorium may be required. The point here is not the details of what should be done, but that the paradigm specifies that something must be done that is deemed to effectively cause the stock to rebuild to a safe level within a reasonable period of time. This is a hard task in single-species management, and it will be more complicated with EBFM.

A stock is considered to be undergoing overfishing if the actual annual harvest is greater than the target harvest level. An important policy element that follows from the concept of overfishing is mandated changes in the actual regulation process if actual harvest exceeds target harvest levels. If the current regulation tools are not controlling harvest, then prudence calls for expanded or stricter regulation. For example, if, despite predictions from current analysis, a two-week closure does not maintain the target harvest level, then it may need to be expanded in space or time. If at first you try and don't succeed, try again. This makes sense in the single-species cases and it will make even more sense in EBFM.

To summarize the discussion so far, the precautionary paradigm for single-species management based on the FAO precautionary approach to fisheries management, and as implemented in the National Standard Guidelines in the United States, are for the most part conceptually sound and have provided the basis for successful management, even though they are sometimes, by necessity, ad hoc in actual implementation. There are also some weaknesses, such as using biomass as the sole metric of success and the lack of formal economic analyses for comparing the benefits and costs of different management actions. Even with these weaknesses, it does provide a useful template for the planning that will be necessary to implement the precautionary paradigm in EBFM. If anything, identifying the weaknesses stresses the work that will need to be done to build EBMM programmes. In fact, the success of the current system, even given its known foibles, should be encouraging. To use these principles as an EBFM framework does not mean we have to shoot for immediate perfection.

The fundamental problem of fisheries management restated in an EBFM framework

To set the stage, consider again the main elements of the precautionary approach paradigm. First, there are the biological reference points, the target and limit stock sizes. The target is what the management process should shoot for, while the limit is an indicator of problems that require changes in management actions. Second, there is the harvest control rule, which determines the time path of harvest that will cause the stock to grow to or remain at the target size. Third, there is the buffer, which reduces the limit harvest level set by the control rule to a target harvest level as a precaution against uncertainty, lack of data, stochasticity, and imperfect enforcement to keep actual harvest at levels such that stock growth path will lead to the target size. Finally, there are the mandates to make corrective management changes if actual harvest surpasses the target harvest. As described above, there are important trade-offs that must be considered in each of these four elements.

It should be noted that while neither the Lenfest task force nor the NOAA road map specifically suggest expanding the dimensionality of the precautionary approach paradigm as part of a fishery ecosystem plan, they do stress important parts of it. For example, the task force argues for 'the use of ecosystem indicators to monitor progress in achieving goals' (Essington et al., 2016: 8) and for the necessity to 'set performance measures, consider a wide range of alternative actions, and explicitly confront trade-offs inherent in selecting an alternative' (Essington et al., 2016: 10). Similarly, two of the guiding principles of the road map are to 'incorporate ecosystem considerations into management advices' and to 'explore and address trade-offs within an ecosystem' (Essington et al., 2016: 3).

The material in this section will describe in graphical terms how the concepts of the precautionary paradigm model must be changed to incorporate the multidimensional aspects of EBFM. The goal will be to take the concepts from the single species and find analogous concepts in the multispecies context. More than just expanding the dimensionality, the issue is to find constructs that capture in explicit terms the analogous concepts that will allow for the same precautionary approach and also will allow for clear consideration of trade-offs that will be inevitable in EBFM. In short, the target stock size becomes the target stock area; the limit stock size becomes the limit stock area; the harvest control rule becomes a multidimensional process that sets simultaneous catch limits for the specified set of stocks; and the concepts of overfishing and overfished and of the buffer between the limit and target harvest levels must be expanded to consider the interconnections and possible trade-offs between stocks.

The graphical analysis will be limited to two dimensions, and that is a serious problem because with EBFM it will be necessary to consider the management of many stocks simultaneously. Nonetheless, it is possible to sketch out a preliminary outline of the way forward, noting obvious points that follow almost directly and identifying issues that will require more work. It is hoped that the discussion in two dimensions helps to encourage thinking about the right issues and does not trivialize the work that needs to be done.

Target stock area

EBFM will require the need to consider many stocks simultaneously. The *predetermined* selection of the stocks or stock complexes to consider and how they can be classified into groups for management is one of the most important decisions of the EBFM problem, and should depend on clearly defined objectives of management that are supported by users, and be based on an understanding of the full range of social, ecological, environmental and technical harvest relationships between the different stocks and the participants that utilize them. It will be necessary to know the ecological and economic relationships between the stocks and how people use and value the sustainable outputs of the various stock combinations. There are many complex layers involved. For example, while two stocks may be fairly close ecological substitutes in the sense that they both can live in the same habitat and can survive on the same amount of primary productivity, they may provide vastly different services to users.

Determining the stocks that will be considered is a first step in the long process of building a fishery ecosystem plan. Specific suggestions on things that must be considered and practices that will ease the work and help ensure that it is complete and successful are provided in the task force report and the road map, and the references cited therein. The discussion here will focus on the elements in the precautionary paradigm.

However, even once these groups of stocks have been defined, implementing EBFM does not mean creating a vector of multiple but independent target stock sizes for the stocks in the group. As a start, at least, it makes sense to transfer the notion of a single linear stock size into the notion of a stock space. As mentioned, the graphical analysis will be limited to two dimensions (see Figure 9.3, where the sizes of stocks 1 and 2 are measured on the axis). Each point in the figure represents a combination of sizes for stocks 1 and 2. To start the discussion, consider first the target stock sizes that would follow from single-stock management, call them $S_1{}^*$ and $S_2{}^*$, respectively. If these two values were to be adopted independently in an EBFM programme, there would be a target stock *point* in (S_1, S_2) space (see point A). However, given the myriad of interdependencies that argue for the need for EBFM, it makes sense to expand this to a target stock *area* in (S_1, S_2) space. A possible example is shown in Figure 9.4. As a start, the concept of an area in (S_1, S_2) space as the target rather than a single point can be based on the notion that society could

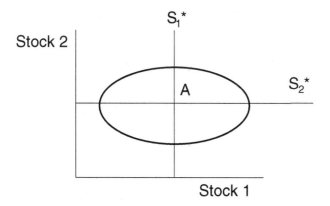

Figure 9.3 In the two-stock case, rather than specifying A as the target point, it may make sense to use an area such as the ellipse as the target.

be indifferent between a little bit less of stock 1 and a little bit more of stock 2 if both stocks provide similar social (market) or ecological services. The concept of the target stock size was based on the fact that the achievement of that size will optimize the benefits from the stock to users. The concept here is that when considering two stocks, it is possible that different combinations will yield similar benefits, and so it is possible to have a larger target. In other words, it is not necessary to focus narrowly on achieving the bull's eye at point A to support a certain level of benefits; that level of benefits can be supported by achieving any point in the specified target area.

This should not be interpreted as meaning that EBFM will be easier because it means aiming at a bigger target. Actually, it is proof that EBFM is a complicated task. It will be necessary to understand the economic and ecological processes that produce the benefits to users, and especially the trade-offs that will be an integral part of the simultaneous management of multiple species.

But as a sidelight, in some ways the larger target could possibly reduce the fear of adopting an EBFM programme. Recall that even in the single-species paradigm, given all of the uncertainties and unknowns, it is considered a management success, or at least not a failure, if regulation can keep the current stock size above the limit and somewhere near the target. The management problems will be exponentially larger in EBFM, and thus it will be more reasonable to measure success in terms of combinations of the sizes of multiple stocks, that is, as a target stock point in stock space.

The specification of the borders of the target stock area will be a difficult task, and it raises the question of the appropriate metric of success in EBFM. Biomass is the most common metric of success in single-species management, and technically it could be used in EBFM. For discussion purposes, consider how the biomass metric could be introduced into the two-stock example.

Again, each point in the figure represents a combination of stock sizes for the two stocks. It follows that at each point, it will be possible to specify the sum of the sustainable yields from the two stocks. If these sums were plotted on the third axis, there would be a surface that would show how total sustainable yield would change with changes in the sizes of the two stocks. Indeed, it would be possible to create shapes similar to the example border of the target stock area by connecting the set of all points with a given sum of yields.

But what information does the sum of biomass yields really provide, and what use is it to fishery managers? Anywhere on the border, the weight of the combined harvest is the same, but it does not say anything about the actual amount of catch from each species, or more importantly the individual values. Given the likely differences in the values or possible benefits from the use of the outputs of the various stocks, it will be necessary to go beyond the concept of the maximization of sustainable biomass yield as a measure of benefits.

But if it is possible to measure the net value of output from each of the stocks (taking into account the issues raised above), the sum of those net values would be a meaningful and useful metric. A dollar of net benefit from harvesting species 1 is comparable to a dollar of net benefit from harvesting species 2.

Further, the border could be drawn based on collections of points with similar net values. It is hard to say *ex ante* what pattern these borders would make, but they would look like the elevation contour lines on a map with smaller areas representing higher and higher values. The meaning of the stock target area border would be that every stock combination on the border has an equal specified value. Further, the meaning of the stock target area specified by the border is that every combination in the area has a value equal to or greater than the specified value on the border.

Conceptually, of course, there could be a single point where the sum of the values is maximized, and a fair question would be if that single point would be an appropriate target. If in fact there is great confidence in the measurement of the net values of the different stocks, there may be some grounds for doing so. On the other hand, given all of the noise in the system, it might be wise to select some net value contour near the maximum as the target stock area.

Perhaps this is a far as this discussion of target stock area can be carried in this very general discussion. There will be many problems involved even in the simple case with two species, not the least of which could be the units of measurement on the two axes if the stocks have large differences in their ranges. And of course, it becomes very difficult to picture the case of the joint management of three or more species. A bull's eye in *n*-dimensional space would be very difficult to specify and even more difficult to obtain, but it may help to think of an *n*-dimensional stock space as a target for EBFM. How to specify the borders of that space is beyond the scope of this discussion. What is necessary is that researchers and managers start thinking in these terms and allocating research effort so as make even small steps towards operationalizing it.

What is to be measured on the *n* + 1 dimension is another critical element. The determination of target stock space requires a clear statement of objectives and acceptable trade-offs. A big part of this will be determining the metric of success.

Limit stock area

The conceptual match for a limit stock size would be a limit stock area, and a possible way to view this in the simple two-dimensional case is shown in Figure 9.4. In the single-stock case, 'overfished' is a fairly simple notion. When stock size falls below the limit stock size, the stock is overfished and there are mandatory predetermined actions that must be taken with respect to future harvest levels. However, with two or more stocks, it is more difficult to delineate situations where mandatory actions can be justified due to issues of stock substitution. Consider line segment *abc* in Figure 9.4, which connects the lowest stock size for stock 1 in the target area and the stock 2 axis. Line segment *def* has an analogous meaning for stock 2. For the moment, assume that point *b* on segment *abc* represents the limit stock size that would apply for stock 1 under the single-species paradigm and that point *e* represents the limit

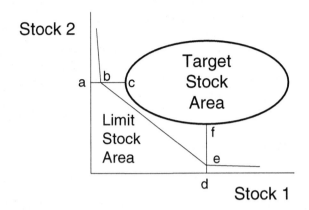

Figure 9.4 The target and limit stock areas.

stock size for stock 2 in that case. One could argue that it is possible to draw a curve between points *b* and *e*, and the area below the curve could be defined as the limit stock area. This has been drawn as a straight line here, but more likely it would be a curve that is convex to the origin. What this means is that a little more of stock 1 will make up for a little less of stock 2, as far as the long-term condition of the two stocks combined is concerned. The shape and position of the boundary curve would depend upon the reproductive capacity of the two stocks, which could be interrelated and will certainly be related to other conditions in the ecosystem.

What the shape of the limit stock boundary should be at higher sizes of both stocks is an interesting question that will depend on the circumstances of a particular case. One could argue that the general shape of the limit stock boundary would be to shift towards the horizontal and vertical axis, as is pictured in Figure 9.4. The logic behind this is that after a while, no matter how much of stock 1 is available, there are reasons for management concern if the size of stock 2 falls lower and lower.

However, perhaps a case could also be made that since the boundary of the target stock area around point *b* moves in a north-easterly direction, it appears that the productive capacity of stock 2 can compensate for lower amounts of stock 1. If this phenomenon is strong enough, this may mean that the limit stock size boundary may have a section with a north-easterly direction as well.

But this is dangerous territory; no assertions about the shape of the limit stock area are being made here. The point is that the limit stock concept makes sense in the single-species case. In EBFM, the limit stock area concept would call for specific action if the group of stocks under management fall into a predetermined limit stock area. The problem, of course, is to develop a meaningful definition of the limit stock area.

A multidimensional control rule

An EBFM control rule would generate a one-to-one mapping from any point in multidimensional stock space to either a vector of specific limit harvest levels for the relevant stocks or an area in the harvest space. In either case, the harvest levels are chosen such that the system is moving towards the target stock area. An argument in favour of selecting a vector of specific harvest levels is its practicality. Given the current way regulation programmes are administered (monitored and enforced) and understood, there must be a strict definition of the limit on harvest. Currently, there is no ground for arguing for having a little less harvest of one stock to make up for a little more harvest of the other, at least as far as the legal administration and enforcement of catch limits. On the other hand, since it is only at the target harvest levels that this becomes an issue, it may be useful to set the harvest limit as an area so that the whole issue of trade-offs can be explicitly considered when setting the harvest targets, which will likely need to be set as specific points of harvest space rather than as areas.

The question of finding the best path from the status quo to somewhere in the target stock space is both a social and an ecological question. The path is important because the amount of benefits that will be produced for the relevant users will depend upon what can or cannot be harvested along the harvest path, as well as on the expected final location in the target stock space. This will require a detailed understanding of the ecosystem connections between the stocks. Both the task force report and the road map stress that these sorts of decisions should be made in a transparent manner with participant input. The point about the almost certain tension between the predetermined control rule and the need for flexibility will be very important in specifying the exact nature of the control rule, and perhaps a description of conditions under which the results can be modified.

A key concept here is the simultaneous determination of a set of allowable annual harvests. In addition to possible ecological and environmental variables, the annual allowable harvest level of any one stock will depend upon its own stock size and characteristics, and on the size, characteristics and annual harvest level of one or more of the other stocks in the group. The annual allowable harvest level for a subset of the stocks may be low or equal to zero, especially in the case of forage species.

Limit and target harvests

While there may be some flexibility in the choice of a limit harvest area versus a limit harvest point, for the reasons discussed above it will likely be necessary to specify the harvest target as a specific point, and not as an area. Transferring the concept of the buffer to set a harvest target point that will help to prevent the harvest limit area or point from being surpassed can be discussed in terms of Figures 9.5a and 9.5b. Figure 9.5a is drawn assuming that the control rule gives the limit

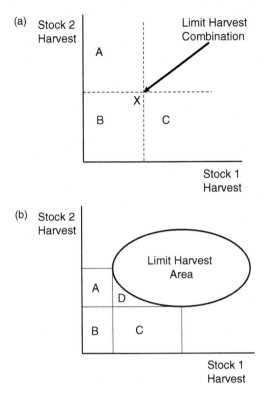

Figure 9.5 With either a specific limit harvest point (a) or a general limit harvest area
(b), only target points in area B will aim below the limit for both stocks,
but it is conceivable that an acceptable target could be in areas A or C.

harvest as a specific point in harvest space (see point X). If the buffer is set such that
the target harvest point is set in area B the target will 'aim' a bit low on the harvest
from both stocks. If the buffer sets the target in either area A or C, the aim will be
such that harvest for one of the stocks may surpass the limit. This could clearly be
a problem in the two-dimensional case shown here but in the analogous case of
many dimensions there may be reasons, either biological or technological dealing
with harvesting techniques or the realities of enforcing catch limits, for choosing a
target harvest point, which surpasses the limit harvest of one or more stocks.

The case where the limit harvest is specified as an area in harvest space is
shown in Figure 9.5b. In this case, if the buffer puts a target harvest point in area
B, this will set harvest levels that are lower than the lowest limit harvest for both
species. Targets harvest points in areas A or C will aim for harvest levels that are
lower than the lowest limit for only one of the species. Targets in area D will
aim for harvest levels that are above the minimum limit for both of the species
but will still be below the harvest limit area. Again, where the target should be

will depend upon the specifics of the particular case, but these are some of the things that should be considered.

It is critical to remember the trade-off that is involved in choosing the size of the buffer. On the one hand, the buffer does lower that chance of overfishing and the inability to achieve the desired growth of the stocks. However, it comes at the cost of foregone current harvest. The concept is the same in EBFM, but the solution is much more difficult because of all of the interactions. It should be clear that work on FEPs should include protocols to undertake the necessary cost–benefit analysis so that there will be a clear and agreed upon basis for making trade-off decisions.

Overfished and overfishing

In concept, determining if the group of stocks undergoing EBFM are overfished is quite simple if a limit stock area can be specified. In the two-dimensional cases, if the current stock size point lies in the limit stock area, the stocks involved are overfished.[4] Following the precautionary approach would then call for a change in the current management rules. It is obvious that there is a connection between determining the limit stock area boundaries and the mandated changes in regulations. It may be necessary to specify different changes for different points in the overfished area.

Now consider the issue of determining if overfishing has occurred. This can be discussed in terms of Figures 9.5a and 9.5b. In either case, only actual harvest points that lie in area B could be certified as having no overfishing on any stock. But then the whole discussion turns on what overfishing means in an EBFM context, and exactly what will be required if overfishing is deemed to have occurred. With many stocks, it may be very difficult to ensure that none will be overfished as judged by its individual target harvest, and even if it does occur it will be hard to interpret what effect it will have on the complex of stocks under management.

Perhaps it would be best to use other procedures to judge if overfishing has occurred. Consider Figure 9.6, which portrays the status quo stock combination and the target stock space. The purpose of the control rule is to keep the stock complex moving towards the target stock space. Therefore, one way to judge if overfishing has occurred is to look at the path along which the complex is growing. If it stays within the bands created by drawing a set of tangents to the target stock space from the status quo point, operationally it appears logical to say that overfishing is not occurring, at least on the level of the whole stock complex. A weaker test would be seeing if the path stayed within the arc created by lines extending vertically and horizontally from the status quo point. Again, these concepts will have to be extended to the multidimensional framework.

Summary and concluding comments

A description of the process of fishery management for the single-species cases based on the precautionary paradigm was provided in the second section

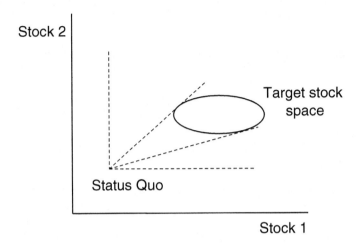

Figure 9.6 Overfishing could be defined with reference to the location of the growth path of the stocks from the status quo towards the target stock space.

above. An analogous description of fisheries management under EBFM based on the above discussion follows.

Ecosystem-based fisheries management (EBFM) is the simultaneous determination of allowable harvest levels for a specified group of stocks (a vector of harvest levels), and it is based on selection of a target stock area and a control rule to determine the time path of the harvest that will cause the collection of current stocks sizes to move into or remain in the target stock area.

The selection of the target stock area and the control rule are conceptually policy rather than scientific decisions, although they should be based on solid biological and socio-economic information. The overall goal in setting the target stock and the control rule is to optimize the stream of net benefits to current and future participants and users.

The success of achieving the target stock area will depend up the validity of the stock assessments, the process used to determine the operational harvest paths, and the success of regulation process in keeping actual harvests equal to desired harvests and in controlling side effects of harvest on by-catch and the ecosystem so as to maximize the net benefits for the current and future users of fisheries output. This should take into account the likely effects such harvests will have on the productivity of the different stocks, taking ecological, technological, oceanographical and climatological effects into consideration.

The Lenfest task force concluded that there are enough basic concepts, tools, knowledge and data to start the process of implementing EBFM immediately. To put it another way, the lack of these elements should not prevent first steps. This chapter has proposed a path to follow based on the precautionary paradigm that can use received knowledge and procedures and help to focus attention on areas where more research will be required.

One identified area of needed research is to find a substitute for biomass as the metric of success or as a means of evaluating trade-offs. While net value of harvest is a good place to start, it will be necessary to measure and compare values for all harvest uses. It will be especially important to elaborate on the distribution of the value of output as well as its total amount. It will also be important to develop methods to allow for rigorous analysis of trade-offs, especially with respect to determining the optimal size of the buffer between limit and target harvest levels. How can the benefit of reducing the risk of overfishing, and hence not achieving desired stock growth, be measured in a way that is directly comparable to the loss of current output?

Another area where research would likely be useful is an expansion of the elements included in limit and target harvest levels. In addition to how much should be caught, current and future direct and indirect benefits will depend on how, where, when and by whom they are caught. Such additions will only be possible if the management objectives address these important issues in clear and operational terms.

An area where considerable research has been undertaken is the choice of general ecological indicators to judge the success of EBFM (Methratta and Link, 2006). The process suggested here proposes using the location of a species group in *n*-dimensional space relative to target and limit stock areas as an indicator of success. While this has the advantage of a direct link between the indicator and the objectives of management, it may indeed be a challenge to implement. It may be better to look for simple and readily available indicators. Perhaps success or failures in the search for operational target stock areas may influence the research objectives relative to these more general indicators.

Acknowledgements

This chapter is based on the author's keynote address at the 2015 Forum of the North American Association of Fishery Economists, and benefited from comments by participants.

Notes

1 Candor requires the acknowledgement that the author was a member of the Lenfest Fishery Ecosystem task force.
2 A complete description of the nature and use of biological proxies is beyond the scope of this chapter, although they will likely to have to be used extensively in EBFM.
3 The general terms from this discussion, *limit harvest level* and *target harvest level*, have been italicized, and are used in place of the analogous terms specific to US law.
4 At this level of discussion, it is important to note that it is not possible to determine the limit stock area unless there is a definition for what overfished means in the EBFM context, which is something that is still being debated in the literature. Perhaps working in terms of a limit stock area (or a limit stock space in *n*-dimensional terms) will help provide suggestions for defining overfished in EBFM.

References

Anderson, L.G. and Seijo, J.C. (2010). *Bioeconomics of Fisheries Management*. Hoboken, NJ: Wiley-Blackwell.

Australian Government (2007). *Commonwealth Fisheries Harvest Strategy: Policy and Guidelines*. Canberra: Department of Agriculture, Fisheries and Forestry. Available at: www.agriculture.gov.au/SiteCollectionDocuments/fisheries/domestic/hsp.pdf (accessed 10 January 2018).

Christie, P., Fluharty, D.L., White, A.T., Eisma-Osorio, L. and Jatulan, W. (2007). Assessing the feasibility of ecosystem-based fisheries management in tropical contexts. *Marine Policy*, 31: 239–250.

Cowan, J.H., Rice, J.C., Walters, C.J., Hilborn, R., Essington, T.E., Day, J.W., et al. (2012). Challenges for implementing an ecosystem approach to fisheries management. *Marine and Coastal Fisheries*, 4: 496–510.

Ecosystems Principles Advisory Panel (1999). *Ecosystem-Based Fishery Management*. Washington, DC: National Marine Fisheries Service.

Essington, T.E., Levin, P.S., Marshall, K.N., Koehn, L., Anderson, L.G., Bundy, A., et al. (2016). *Building Effective Fishery Ecosystem Plans: A Report from the Lenfest Fishery Ecosystem Task Force*. Washington, DC: Lenfest Ocean Program. Available at: www.lenfestocean.org/EBFM (accessed 10 January 2018).

FAO (Food and Agriculture Organization) (1996). *Precautionary Approach to Capture Fisheries and Species Introductions*. FAO Technical Guidelines for Responsible Fisheries, No. 2. Rome: FAO.

FAO (Food and Agriculture Organization) (2009). *Report of the Workshop on Toolbox for Applying Ecosystem Approach to Fisheries*. Rome, Italy, 29 February. Rome: FAO.

Frid, C., Paramor, O. and Scott, C. (2006). Ecosystem-based management of fisheries: is science limiting? *ICES Journal of Marine Science*, 63: 1567–1572.

Hilborn, R. (2004). Ecosystem-based fisheries management: the carrot or the stick? *Marine Ecology Progress Series*, 274: 275–278.

Hilborn, R. (2011). Future directions in ecosystem based fisheries management: a personal perspective. *Fisheries Research*, 108: 235–239.

Link, J.S. (2010). *Ecosystem Based Fisheries Management: Confronting Tradeoffs*. New York: Cambridge University Press.

Magnuson-Stevens Act (2017) National Standards 16 U.S.C. 1851(a)(1).

Methratta, E.T. and Link, J.S. (2006). Evaluation of quantitative indicators for marine fish communities. *Ecological Indicators*, 6: 575–588.

NMFS (National Marine Fisheries Service) (2016). *NOAA Fisheries Ecosystem-Based Fisheries Management Road Map*. Available at: www.st.nmfs.noaa.gov/Assets/ecosystems/ebfm/EBFM_Road_Map_final.pdf (accessed 10 January 2018).

Pikitch, E.K., Santora, C., Babcock, E.A., Bakun, A., Bonfil, R., Conover, D.O., et al. (2004). Ecosystem-based fishery management. *Science*, 305: 346–347.

Sanchirico, J.N., Smith, M.D. and Lipton, D.W. (2008). An empirical approach to ecosystem-based fishery management. *Ecological Economics*, 64: 586–596.

10 Fishery bio-socio-economics

Anthony Charles

Introduction

The reality of fish as both a scarce resource and a public resource has meant that the practice of fishery management always involves the balancing of multiple objectives. This is a long-standing truth (Lawson, 1984; Charles, 2001), though one not necessarily incorporated into conventional fishery economics analyses, such as those focused on rent maximization. Another key reality of real-world fisheries is that their assessment and effective management requires going far beyond the simplified 'bioeconomic' essence of fish and fishing fleets to see them as 'fishery systems', with complex interactions not only between fish stocks and ecosystems, but also between fishers and fishing communities (Garcia and Charles, 2008). Indeed, more broadly, fishery systems also include social, economic, biological, environmental and regulatory components, as well as the surrounding social, economic and ecological environments. A third reality in fisheries is their inherent (yet often uncertain) dynamics. While the population dynamics of fish have received considerable attention, the dynamics of fishers and human communities utilizing the fishery are equally important in driving change and influencing the appropriateness of management policies.

To assess and to attempt to manage fisheries – within this context of multiple objectives, systems structure and inherent dynamics – requires a more comprehensive, more integrated framework than was typical in the past. This chapter highlights the shift to a bio-socio-economic framework that links bioeconomic and socio-economic approaches to fishery analysis.

The term 'fishery bio-socio-economics' is used here to incorporate those aspects of the fishery system in which human and social elements influence fishery objectives, practice, management and policy. This includes: (1) explicitly recognizing multiple objectives for fishery management, to incorporate both societal goals and those of the fishery participants; and (2) focusing on the distribution of benefits and costs, on behavioural and labour dynamics of people in the fishery (going beyond the more usual focus on fishing vessels or 'fishing firms'), on issues of fishery governance, and on the interaction of fisheries with fishing communities. To put it another way, broadening bioeconomics to a bio-socio-economic approach explicitly adds consideration of the objectives and dynamics of fishers and fishing communities, with joint treatment of biological, social and economic structures, as well as aspects of human and institutional behaviour.

This conception of fishery bio-socio-economics is expanded upon in the next section, which provides a sense of the specific major themes incorporated within bio-socio-economics. The third and fourth sections then describe two specific examples of bio-socio-economic analysis, based on model frameworks – one involving a combination of multiple objectives and labour dynamics, the other the dynamics of fishing communities and the nature of distributional impacts. The fifth section turns from model-based analysis to fishery policy analysis, showing how a broader bio-socio-economic perspective can result in improved fishery policy. The chapter closes in the sixth section with conclusions about the future potential and role for fishery bio-socio-economics.

Ingredients of fishery bio-socio-economics

In this section, some key ingredients of fishery bio-socio-economics are described, expanding on an earlier analysis (Charles, 1988), with the goal of broadening bioeconomic thinking (focused on fish stocks and fishing fleets) to a more comprehensive bio-socio-economic approach.

Multiple objectives and fishery conflicts

As noted above, a wide variety of objectives are important practically within real-world fisheries, whether or not they are expressed explicitly in fishery policy. These can include employment, fair distribution of fishery benefits, the generation of resource rents, and more (Lawson, 1984). It is important to recognize the general impossibility of simultaneously maximizing across multiple objectives, which implies that objectives are likely to be conflicting (for a typology of the many forms of resulting fishery conflicts, see Charles, 1992). Success in managing fisheries will then require three major ingredients:

(1) Mechanisms for determining the desired weighting of the legitimate societal objectives, usually through a political process, led by policymakers but benefiting from broad discussion.
(2) Application of suitable policy and regulatory instruments to achieve the 'desired' balance or blend of objectives, whether the fishery is *explicitly* managed on a multi-objective basis, or by means of an *implicit* balancing of divergent single-objective user groups.
(3) The use of mechanisms for resolving the inevitable and often ubiquitous conflicts, recognizing that choices made by policymakers, including in the types of management instruments, likely result in 'winners' and 'losers' across the fishery sector. This point is elaborated in the discussion below.

Distribution of benefits and costs

In selecting acceptable regulatory alternatives, fishery policymakers need to be aware that distributional implications must be considered, notably issues of who are the 'winners' and 'losers' from certain policy choices, as above. This practical interest in the distribution of benefits (notably income and employment) and associated costs is matched by its theoretical relevance to determination of socially optimum fishery arrangements. For example, Bromley and Bishop (1977) suggested long ago that for both practical and theoretical reasons, interactions of fishery management and income distribution should be highlighted explicitly. Increasingly, this attention to distributional impacts must go beyond the fishery per se to include such impacts arising from a range of competing ocean uses – fisheries, but also sectors such as aquaculture, shipping and mining, as well as coastal economic development – and increasing implementation of new ocean conservation measures such as marine protected areas (Charles, 2010).

Fisheries governance, rights and the commons

As noted above, the existence of multiple fishery objectives, and the choice of priorities among these, interacts directly with the choice of appropriate management approaches and regulatory instruments. Certain fishery policies may be entirely incompatible with declared objectives, while with others it may not be possible to 'get there from here' in terms of achieving fishery goals. Thus, it is important, from a bio-socio-economic perspective, to assess the relevance of management alternatives, and for this it is relevant to explore two key areas:

(1) The nature of fishery rights (e.g. Pinkerton, 1989; Charles, 2009, 2011) covering a wide range of use rights and management rights in fisheries, including critiques of conventional methods (such as regulated property rights and limited entry schemes) and studies of alternatives (e.g. informal rights, cooperatives, co-management and community property rights).
(2) The realities of 'commons' management (e.g. Berkes, 1989; Berkes et al., 1989; Ostrom, 1990, 1992), with abundant research over the past several decades, notably on how fishers' organizations and fishing communities are involved in regulating the fishery in which they have community self-interest (e.g. see Copes and Charles, 2004).

Behavioural and labour dynamics

The 'socio' in a bio-socio-economic perspective focuses on the people in fishery systems. A key element of this is the behaviour and decision-making of fishers, including aspects ranging from the fundamental long-term issue of whether to remain as a fisher occupationally, through to short-term day-to-day decisions about where to fish and what species to fish. A major rationale for bio-socio-economic analysis is the realization that fishery management requires a suitable understanding of the behavioural dynamics of fishers, both individually and collectively, as well as overall decision-making structures, in fishing and post-harvest activities. Early efforts to model and predict fisher behaviour, from an economic perspective, include the work of Wilen (1979) and Opaluch and Bockstael (1984: 107) – with the latter arguing for 'a change in research focus from the behaviour of fish to the behaviour of fishermen'. Since then, behavioural analyses in fisheries have expanded (e.g. Charles et al., 1999; Wilen et al., 2002; Salas and Gaertner, 2004), although there still is much less attention here relative to studies of fish population dynamics.

Another key ingredient from a bio-socio-economic perspective is the fishery labour force – the fishers as well as the post-harvest (e.g. processing) workers. The structure and dynamics of labour markets, labour supply and participation in the fishery all play a major role in fishery systems, and specifically in the determination of suitable management policies. Key issues include labour mobility (both geographical mobility, i.e. shifts of labour between locations, and occupational mobility, i.e. shifting between employment types), the resulting extent of migration into and out of the fishery, and work conditions (e.g. measured by work satisfaction indices, and the relationship between work environment and corresponding productivity levels).

The opportunity cost of labour is also important in considering fishery policy. A low opportunity cost of labour, as often seen in isolated fishing communities with few alternative employment possibilities, can drive the feasibility and equity of management options. For example, fishery policies based on 'rationalization' measures that reduce the number of fishers may be counterproductive if, as in many fisheries, there are effectively no alternative local sources of livelihood, and surplus labour cannot be absorbed elsewhere in a high-unemployment economy. The fact that such measures may produce disastrous results both in and beyond the fishery, and thus fail from a practical perspective, can be explained through suitable bio-socio-economic analysis. As a result, a key issue in fishery policy involves the extent to which the opportunity cost of fishing can be raised by providing non-fishing employment alternatives as a more sustainable approach.

Fishing communities

Many social scientists over the years have explored the nature of fishing communities, including both place-based communities (i.e. discrete and usually small, local places in which fishing is a dominant occupation – ones that, for the public, are seen to be actual 'fishing communities') and 'communities of interest' (e.g. fisher associations and cooperatives). In the past, this level of analysis received little attention in economic-focused studies, but more recently the importance of understanding the structure, dynamics and objectives of fishing communities has been more broadly recognized. This may be due to the reality that fishing communities form a key part of the fishery's human environment, just as aquatic ecosystems form the environment of fish stocks (Charles, 2001). If ecosystem-based management and an 'ecosystem approach' (Bianchi and Skjoldal, 2008; De Young et al., 2008) are to be adopted in fisheries, so that the ecosystems in which the fish live are better incorporated, then we should consider the human side of the fishery system equally (i.e. where the people live, notably fishing communities).

Accompanying this logic are two further realities. First, the nature of and challenges within fishing communities may dramatically affect the feasibility and success of fishery management. For example, poverty, food insecurity and negative health impacts (such as HIV) in fishing communities can be detrimental to stewardship and conservation efforts. Second, on a positive angle, community cohesion, empowerment and social capital in fishing communities can be crucial factors leading to efficient fishery conservation – a point made strongly by Ostrom (1990, 1992) and many others, in terms of managing the 'commons'. Hence, the realities of communities may be key drivers of fisher behaviour and key factors affecting success of fishery governance. Fishery bio-socio-economics must thus pay close attention to the underlying values and objectives, the knowledge and local institutions, and the overall nature and functions of communities (Graham et al., 2006; Charles et al., 2010).

The topics outlined in this section provide the basis for a bio-socio-economic framework that permits more complete assessment of fishery management options, the extent to which these choices will meet multiple objectives, the rate at which desired outcomes will be approached, and challenges and trade-offs likely to arise along the way. This, it is argued, poses short-term challenges (to be discussed at the end of the chapter), but may well ultimately improve the efficiency of fishery governance, policy and management by making management measures better suited to the given human context, increasing the participation of fishers and fishing communities in decision-making, and thereby increasing the likelihood that fishery objectives can be achieved in practice.

In the following two sections, examples of bio-socio-economic analysis are provided, in the form of conceptual models, used not to obtain specific numerical results, but rather to generate insights about bio-socio-economic dynamics and outcomes. These examples seek to illustrate how the success and efficiency of fisheries management can be affected by bio-socio-economic aspects, how the results can vary between the short run and the long run, and how the choice of fishery management instruments interacts with bio-socio-economic structure and dynamics. The first example focuses on dynamics of *fishery labour*, in conjunction with fishing effort and fish stocks, and the interaction of *multiple objectives* in the fishery. The second example focuses on fishing and *fishing communities*, and in particular the *distribution of benefits and costs* among fishing communities as a result of implementing a major conservation tool, marine protected areas.

Example: multiple objectives and labour dynamics

Fisheries often form the core of a fishery-dependent local economy (e.g. a specific place-based community, set of communities, or relatively small stretch of coastline) operating within a larger multi-sector regional economy. Let us assume that in such a situation, the fishery is sufficiently dominant that the dynamics of the local population are approximately proportional to its fishery labour force: as the fishery goes, so goes the community. There is some *labour mobility*, so those in the labour force of the *regional* economy can move into and out of the *local* fishery economy, in response to both internal conditions (the state of the fishery, e.g. per capita income and employment rates) and external conditions (i.e. the attractiveness of employment elsewhere in the region). Changes in the aggregate fishery labour force are determined, then, by the decisions of individual fishers, in response to these realities. Given this scenario, a bio-socio-economic model can explore the dynamics of the fishery system. The present discussion presents such a model, adapting the analysis in several earlier articles (Charles, 1989, 1991, 1995).

Consider a simple model with two dynamic variables, the *fish stock* and the *fishery labour force*, and subject to their dynamics, the task of fishery management is to balance multiple objectives such as income, employment and community stability. Consider a fish stock denoted, at any time t, by x_t. This stock is assumed to be driven jointly by natural reproductive dynamics and human impact on the resource – the harvesting activity. The rate of harvest is $h_t = qE_t x_t$, where E_t is the level of fishing effort, and q is the catchability coefficient. Here, E_t is assumed to be regulated by the fishery management process. The rate of change in the fish stock is $\dfrac{dx}{dt} = F_x - h$, where F_x is the fish stock's natural growth rate, assumed given by logistic population dynamics, $F_x = sx\left(1 - \dfrac{x}{K}\right)$, where s is an intrinsic growth rate and K a carrying capacity. Then the overall population dynamics are:

$$\frac{dx}{dt} = sx\left(1 - x / K\right) - qEx \tag{10.1}$$

In the examples presented below, the parameter s will be set appropriately for the different cases, while the values $K = 1$, and $q = 1$ are fixed.

The fishery labour force L_t is also assumed to adjust continuously to changing conditions over time. In analogy with natural population dynamics, the labour force dynamics are assumed to be driven by a maximum per capita growth rate r, reflecting the sum of natural growth and immigration, and a carrying capacity L_t representing the maximum sustainable level for L_t, given internal and external conditions as determined by the state of the external economy and the internal conditions in the local economy (i.e. the attractiveness of the fishery itself).

These assumptions produce a 'logistic' growth pattern, with the carrying capacity as a 'natural' level that the labour force tends towards over time. However, here the carrying capacity $\bar{L}_t$ is a function of time, so unlike a basic logistic equation, in which the state variable tends towards a constant level, in this case as conditions change, so too does the carrying capacity $\bar{L}_t$. Thus, the labour force L_t adjusts continuously towards a 'moving target' $\bar{L}_t$, in a manner analogous to a population dynamics model in which carrying capacity varies with environmental factors. If the local labour force is relatively low, $L_t < \bar{L}_t$ (given current conditions in the fishery compared with elsewhere in the economy), the labour force expands, since the fishery seems relatively attractive to potential fishers (cf. Smith, 1968). Conversely, if the labour force is relatively high, $L_t > \bar{L}_t$, then it would be expected to decline.

Thus, the labour force dynamics are such that the per capita growth rate at time t is given by the product of r and a term involving the ratio $L_t / \bar{L}_t$, so the overall rate of change is given by:

$$\frac{dL}{dt} = rL\left(1 - \frac{L}{\bar{L}}\right) \tag{10.2}$$

On the one hand, the better the employment situation in the external economy, the greater the tendency for labour movement away from the fishery, and thus the lower the carrying capacity for labour in the fishery. For the present discussion, the state of the external economy will be treated as constant, to focus on changes within the fishing economy. Note as well that the extent to which labour will exit the fishery will depend not only on economic aspects (employment, wages), but also on sociocultural factors such as local tradition, family ties and employment sharing; these factors are also treated as constant in this analysis.

The attractiveness of the local fishery to both current and potential participants, relative to other employment options, is assumed to depend on several factors, with two of these considered here (for other options, see Charles, 1989).

First, following Smith (1968), we assume that a key factor is how lucrative the fishery appears, measured by the *average per capita income* received by fishers. This is captured by the term $(\pi + T) / L$, where π is the fishery rents and T represents the level of net non-fishery transfers to fishery participants from the external economy (assumed constant). Here, π is given by total fishery revenue minus operating costs, minus the opportunity costs of labour. Assuming linear costs, with c_E and c_L being unit costs of effort and labour, and constant price p, then the rents can be written $\pi = \pi(x, L, E) = p(qEx) - c_E E - c_L L$ using the relationship $h = qEx$. In the examples presented below, the economic parameters in this equation are set at $p = 1$, $c_E = 0.01$ and $c_L = 0$.

Second, we assume that the fishery is considered attractive if there is a high *employment* level (i.e. if the level of allowable fishing effort is high relative to the labour available), so that each fisher faces few restrictions on fishing activity. A measure of the rate of employment in the fishery is E_t / L_t. Note that if $E_t = L_t$, the fishery is operating with full employment of its labour force. On the other hand, if $E_t < L_t$, the labour force is underutilized, and if $E_t > L_t$, the available work force is overextended.

The higher the average per capita income and aggregate employment levels, the more attractive the fishery is to fishers, inducing expansion of fishing effort. This is modelled here with a Cobb–Douglas function, in which the labour force carrying capacity $\overline{L}_t$ reflects the attractiveness of the fishery, as the product of the two terms discussed above, each raised to a constant power (α and β, respectively). Thus, the carrying capacity of the labour force is given by:

$$\overline{L}_t = M \left(\frac{E}{L} \right)^{\alpha} \left(\frac{\pi + T}{L} \right)^{\beta} \tag{10.3}$$

Here, M is a constant that incorporates the (assumed constant) state of the external economy, and reflects the maximum labour force under historical conditions. This expression for the carrying capacity is inserted in the labour

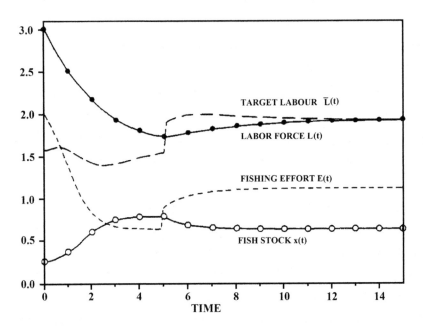

Figure 10.1 Fishery system dynamics are shown for the case of an initially small fish stock and a large labour force. Maximum intrinsic growth rates are $s = 3$ for the fish population and $r = 0.25$ for the labour force. For this simulation, the harvest level h, given as a percentage of the fish stock carrying capacity, is set at 50 per cent for the first five years, and 70 per cent thereafter. The labour force L_t continuously approaches its target level $\overline{L}$, but this quantity varies over time, depending on profit rates, effort levels and the size of the labour force itself.

Source: Charles (1989).

dynamics described above. In the examples presented below, the parameter r will be set appropriately for the different cases, while the values $M = 2.12$, $T = 2$ and $\alpha = \beta = 0.5$ are fixed.

Thus, for any given set of initial conditions, and given the above dynamics and values for the parameters, the fishery system will evolve over time, driven by the dynamics of x and L, and the choice of fishing effort E_t at each time t. The latter may be specified a priori to simulate the evolution of the fishery for specific choices of effort E_t. To illustrate this, using simulation, consider the continuous time fishery 'discretized' (using a small time increment, in this case 0.1 years) and the fishing effort set at each point in time. Suppose we assume the labour force is initially relatively large, while the fish stock is significantly depleted, and the parameter values are as given above. If fishery managers set effort to rebuild the depleted stock by harvesting at a modest level initially (for the first five years), then increasing that level thereafter, Figure 10.1 shows the evolution of the resulting fishery. Note in Figure 10.1 how the labour force varies over time, with a tendency at each time step towards its constantly shifting carrying capacity.

Now consider an optimization approach involves determining the fishing effort E_t over time as a control variable to optimize the fishery, given certain objectives (i.e. maximize the discounted sum of net social benefits over time) and constraints, including the inherent dynamics above. In a bio-socio–economic framework, typically the net benefits function must capture the multiple objectives in fisheries. While there are many possible objectives to include, for concreteness we focus on jointly optimizing two objectives:

1   *Economic wealth (rent generation).* This is the conventional goal in bioeconomic fishery models, based on the resource rent accruing directly from the fishery (π), assumed to be given by $\pi = \pi\left(x, L, E\right) = p\left(qE_x\right) - c_E E - c_L L$, where the various parameters and variables are as above.

2   *Community 'health'.* Fishing community viability (or health) is an important factor in determining social welfare, although often neglected in many jurisdictions' fishery management. While there are various options for assessing community viability, in this case we focus on the trend in population of the relevant community. The assumption is that in a fishery-dependent area, a growing labour force (or population) tends to reflect a healthy, more prosperous community, and thus is preferred to a shrinking one, other things being equal. Accordingly, the objective of community health is modelled by the rate of change of the fishery labour force, dL / dt. It is important to note two caveats. First, there may in fact be negative effects of an increasing labour force (and community population), e.g. in terms of higher unemployment and lower per capita fisher incomes, but such negative aspects are already incorporated in the second and third objectives above, and thus do not need to be considered here. Further, the preference for a growing labour force (and community population) may be valid for unchanging external conditions, but this could be different if there are positive

changes in the external economy (e.g. better opportunities). Despite these caveats, other things being equal, this measure of community health seems appropriate.

The objective function combines the two goals, in this case as a 'weighted sum' of the objectives with each multiplied by a constant weighting term (a_1 and a_2, respectively). Care is needed in doing this since, as discussed in Charles (1989), the objectives are measured in very different units. Given this multi-objective function, the overall goal is to choose a fishing effort policy $\{E_t\}$ to maximize a discounted sum over time:

$$\underset{\{E_t\}}{Maximize} \int_{t=0}^{\infty} e^{-\delta_t}\left[a_1\left(\pi_t\right)+a_2\left(\frac{dL}{dt}\right)\right] \tag{10.4}$$

where $e^{-\delta\tau}$ is a discount factor, with $\delta = 10$ per cent, and an indefinite time horizon assumed here.

We focus here on approximately optimal solutions using simulation methods. This allows us to examine the bio-socio-economic dynamics, driven by the objective function above, in this case using a 30-year time horizon. Constraints are placed on 'allowable' harvest strategies, such that the effort choices considered allowable are assumed to be constrained by requiring that: (1) harvest policies must result in a long-term sustainable fish stock, so sustainability of the resource is imposed as a firm constraint; (2) the overall income level must be at least 0 in any period, assuming that positive income is needed at each time step for a strategy to be acceptable; (3) the per capita rate of decline in the labour force (and fishery population) cannot exceed 20 per cent, reflecting the idea that too fast a decline is politically unacceptable; and (4) fishing effort E cannot exceed the available labour force L; $E_t \leq L_t$ at each time t. Further, to simplify the calculations required, the harvest policy is discretized into a set of five harvest levels, one for each of years 0–5, 5–10, 10–15, 15–20 and 20–30 (rather than allowing separate choices for each year). With these assumptions, a strategy is chosen to maximize the given objective function, though it must be noted that the results are only optimal relative to the set of possibilities considered.

Two scenarios are considered here, each with certain levels of the initial conditions, choices of the management objectives, and choices of the intrinsic growth rates (s and r), holding all other parameters fixed.

In the first scenario (see Figure 10.2), a single objective is assumed – *maximizing* the sum of discounted rents (so $a_2 = 0$). This is subject to relatively fast adjustment dynamics for both the fish stock and the labour force ($s = 3$ and $r = 1$), and starting with a relatively small initial fish stock size, $x_0 = 0.25$. The resulting 'optimal' fishing effort policy calls for initial recovery of the stock through a low harvest level in the first five years, increasing to an equilibrium level thereafter. In fact, however, the actual harvest level in this case lies initially below its optimal level, since fishing effort is constrained by the size of the labour force ($E \leq L$). This leads to an increase in the fish stock, while a high profit rate leads to gradual expansion in the labour force, and a corresponding increase in the fishing effort level. However, once the fish stock has grown to a certain extent, effort must decrease to maintain the desired harvest. When in year 5 the optimal rate of harvest rises, this produces jumps in both the effort and the natural labour force. Labour and the fish stock then gradually adjust towards a new long-term equilibrium.

The second scenario (see Figure 10.3) involves an objective function that places equal weight on rent generation (π) and community health (dL / dt), so $a_1 = a_2$. There are relatively slow adjustment dynamics for the fish stock and the labour force ($s = 1.5$, $r = 0.25$) and a high initial stock, $x_0 = 1$. In this case, the optimal harvest changes to a greater extent over time, producing fluctuations in both the fish stock and the labour force. Initially, the large fish stock and low labour force produce incentives for entry into the fishery, indicated by the high

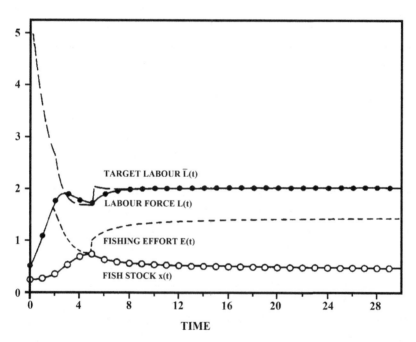

Figure 10.2 The optimal dynamics of the fish stock x_t, fishing effort E_t, fishery labour L_t and the target labour force $\bar{L}_t$ are shown for a 30-year time horizon, with initial conditions $x_0 = 0.25$ and $L_0 = 0.50$. Maximum intrinsic growth rates are $s = 3$ for the fish population and $r = 1$ for the labour force. The optimal harvest level h is 55 per cent for the first five years, and 75 per cent thereafter. Note that the constraint $E_t < L_t$ restricts the fishing effort, and hence the actual harvest level, in the first few years until the labour force has increased sufficiently.

Source: Charles (1989).

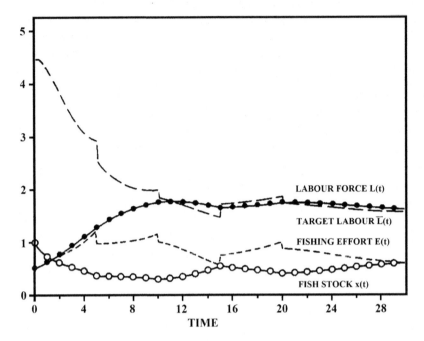

Figure 10.3 The optimal dynamics of the fish stock x_t, effort E_t, labour L_t and the
target labour force are shown for a 30-year time horizon, with initial
conditions $x_0 = 1.00$ and $L_0 = 0.50$. Maximum intrinsic growth rates
of $s = 1.5$ for the fish stock and $r = 0.25$ for the labour force are lower
than those used in Figure 10.1, producing a more gradual approach to
equilibrium. However, shifts in the desired harvest level h, which ranges
from 45 per cent to 35 per cent, lead to periodic jumps in effort E and
target labour $\bar{L}$, and corresponding dynamics in the labour force L.

Source: Charles (1989).

natural labour force L_t. This leads to expansion of both L and the fishing effort
E, as well as a corresponding decline in the fish stock, and thus a decrease in
the desirability of the fishery (L). Eventually, the actual labour force (L) rises
to meet its target level, and thereafter 'tracks' changes in the target L caused by
jumps in the harvest level.

These scenarios illustrate how the labour force L is continually approaching
its target level, albeit with this 'tracking' being subject to delay. In addition,
since periodic jumps are assumed to occur in the harvest, given the discrete time
steps, the optimal fish stock dynamics are not monotonic, but rather under- and
overshooting of the eventual stock equilibrium can occur. The examples here
have also illustrated how multiple objectives (in this case, rent maximization and
labour force stability) are included explicitly in the optimization process, how
approximately optimal harvest levels vary over time, and how labour dynamics
can depend significantly on the constraints placed on fishing effort, in particular
if effort is restricted by the size of the labour force itself.

Example: distribution of benefits and costs across fishing communities

The second example of bio-socio-economic analysis focuses on the interaction of fisheries (and fishing communities) with marine protected areas (MPAs). When an MPA is implemented within a designated ocean space, the area inside the MPA is regulated more stringently than outside. As a result, choices about the size, location and overall implementation of an MPA are likely to imply differential impacts on the various groups of fishers and communities, with resulting 'winners' and 'losers' (Brown et al., 2001; Sanchirico, 2004; Pomeroy et al., 2007; Charles and Wilson, 2009). For example, those fishing just out-side an MPA may reap the benefits of more abundant fish, while those dis-placed from their traditional local fishing grounds, as a result of the new MPA, may face higher costs, or even a loss of livelihood. This potential dichotomy between winners and losers has implications for the interaction of fisheries and MPAs (Charles and Sanders, 2007), in particular relating to: (1) overall net benefits; and (2) acceptance and long-term viability (which will be affected by a perceived unfair distribution of benefits and costs).

To address the distribution of benefits and costs across fishing communities when an MPA is implemented, a spatially explicit bioeconomic model is used; the discussion here draws strongly on the analysis in Charles (2010). Consider the situation of a fishery carried out by multiple fishing communities (with the ith denoted C_i) on multiple fish stocks (with the ith denoted S_i). To be con-crete, assume there are 10 communities and 10 stocks, equally spaced along the coastline (denoted as the interval [0,1] along a line) (see Figure 10.4). The fish stocks are assumed to be all part of a single population, but each has its own independent dynamics from year to year. Intermingling (mixing) takes place among the stocks, so they are not truly independent of one another (since fish from one stock are able to join, and reproduce with, a neighbouring stock).

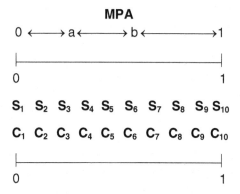

Figure 10.4 Placement of an MPA in the set of fish stocks and fishing communities along a coastline.

Source: Charles (2010).

Each stock *i* is assumed to lie a distance *d* offshore from the corresponding community *i*, as depicted in Figure 10.4. The fishing communities are assumed traditionally to harvest only the stock 'adjacent' to that community – whether due to a lack of mobility, a preference of the fishers, safety or cost minimization, a regulatory system (e.g. 'area licensing'), or a form of formal or informal rights. Thus, it is assumed that those in community C_1 harvest stock S_1, and so on.

Now consider the introduction of an MPA, as a no-take area in which no fishing is allowed. Suppose the MPA is placed between points 'a' and 'b' on the interval [0,1] (the coastline). Note that for simplicity, it is assumed that each stock, each community, and thus each community's fishing area, lies either inside the MPA or outside it. With these assumptions, the choice of 'a' and 'b' determines: (1) the MPA location, given by its left-hand coordinate, 'a'; and (2) the MPA size, b–a, as well as specifying which fish stocks, and fishing communities, will be directly affected by the MPA. The configuration is depicted in Figure 10.4.

Given the assumed interaction of each fishing community with its 'local' fish stock, if an MPA is introduced that includes stock S_1, the fishers most directly affected include those in community C_1. Indeed, since this MPA is no-take, fishers in communities associated with fish stocks located inside the MPA will no longer have access to 'their' stocks. What is to become of these fishers?

This is a fundamental issue faced in establishing MPAs, and a variety of options can be envisioned. At one extreme, all those located 'within' the new MPA could lose their fishing rights, absorbing the full negative impact of the MPA (though the government could provide compensation or alternate employment) – even while the MPA may benefit those remaining in the fishery. At the other end of the spectrum is the option of allowing fishers located near the MPA to continue fishing even within the no-take zone (perhaps recognizing historical rights). Intermediate between the above two possibilities is the option modelled here, of shifting the fishing of those displaced into the nearest areas outside the MPA, thus maintaining the 'no-take' nature of the MPA but allowing for continued fishing by those now inside the MPA.

The conservation and socio-economic implications of the latter approach will be explored in this model. In particular, three negative impacts on the displaced fishers' profits can be anticipated: (1) extra costs in travelling further to their new fishing grounds; (2) less time available for fishing due to greater travel times; and (3) sharing fishing grounds with those traditionally located there, as well as with other displaced fishers, leading to increased aggregate effort and lower catchability (i.e. a congestion effect). An additional negative factor that may be faced by displaced fishers arises if they are unwelcome in the 'new' area, where they will be fishing alongside others holding longer-standing rights, and will be adding additional harvesting pressure on the stock in that area. While this may arise as a critical problem in various situations, it is not included in this model.

The balance of the above negative factors with positive ones will affect the distribution of benefits from the MPA, which in turn can be expected to affect the acceptability of the MPA to fishers. A notable aspect of the model here is that not only are the benefits from expanded fish stocks likely to grow with the size of the MPA, but the cost components will tend to do likewise – in other words, a larger MPA will imply increased costs, because of the above mechanisms.

In this analysis, we assume that the fishery is managed not through catch quotas, but with limits on fishing effort, specifically on the available time for fishing. While the limit could arise based on natural constraints on fishing (e.g. tides or currents), here it is treated as a decision variable, set either culturally (e.g. if fishing traditionally takes place only on certain days) or institutionally (with government regulations). In either case, assume that this specifies the time T (potential fishing effort) that fishers have available per fishing trip. If fishers from the jth community require a travel time $t_{travel\,(i,j)}$ for a return trip to and from fishing ground i, then the actual fishing time (effort) per trip is $T - t_{travel\,(i,j)}$. Assuming a total of N fishers in each community, with each fisher making f trips per year, the total annual fishing time is $N \cdot f \cdot (T - t_{travel\,(i,j)})$. The resulting harvest is assumed to be proportional to this total annual fishing time and to the stock size ($X_{i,n}$ = stock size for S_i in year n) with the proportionality constant being the catchability coefficient (q). The harvest of the ith stock by fishers of community j in year n is then given by:

$$h_{i,j,n} = q \cdot X_{i,n} \cdot N \cdot f \cdot \left(T - t_{travel(i,j)} \right) \tag{10.5}$$

The *total* harvest of the ith stock in year n is then the sum over all communities j fishing on stock i:

$$h_{i,n} = q \cdot X_{i,n} \cdot N \cdot f \cdot \sum_{j}(T - t_{travel(i,j)}) \tag{10.6}$$

The value of this harvest, net of fishing costs, represents the profit from fishing, to be discussed below, following a discussion of the fish stock dynamics.

We assume here that within each year, the fishing season is followed by a reproductive period, and that migration occurs over the remainder of the year (along with natural mortality processes). So, in year n, the stock size $X_{i,n}$ is reduced by the harvest $h_{i,n}$ and the remainder $X_{i,n} - h_{i,n}$ is available for reproduction. The latter is assumed to follow a basic logistic–type relationship in which recruitment of stock i in year $n + 1$ is given by the product of three terms: an intrinsic growth rate r, the stock size remaining after harvesting, i.e. $(X_{i,n} - h_{i,n})$, and a linear scaling factor that reflects the stock's growth potential, depending on the carrying capacity, which, in the absence of an MPA, is assumed to be constant (K). On the other hand, if the particular stock lies within an MPA, we allow for the possibility that the MPA could improve ecosystem functioning, and thereby increase the reproductive capability of the fish stocks, leading to an increase in the carrying capacity. In the present model, the carrying capacity in such circumstances is increased by a multiplicative factor $1+ k$, where k is a constant ($k = 0$ if no such benefit of the MPA exists).

We assume a constant survival rate s, so that a biomass $s(X_{i,n} - h_{i,n})$ of stock i survives from year n to $n + 1$. There is some intermingling of stocks so stock S_i in year $n + 1$ will be composed of two parts: fish from S_i in year n that survive and *do not* migrate away, plus a fraction m of each neighbouring stock that survives from year n *and* migrate *into* the stock (S_i). Note that this model restricts migration to occurring between neighbouring stocks in a given year.

With this structure, the overall population dynamics are as follows:

$$X_{i,n+1} = \left(1 - 2m\right)s\left(X_{i,n} - h_{i,n}\right) + ms\left(X_{i-1,n} - h_{i-1,n}\right)$$

$$+ ms\left(X_{i+1,n} - h_{i+1,n}\right) + r\left(X_{i,n} - h_{i,n}\right)\left[1 - \frac{X_{i,n} - h_{i,n}}{K\left(1 + k\delta_{MPA}\right)}\right] \qquad (10.7)$$

where s is the inter-annual survival rate, m is the inter-area migration rate, r is the intrinsic growth rate, K is the 'carrying capacity', and k is the fractional increase in carrying capacity if the stock lies inside the MPA ($\delta_{MPA} = 1$).

Assume: (1) fishing times are as discussed above; (2) the cost per unit time for travel and for fishing are c_{travel} and $c_{fishing}$, respectively; (3) an additional fixed cost c_{fixed} is incurred annually by each fisher; and (4) there is a constant fish price p. Then the total profits obtained in year n by fishers in community j, fishing on stock i, are given by:

$$\Pi_{i,j,n} = p \cdot h_{i,j,n} - c_{travel} \cdot N \cdot f \cdot t_{travel(i,j)}$$

$$- c_{fishing} \cdot N \cdot f \cdot \left(T - t_{travel(i,j)}\right) - N \cdot c_{fixed} \qquad (10.8)$$

The bioeconomic model was analysed to determine the impacts of the MPA on conservation and distributional aspects in the fishery, based on specific fishery configurations (described in Charles, 2010) and particular choices of MPA location and size, then using simulation (with a 100-year time frame). Impacts on the fishers depends on whether they are displaced (e.g. new travel and fishing costs), as well as the fishing pressure on each stock and the consequent population dynamics. Finally, the biological and economic outputs of the simulation are determined, as described below.

The dynamics of fish stock sizes and economic performance of the fishing communities are examined over time to compare the effects of the MPA with the base case of no MPA. The results are given in terms of two major decision variables: (1) the intensity of fishing activity, measured in terms of fishing time T; and (2) the configuration of the MPA (i.e. location and size), as well as two model parameters: (1) the 'spillover' of fish to areas outside the MPA, as specified by the migration rate; and (2) the existence of benefits from the MPA in providing increased ecosystem health, measured by the carrying capacity adjustment factor k.

Three examples are shown here, all for the same MPA configuration, namely an MPA covering stocks 6 and 7 of the 10 stocks ($a = 0.5$, $b = 0.7$), and thus 20 per cent of the total coastal region. In each example, two figures are shown. The first ('a') indicates how final fish stock sizes vary across the 10 stocks, and how the two economic indicators – the net present value (over the 100-year period of the simulation) and the average annual net revenue (over a 10-year period) – vary across the 10 communities. The second figure ('b') shows the evolution of net revenue (profit) over time, one line depicting the dynamics of net revenue for a 'displaced' community that must shift its fishing from inside to outside the MPA, and the other a 'distant' community located well away from the MPA.

Two points should be made here. First, the results can be contrasted with a base case of no MPA. In such a situation, the fish stocks and their dynamics are all identical, as are the fishing communities, so there is no difference in results between stocks or between communities. This implies no distributional impacts, so that the figure 'a' in such a case will consist of horizontal lines. Second, while all examples below involve the same MPA configuration, further simulations, not shown here, demonstrate that the main effect of varying the size of the MPA is to change the extent to which economic performance between communities differs between inside and outside the MPA.

Well-managed fishery and moderate fish migration

First, suppose the fishery is 'well-managed' prior to the MPA introduction. Figure 10.5 shows a case in which the total possible time at sea, T, is set to achieve the economic goal of maximizing long-term net present value ($T = 16.3$), and this effort level is maintained with the introduction of the MPA. A migration rate of 20 per cent ($m = 0.2$) is used, with no ecosystem benefits of the MPA ($k = 0$). The results show that within the MPA, stocks grow to a higher biomass relative to no MPA, but the economic performance of communities within the MPA is lower than in the absence of the MPA (shown by a ratio <1). Those communities are also worse off than more distant communities, since they incur extra travel costs to reach new fishing areas, consequent reduced fishing time, and lower catch rates since they harvest from stocks depleted due to increased fishing pressure outside the MPA, resulting from harvesting by traditionally resident fishers and those from displaced communities. These negatives for displaced communities are not compensated for by increased migration of fish into the neighbouring areas where they are now fishing. Note as well that the 'border' communities just outside the MPA are also worse off than those distant from the MPA, though not in as bad a situation economically as those displaced.

Well-managed fishery and no fish migration

Suppose we have the same MPA configuration as above, but there is *no* fish migration (an extreme case adopted for illustrative purposes). This implies there are 10 independent fish stocks with no mixing between them.

Figure 10.6 provides a cautionary note concerning the potential impacts of an MPA in a situation of low fish migration. The stocks within the MPA grow to carrying capacity, as there is no out-migration, so all ecological benefits of ending fishing inside the MPA stay there. However, as in other scenarios, displaced fishers shift spatially to fish on neighbouring stocks just outside the MPA, joining others already there. Since there is no input of fish from the MPA into these areas, this leads to heavy depletion (under the limited fishery management assumed here). Indeed, in this example, the 'border' stocks (5 and 8) are reduced to zero within the simulation time frame, and net revenues for both displaced and border communities (5, 6, 7 and 8) drop to zero within 20 years. Thus, the message here is that if an MPA induces displacement of effort but there is insufficient fish migration to compensate (and insufficient management measures in place), this can lead to stock collapses outside the MPA.

Over-exploited fishery and ecosystem benefits

Figure 10.7 shows a very different scenario. Here, the MPA is configured as in the above examples ($a = 0.5$ and $b = 0.7$), and all the model parameters are the same, except for two key features. First, the initial situation is one of an over-exploited stock, and there is high fishing effort ($T = 25$ rather than the economically optimal $T = 16.3$), which, in the absence of an MPA, would lead to systematic depletion of the fish stocks. Second, the presence of an MPA is assumed to improve ecosystem health within it, thereby increasing the carrying capacity for fish stocks inside the MPA, specifically a doubling of the carrying capacity relative to the no MPA situation ($k = 1$). The effect of the MPA is greater in this situation of high fishing effort than when the effort was set at an economically optimal level. In particular, the MPA protects stocks that would otherwise become severely depleted (the ratio of stock sizes, 'with MPA' versus 'no MPA', is very high; see Figure 10.7). With ecosystem benefits, displaced fishers are better off than those distant from the MPA, with the long-term present value greater for displaced and border communities than for those distant from the MPA. The economic outcomes (e.g. net revenue) for the displaced communities, with the MPA in place, not only recover from an initial drop, but grow to a strong equilibrium (see Figure 10.7b), significantly surpassing that of the 'distant' community after a few years. Thus, the message here is that positive distributional impacts (relatively greater benefits for those displaced by the MPA) are more likely when ecological sustainability is threatened (e.g. cases of high fishing effort). This situation is a desirable one from the perspective of MPA implementation, since those fishers forced to move and face higher costs actually end up 'winners' in the process, at least over the long term. Such a result was only seen clearly in scenarios involving 'ecosystem benefits'.

In summary, this analysis focuses on fishing communities and the distribution of benefits and costs across those communities, when an MPA affects fishing activity. While those in fishing communities that are displaced will face

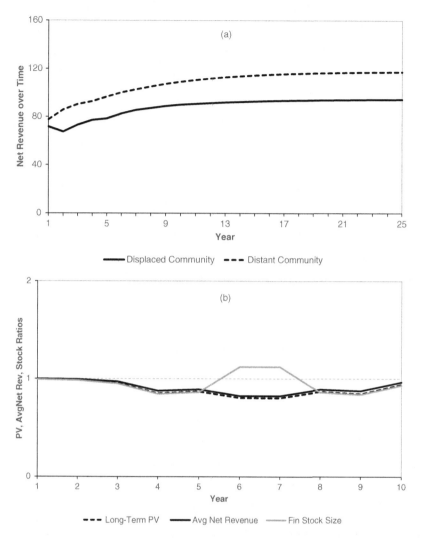

Figure 10.5 An MPA is in place covering stocks 6 and 7 (i.e. $a = 0.5$, $b = 0.7$) with migration rate $m = 0.2$ and fishing effort set at the (no MPA) economic optimum $T = 16.3$. Figure 10.5a shows the distribution of final stock size, 10-year average net revenue and long-term discounted present value across the 10 communities/stocks. Figure 10.5b shows the time series of net revenue for a community 'distant' from the MPA, and one displaced from its fishing ground by the MPA.

Source: Charles (2010).

the costs of decreased fishing time and increased travel costs to neighbouring grounds, and must always deal with a decrease in net revenues in the short term, the *net* distributional outcomes depend profoundly on the ecological responses

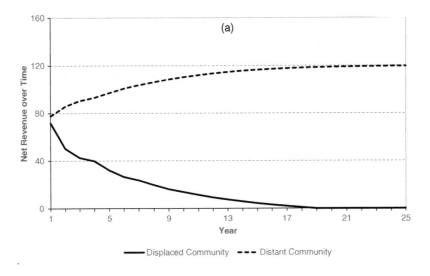

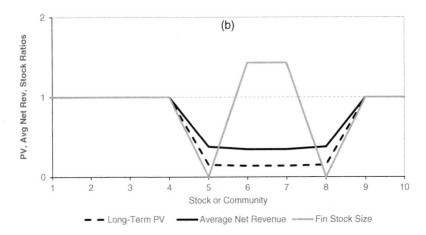

Figure 10.6 The same MPA is in place as in Figure 10.5 (covering stocks 6 and 7), and again fishing effort is set at the (no MPA) economic optimum $T = 16.3$, but in this case there is no migration of fish between stock areas ($m = 0$). See the caption of Figure 10.5 for descriptions of graphs shown in Figures 10.6a and 10.6b.

Source: Charles (2010).

within the MPA, and on the biological realities of the fish stocks. If there are no significant ecological improvements that occur within the MPA, and low migration rates, then in this model economic performance will be lower for displaced fishers than for others. On the other hand, displaced fishers can be better off than others if ecosystem health within the MPA improves, such that fish

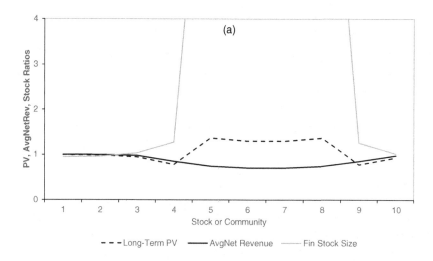

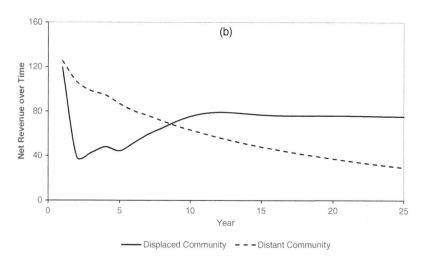

Figure 10.7 The same MPA is in place as in Figure 10.5 (covering stocks 6 and 7), with the same migration rate (*m* = 0.2), but now fishing effort is at a high level (*T* = 25) and the MPA generates ecosystem benefits (carrying capacity adjustment factor *k* = 1). See the caption of Figure 10.5 for descriptions of graphs shown in Figures 10.7a and 10.7b. Note that here, stocks inside and bordering the MPA are far higher than the case of no MPA – off the graph at 10.5 for stocks 5 and 8, and 55.2 for stocks 6 and 7.

Source: Charles (2010).

stock carrying capacities increase. Overall, this bio-socio-economic analysis has demonstrated the reality that spatial measures such as MPAs can strongly affect the distribution of benefits and costs to fishing communities.

Bio-socio-economics and fishery policy

The preceding two sections of this chapter used modelling analysis to show how some of the key ingredients of a bio-socio-economic approach to fisheries – specifically multiple objectives, labour dynamics, distributional impacts and fishing communities – help to inform management decision-making. These models have the benefit of providing a transparent mechanism to show structure and dynamics of the fishery system, but at the same time they may well require data that are not necessarily available in a given fishery. Fortunately, models are not required for a bio-socio-economic approach, since instead the use of policy analysis that is interdisciplinary and integrated (holistic) can be effective, drawing on multidimensional conceptual frameworks:

1   One class of such policy-oriented work involves comparative analysis of multiple case studies. For example, Garcia et al. (2014) examine the complex interactions between fishery management and marine biodiversity conservation, at levels from the local to the global, through an integrated bio-socio-economic analysis. A range of studies in that volume all share a common conceptual framework but vary across multiple scales (spatial, organizational and institutional). Along similar lines, Salas et al. (2011) examine coastal fisheries of Latin America and the Caribbean, including a set of cases all taking the same interdisciplinary and integrated perspective on coastal fishery systems, with their assessment and governance, but organized on a jurisdictional (nation-by-nation) basis. These comparative analyses, based on a common analytical framework, can provide emergent insights into appropriate policy directions ('what works and what does not') in a holistic manner.

2   Another class of integrated bio-socio-economic policy-focused analysis involves providing a systematic and multifaceted approach to a certain major fishery policy theme. Examples of this include development of suitable frameworks to assess: (1) ecosystem-based management, and specifically the ecosystem approach to fisheries (De Young et al., 2008); and (2) comprehensive examination of financial support to fisheries, i.e. subsidies (Charles, 2006) and of structural change in fisheries (Charles, 2007). While these policy analyses are not usually labelled 'bio-socio-economic', their defining feature is a balanced coverage of biological, social and economic factors, as befits fishery bio-socio-economics. Such integrated approaches can lead to policy that reflects a more realistic understanding of the values, structures and dynamics of fishery systems.

3   A bio-socio-economic perspective is also relevant to policy formation itself. Taking an integrated (holistic) approach to policy avoids the trap of governmental policy failing to reflect the goals of resource communities, or failing to incorporate the dynamics of human behaviour, or failing to be developed in a manner in keeping with the realities of the real-world fishery system. The following are three examples in which applying a bio-socio-economic approach to policy can be a potentially important ingredient of success.

Values

The underlying values of those in fisheries (i.e. resource users, fishing communities, industry sectors and fishery managers themselves) is not a topic common in conventional bioeconomics. Yet these aspects can be important to build into fishery policy (Charles et al., 2010). Such common values include the importance of 'place' (i.e. stewardship of a fisher's home area), intergenerational respect (i.e. protecting the environment for one's children), valuing healthy communities (linking community and ecological wellbeing), respect for human rights (including equity and fairness), and respect for local knowledge.

Participatory governance

An integrated, bio-socio-economic approach to policy can provide the breadth of thinking to properly develop effective governance arrangements (Garcia et al., 2014) to include meaningful participation of fishers, and appropriate co-management, thus making the difference between success and failure of management.

Costs and benefits

A bio-socio-economic approach to policy recognizes that costs and benefits are not necessarily monetary, and takes a broader perspective that considers social, economic and ecological costs together. For example, a policy measure, such as a marine protected area, which could lead to displacement of fishers from certain geographical areas, would need to be assessed, before implementation, through a suitably integrated process (Charles et al., 2016) so that the balance of costs and benefits, and their distribution, are properly considered.

Taking these and other aspects into account, the integrated perspective of bio-socio-economics provides better understanding of fishery systems, enabling development of policy – and fishery governance – more appropriate for the specific human context, and with better support of fishers and fishing communities. In doing so, it is crucial to recognize that high-level policy has different impacts at different spatial and temporal scales (e.g. from a local community to a region to a nation). Thus, assessment of the implications of policy measures is needed at each relevant scale (Charles, 2001). In this way, there is a better chance of ultimately meeting fishery objectives in practice.

Conclusions

A defining feature of fishery bio-socio-economics, relative to bioeconomic analysis, is the focus on ensuring that social, cultural and other 'human dimensions' are included equally with biological and economic factors, including comprehensive incorporation of social, community and behavioural aspects, so as to provide a framework for analysing joint ecological and socioeconomic dynamics inherent in fishery systems. This chapter has emphasized five key elements of bio-socio-economics: (1) incorporating and assessing multiple fishery objectives, and dealing with the resulting conflicts; (2) recognizing and analysing distributional impacts of fishery policy and practice; (3) human dimensions of fisheries governance and rights, in the commons; (4) consideration of behavioural and labour dynamics in fisheries, including fisher response to regulations and the role of labour markets; and (5) interactions of fisheries and fishing communities (including underlying values, objectives, knowledge, institutions and functions). We have seen that insights into these bio-socio-economic considerations can be obtained both through modelling analysis and through policy analysis.

These elements of a fishery bio-socio-economic framework, taken together, can help us better understand human and institutional behaviour in fisheries, expand the breadth of thinking in fishery management, and build that broader knowledge into fishery decision-making. This in turn can improve the buy-in of stakeholders, improve the feasibility and likelihood of success in fishery management initiatives, and thereby improve the chances of meeting the new UN Sustainable Development Goals.

There is, however, further work needed to build an integrated bio-socio-economic fishery analysis – bringing together relevant social, economic and socio-economic components in a form suitable for developing and analysing practical fishery management plans. From a knowledge perspective, it is important to determine priorities for further bio-socio-economic data collection and research activity. There is a notorious bias in most jurisdictions towards natural science data in fisheries, with relatively little economic data, and almost no social data, being collected. This is especially the case in terms of regular annual processes. For example, it is rare for time series of data on fishery labour forces, fishing community populations and fishery participation rates.

There are also challenges to overcome, in broadening the use of bio-socio-economics, arising in the difficulties of bringing people together – whether this be specialists from a variety of fields, notably linking natural science approaches with the human dimensions of fisheries, or the range of fishery stakeholders (since, given the reality of a multi-objective world, differences exist in the weights placed on fishery objectives by various groups). Indeed, the matter of which fishery objectives are considered legitimate will affect the very extent to which bio-socio-economic factors are seen as relevant to actual fishery management decisions. Overall, the complexities of multiple objectives in a multidimensional fishery system ensure that building and applying a full bio-socio-economic framework for fisheries will remain an important challenge into the future.

Acknowledgements

This chapter has benefited from helpful comments provided by numerous colleagues, notably Fikret Berkes, Derek Armitage and Keith Criddle, as well as research assistance from Ashley Shelton, Meagan Symington, Patrick Larter, Jieni Muaror-Wilson and Chris Burbidge. The useful comments of an anonymous referee improved the chapter. Financial support for this research is acknowledged from the Natural Sciences and Engineering Research Council of Canada, and the Social Sciences and Humanities Research Council of Canada, through the Community Conservation Research Network (www. communityconservation.net).

References

Berkes, F. (ed.) (1989). *Common Property Resources: Ecology and Community-Based Sustainable Development.* London: Bellhaven Press.

Berkes, F., Feeny, D., McCay, B.J. and Acheson, J.M. (1989). The benefits of the commons. *Nature,* 340: 91–93.

Bianchi, G. and Skjoldal, H.R. (eds) (2008). *The Ecosystem Approach to Fisheries.* Oxford: CABI.

Bromley, D.W. and Bishop, R.C. (1977). From economic theory to fisheries policy: conceptual problem and management prescription. In: L.G Anderson (ed.), *Economic Impacts of Extended Jurisdiction.* Ann Arbor, MI: Ann Arbor Science.

Brown, K., Adger, N., Tompkins, E., Bacon, P., Shim, D. and Young, C. (2001). Trade-off analysis for marine protected area management. *Ecological Economics,* 37: 417–434.

Charles, A. (1988). Fishery socioeconomics: a survey. *Land Economics,* 64: 276–295.

Charles, A. (1989). Bio-socio-economic fishery models: labor dynamics and multi-objective management. *Canadian Journal of Fisheries and Aquatic Sciences,* 46: 1313–1322.

Charles, A. (1991). Bio-socio-economic dynamics and multidisciplinary models in small-scale fisheries research. In: J.R. Durand, J. Lemoalle and J. Weber (eds), *Research and Small-Scale Fisheries.* Paris: ORSTOM, pp. 603–608.

Charles, A. (1992). Fishery conflicts: a unified framework. *Marine Policy,* 16(5): 379–393.

Charles, A. (1995). Sustainability assessment and bio-socio-economic analysis: tools for integrated coastal development. In: M.A. Juinio-Meñez and G. Newkirk (eds), *Philippine Coastal Resources Under Stress.* Halifax: Coastal Resources Research Network and Quezon City, Philippines: Marine Science Institute, pp.115–125.

Charles, A. (2001). *Sustainable Fishery Systems.* Oxford: Wiley-Blackwell.

Charles, A. (2006). Subsidies in fisheries: an analysis of social impacts within an integrated sustainable development framework. AGR/FI(2004)6. OECD. Also published as: Social impacts of government financial support of fisheries. In: OECD (ed.), *Financial Support to Fisheries: Implications for Sustainable Development.* Paris: OECD, pp. 225–260.

Charles, A. (2007). The human dimension of fisheries adjustment: an overview of key issues and policy challenges. Keynote Paper, Expert Meeting on the Human Side of Fisheries Adjustment. 19 October 2006. Paris, France. Published as Chapter 1 in: OECD (ed.), *Structural Change in Fisheries: Dealing with the Human Dimension.* Paris: OECD.

Charles. A. (2009). Rights-based fisheries management: the role of use rights in managing access and harvesting. In: K.L. Cochrane and S.M. Garcia (eds), *A Fishery Manager's Guidebook.* Oxford: Wiley-Blackwell, pp. 253–282.

Charles, A. (2010). Fisheries and marine protected areas: a spatial bioeconomic analysis of distributional impacts. *Natural Resources Modeling*, 23: 218–252.

Charles, A. (2011). Human rights and fishery rights in small-sale fisheries management. In: R.S. Pomeroy and N.L. Andrew (eds), *Small Scale Fisheries Management*. Oxford: CAB International, pp. 59–74.

Charles, A. and Sanders, J. (2007). *Issues Arising on the Interface of MPAs and Fisheries Management*. Report and Documentation of the Expert Workshop on Marine Protected Areas and Fisheries Management: Review of Issues and Considerations. Rome, Italy, 12–14 June 2006. FAO Fisheries Report, No. 825. Rome: FAO, pp. 301–332.

Charles, A. and Wilson, L. (2009). Human dimensions of marine protected areas. *ICES Journal of Marine Science*, 66: 6–15.

Charles, A., Mazany, R.L. and Cross, M.L. (1999). The economics of illegal fishing: a behavioral model. *Marine Resource Economics*, 14: 95–110.

Charles, A., Wiber, M., Bigney, K., Curtis, D., Wilson, L., Angus, R., et al. (2010). Integrated management: a coastal community perspective. *Horizons*, 10: 26–34.

Charles, A., Westlund, L., Bartley, D.M., Fletcher, W.J., Garcia, S., Govan, H., et al. (2016). Fishing livelihoods as key to marine protected areas: insights from the World Parks Congress. *Aquatic Conservation: Marine and Freshwater Ecosystems*, 26: 165–184.

Copes, P. and Charles, A. (2004). Socioeconomics of individual transferable quotas and community-based fishery management. *Agricultural and Resource Economics Review*, 33: 171–181.

De Young, C., Charles, A. and Hjort, A. (2008). Human dimensions of the ecosystem approach to fisheries: an overview of context, concepts, tools and methods. *Fisheries Technical Paper No. 489*. Rome: FAO.

Garcia, S.M. and Charles, A. (2008). Fishery systems and linkages: implications for science and governance. *Ocean and Coastal Management*, 51: 505–527.

Garcia, S.M., Rice, J. and Charles, A. (2014). *Governance of Marine Fisheries and Biodiversity Conservation: Interaction and Co-evolution*. Oxford: Wiley-Blackwell.

Graham, J., Charles, A. and Bull, A. (2006). *Community Fisheries Management Handbook*. Gorsebrook Research Institute, Saint Mary's University, Halifax, Canada. Available at: www.communityconservation.net/resources/coastal-cura/ (accessed 25 January 2018).

Lawson, R. (1984). *Economics of Fisheries Development*. London: Frances Pinter.

Opaluch, J.J. and Bockstael, N.E. (1984). Behavioral modelling and fisheries management. *Marine Resource Economics*, 1: 105–115.

Ostrom, E. (1990). *Governing the Commons*. Cambridge: Cambridge University Press.

Ostrom, E. (1992). The rudiments of a theory of the origins, survival, and performance of common-property institutions. In: D.W. Bromley, D. Feeny, M.A. McKean, P. Peters, J.L. Gilles, R.J. Oakerson, et al. (eds), *Making the Commons Work: Theory, Practice and Policy*. San Francisco, CA: Institute for Contemporary Studies, pp. 293–318.

Pinkerton, E.W. (1989). *Cooperative Management of Local Fisheries*. Vancouver: University of British Columbia Press.

Pomeroy, R., Mascia, M. and Pollnac, R. (2007). Marine protected areas: the social dimension. In FAO (ed.), *Report and Documentation of the Expert Workshop on Marine Protected Areas and Fisheries Management: Review of Issues and Considerations*. 12–14 June 2006. FAO Fisheries Report No. 825. Rome: FAO, pp. 149–181.

Salas, S. and Gaertner, D. (2004). The behavioral dynamics of fishers: management implications. *Fish and Fisheries*, 5: 153–167.

Salas, S., Chuenpagdee, R., Charles, A. and Seijo, J.C. (2011). *Coastal Fisheries of Latin America and the Caribbean*. Washington, DC: FAO.

Sanchirico, J.N. (2004). Designing a cost-effective marine reserve network: a bioeconomic metapopulation analysis. *Marine Resource Economics*, 19: 41–65.

Smith, V.L. (1968). Economics of production from natural resources. *American Economic Review*, 58: 409–431.

Wilen, J.E. (1979). Fishermen behavior and the design of efficient fisheries regulation programs. *Journal of the Fishery Research Board of Canada*, 36: 855–858.

Wilen, J., Smith, M., Lockwood, D. and Botsford, L. (2002). Avoiding surprises incorporating fisherman behaviour into management models. *Bulletin of Marine Science*, 70: 553–575.

11 Synthesis

Theory, policy and contemporary challenges for bioeconomics

Jon G. Sutinen and Juan Carlos Seijo

The chapters in this book have demonstrated how modern bioeconomics can be applied to address an emerging set of complex environmental and fisheries management issues. The authors have provided innovative approaches to these issues with some novel approaches to fisheries management and challenged conventional paradigms. The findings are briefly summarized below, followed by suggestions for future research.

Will more countries deplete a fishery?

In his analysis of the effect of number of players in a non-cooperative fisheries game, Hannesson (Chapter 2) shows that as the number of players increases, it is increasingly likely for the fish stock to be depleted to extinction from a game theoretic perspective. As the number of players increases, it becomes less likely that the any single player will be sufficiently dominant to have an incentive to conserve the fish stock in its own interest. While theoretical adherents may conclude that a large number of countries sharing a fish stock is a recipe for disaster, Hannesson argues it is not necessarily the case. Instead, countries might cooperate due to the risk of common ruin in an infinitely repeated game. He presents evidence from the Northeast Atlantic mackerel fishery, where there is no formal cooperation but countries have set cautious quotas to conserve the stock. Hannesson concludes that assured mutual destruction may prompt the parties sharing a fish stock to cooperate, at least informally, even if no single party is dominant enough to conserve the stock in its own interest.

Does it matter how fisheries management is paid for?

Sutinen and Andersen (Chapter 3) develop and use a static bioeconomic model of fisheries law enforcement to derive the economic, biological and fishery management policy consequences of a royalty to recover the costs of enforcement in a fishery. They find that using a royalty has multiple advantages, including a conservation benefit that has not been explicitly noted in studies of cost recovery mechanisms. This result is further evidence that who pays and how they pay for management services influences policies and the economic performance of a fishery.

Is it best to harvest only mature fish?

Caddy (Chapter 4) presents a paradigm shift in fisheries management away from the conventional Beverton and Holt approach that assumes it is inappropriate to harvest fish before a cohort has matured and spawned at least once. An alternative approach to managing fisheries is suggested where immature fish are marketable, which harvests juveniles and protects mature fish by closures or gear/area refugia. This approach is developed for the Mediterranean hake fishery, and multi-gear allocations are suggested that predominantly harvest juveniles as well as a very restricted quantity of older fish.

From a bioeconomic perspective, the capture of a mature female terminates a train of future benefits from population replenishment by its offspring. A limited harvest of these could in total exceed the value of the parental generation available for capture. Yield calculations using estimates of the declining rates of natural mortality (M-at-age) and increases in F-at-age suggest that delaying exploitation until age at maturity is unlikely to increase the overall yield and corresponding resource rent. It risks reducing the intergenerational ratio of recruit numbers below unity, leading to stock declines. If the spawning stock offshore is heavily targeted, this will also adversely affect population fecundity.

How should fishery management deal with ocean acidification?

In their dynamic bioeconomic decision analysis of ocean acidification, Seijo and Villanueva (Chapter 5) conclude that adapting to ocean acidification can be achieved when fishing at maximum economic yield harvesting rates, combined with decision criteria reflecting different decision-makers' attitudes towards risk. In sum, they demonstrate that well-established methods of bioeconomic modelling and decision analysis in data-limited situations can be applied to aid fishery participants in responding to the potential impacts of ocean acidification on fisheries using appropriate precautionary bioeconomic reference points. Three species groups were examined here with different renewability capacities: low ($r = 0.2$), medium ($r = 0.4$) and high ($r = 0.6$). The bioeconomic simulation experiments developed in this chapter demonstrate that bioeconomic ocean acidification effects on fisheries targeting calcifier species will depend on species life cycle and relative abundance. Results from the dynamic bioeconomic decision analysis indicate that focusing on adaptation to possible effects of OA can be accomplished using, as a precautionary measure, a level of fishing mortality (F) that maximizes the net present value (NPV) of the fishery, with an appropriate decision criteria reflecting the decision-maker's degree of caution.

Is a discard ban a good way to deal with unwanted by-catch?

In their theoretical analysis of a landing obligation, Andersen and Ståhl (Chapter 6) conclude that in a simple one-species, two-cohort model, the regulation changes stock size under both open access and an economic optimum management. The direction of the change in stock size depends on prices and costs in the open-access case, and on the initial stock size in the optimal case. The empirical analysis of the Danish multispecies fishery indicates that implementing the landing obligation without quota uplifts (increases) would reduce revenues and profitability in the fishery. These losses can be mitigated with decreases in the minimum size and/or increases in quotas.

Are subsidies helping small-scale fishers?

Sumaila and Schuhbauer (Chapter 7) emphasize three key findings in their study of fisheries subsidies. First, it is clear that harmful subsidies are the big problem, consuming close to 60 per cent of the estimated US$35 billion total subsidies, with large-scale industrial fisheries receiving a higher proportion of these harmful subsidies. Second, only a small fraction of fisheries subsidies goes to small-scale fishers, limiting their ability to be economically viable. This is bound to undermine the lofty United Nations Sustainable Development Goals of eliminating poverty, hunger and reducing inequality. Third, even in the case of 'beneficial' subsidies, the use of public funds that could go elsewhere in society needs to be examined. For instance, are managing fisheries and creating MPAs, as two kinds of good subsidies, better than building hospitals or roads? Sumaila and Schuhbauer conclude by urging the global community to work relentlessly to eliminate harmful subsidies.

Who is being helped and hurt by eco-labelling and eco-certification schemes?

In his discussion of eco-labelling schemes, Cochrane (Chapter 8) concludes that eco-labelling and certification have significantly impacted several fisheries, leading to the economic and sustainability benefits that theory predicts. He expects this to expand for the foreseeable future, with opportunities lying in increasing awareness of the environmental value of eco-labelling and certification in those countries that have the wealth to make environmentally responsible choices but currently have limited knowledge of or access to eco-labelled products at present, such as Japan, Australia, New Zealand and others. Cochrane argues that eco-labelling schemes need to ensure that well-managed fisheries in developing countries need equitable and cost-effective access to eco-labelling for their full potential to be realized. For most fisheries, particularly small-scale fisheries and fisheries of low or moderate value in developing countries, eco-labelling is unlikely to be a useful tool and incentive in helping them to achieve sustainability and improved benefits for their stakeholders. In his opinion, those fisheries, governments, development agencies, and development and conservation NGOs should not be distracted by the high interest in eco-labelling, and instead should focus on management measures and incentives that are more appropriate and more likely to be effective.

How can economics be used in the ecosystem-based fisheries management approach?

Anderson (Chapter 9) has proposed a systematic process to follow for moving from single-species management to ecosystem-based fisheries management (EBFM). In his view, EBFM is the simultaneous determination of allowable harvest levels for a specified group of stocks (a vector of harvest levels), based on selection of a target stock area (set of desired or acceptable stock size combinations) and control rules to determine the time path of the harvests that will cause the collection of current stock sizes to move into or remain in the target stock area. The selection of the target stock area and the control rule are conceptually policy rather than scientific decisions. The overall goal in setting the target stock and the control rule is to optimize the stream of net benefits to current and future participants and users. Anderson further argues that studies have shown that the basic concepts, tools, knowledge and data are sufficient enough that implementation of EBFM can start immediately, even if it is only with baby steps initially. Certainly, the lack of these things cannot be used as an excuse to delay starting.

How can human and social elements be incorporated in bioeconomics analysis?

Charles (Chapter 10) argues that if ecosystem-based management and an 'ecosystem approach' are to be adopted in fisheries, so that the ecosystems in which the fish live are better incorporated, then we should consider the human side of the fishery system equally, i.e. where the people live (notably fishing communities). Bio-socio-economics accomplishes this with its focus on ensuring that social, cultural and other 'human dimensions' are included equally with biological and economic factors. Charles makes the case that important insights into these bio-socio-economic considerations can be obtained both through modelling analysis and through policy analysis. The use of a fishery bio-socio-economic framework can help policymakers better understand human and institutional behaviour in fisheries, expand the breadth of thinking in fishery management, and inject broader relevant information into fishery decision-making. This in turn can improve the buy-in of stakeholders, improve the feasibility and likelihood of success in fishery management initiatives, and thereby improve the chances of meeting the new UN Sustainable Development Goals.

Challenges and future directions

The basic model used by Sutinen and Andersen for their analysis of cost recovery produces results only for long-run, static equilibriums. A more appropriate model for practical policy analysis should consider short-run outcomes in a dynamic setting. For this purpose, a dynamic model will be required to consider short-run consequences of applying a royalty or other cost recovery methods. In addition, models of cost recovery for cases where fishery user groups are managing their fisheries should be developed and tested. Empirical analysis would be useful to determine whether and to what extent cost recovery user charges are significantly influencing bioeconomic outcomes. If not, many of the issues examined here are irrelevant.

Seijo and Villanueva note that there are additional complexities to be considered in future research on ocean acidification, notably building spatial considerations in fisheries targeting low-mobility resources in areas with significant changes in ocean acidification.

To better understand the consequences of a landing obligation, Andersen and Ståhl suggest that future research should examine changing behaviour with regard to selectivity, substitution, economic viability of fleets, learning across fleets and fisheries, and investment decisions and disinvestment. As part of a European Union project, future work will focus on impacts of stock effects and biodiversity, technology changes and selectivity, complex behavioral changes, and imperfect control and enforcement of the landing obligation.

To improve applications of EBFM, Anderson identifies the following areas for future research: (1) find a substitute for biomass as the metric of success or as means of evaluating trade-offs; (2) develop methods to allow for rigorous analysis of trade-offs, especially with respect to determining the optimal size of the buffer between limit and target harvest levels; and (3) expand the elements considered when setting limit and target harvest levels beyond how much should be caught, to how, where, when and by whom they are caught.

Charles emphasizes the need for future work to build an integrated bio-socio-economic fishery analysis that brings together relevant social, economic and socioeconomic components in a form suitable for developing and analysing practical fishery management plans. From a knowledge perspective, it is important to determine priorities for further bio-socio-economic data collection and research activity. There is a notorious bias in most jurisdictions towards natural science data in fisheries, with relatively little economic data, and almost no social data, being collected. This is especially the case in terms of regular annual processes. For example, it is rare for time series of data to be collected on fishery labour forces, fishing community populations and fishery participation rates.

He also notes that there are other challenges to overcome in broadening the use of bio-socio-economics that arise from the difficulties of bringing people together – whether this be specialists from a variety of fields, notably linking natural science approaches with the human dimensions of fisheries, or the range of fishery stakeholders (since, given the reality of a multi-objective world, differences exist in the weights placed on fishery objectives by various groups). Indeed, the matter of which fishery objectives are considered legitimate will affect the very extent to which bio-socio-economic factors are seen as relevant to actual fishery management decisions. Overall, the complexities of multiple objectives in a multidimensional fishery system ensure that building and applying a full bio-socio-economic framework for fisheries will remain an important challenge into the future.

Index

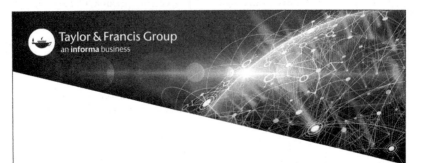